I0521048

PUT SOME GRAVY ON IT

ASHLEIGH BILLS

Put Some Gravy On It
The Mud, The Blood and 40 Years of Nine Pound Hammer

Interviews in this book have been edited for length and clarity.

Copyright © 2025 by Ashleigh Bills

All rights reserved. No part of this book may be reproduced in any form without permission from the author, with the exception of brief passages embodied in critical articles and reviews.

Cover design by Brittany Chapman

Interior photo retouching and layout by Brittany Chapman and Ashleigh Bills

Proofed by Heather Fuhrmann

Special thanks to Troy Burkhart, Brittany Chapman, Brian Moore and Kelly and Scott Chambers for additional photos, gig flyers and artwork.

A product of Heavy Chevy, LLC

ISBN: 979-8-9936241-0-5

To my parents, my wife and every friend
who pitched in and helped out.

Smooches.

CONTENTS

<u>PROLOGUE</u>

Kentucky is a contradiction.

A commonwealth with an identity crisis. The northernmost southern state that's almost Midwestern in certain parts and in certain ways. Fortunately, Kentucky still serves up enough "Please and thank you, ma'ams," fried chicken, and biscuits and gravy to keep our seat at the Southern dinner table.

We're equal parts bourbon and bibles. *"Lord, gonna send you to hell for drinking on Saturday night. Lord, gonna save your soul for tossing on a navy blazer and khakis and pouring yourself into a pew on Sunday morning."*

While parts of Kentucky are flush with horse money, other parts are full of seemingly inescapable, generational poverty. We're also home to several industrious cities – but those are outnumbered by the state's 120 counties and a lot of old-school, stuck-in-the-mud ideas. Progress doesn't happen easily or quickly around here.

Most people in this state are the kindest souls that have ever walked the earth. Rolling hills, gigantic state and national parks, caves, caverns and lakes – Kentucky is beautiful. I'm proud to call it home now, but not so much as a teenager growing up in Paris, Kentucky, in the mid-90s. Many of the things that made it seem idyllic to a lot of people felt out-of-step and out-of-time to me.

I grew up around generations of people who were born, lived, worked and died in the same 10,000-person town. Sure, family is important, and there's comfort in the familiar. But there's a giant world out there and unfortunately, I wasn't going to see it all with the few free hours I was granted by the America Online CD-ROM in my mailbox. But what I did see in between chat rooms and instant messages to friends made me want to see more.

Another thing that made me want to see more of the world was a cowpunk band from Owensboro.

I became a fan of Nine Pound Hammer in the summer of 1992 when a friend passed me a homemade copy of *The Mud, The Blood and The Beers* and *Smokin' Taters* on one cassette. That tape didn't leave my Sony Walkman for a year – except for an occasional Beastie Boys *Check Your Head* break.

So many of the songs on Nine Pound Hammer's first two albums were instantly relatable to my experience growing up in Bourbon County. My friends and I could see the sequel to "Redneck Romance" occurring in front of our eyes as braindead jocks and cheerleaders coupled up in high school.

We didn't have book burnings, like in "Runaway Train," but my friends and I sure as hell got our own taste of censorship with the "Tipper Sticker." Yeah, that little annoying black and white "Parental Advisory Explicit Lyrics" sticker that Tipper Gore and the Parents Music Resource Center forced record companies to slap on albums meant my friends and I had to figure out new ways to sneak suggestive and swear-filled CDs and tapes into our homes. We also had to find new places to hide them from our parents.

"He's Gone" made me want to steal my dad's two-tone brown-and-cream 1979 Ford XLT pick-up truck, hit the road and cure my case of small-town escapism. But, being 16 in 1993, that was impossible, because I wasn't allowed to leave the county. Honestly, it was probably for the best. No 16-year-old needs grand theft auto on their record. That's not going to get you into many colleges.

We had a "Drive-In" in Paris, Kentucky. We knew more than one "Headbangin' Stockboy." And we had our share of people who we called "The Weasel" or were at the very least weasel-y.

For me, the songs on those first two albums didn't feel just like songs. They felt like warning signs. Notes left in lockers from classmates who graduated a few years before. Inscriptions in yearbooks that laid out the dangers of getting too comfortable and staying in one spot for too long.

Those songs were also full of wit and humor, which wasn't something my friends and I were getting from the only rock station we could pick up in Paris. Buried between burned-out BTO jams and tired-ass Eagles songs was grunge – and there wasn't anything funny about that style of music. Guess it's hard to laugh on heroin.

Nine Pound Hammer showed me that you could be successful – at least that's what my friends and I assumed – being funny and satirical. We had no idea that the members of the band were barely making rent, constantly getting fired from jobs, on the road sleeping next to cat litter boxes and from time-to-time surviving on oranges and "free" sandwiches.

They might not have been in *Rolling Stone* or *Entertainment Weekly*, but Nine Pound Hammer was in the *Lexington Herald-Leader* newspaper frequently. We'd also heard at Cut Corner – Lexington's legendary record store, which sat across the street from the University of Kentucky – that the Hammer was killing it in Europe. Those same people at Cut Corner told us about all-ages shows on Sunday nights at a bar called The Wrocklage. That sent my friends and I racing to the *Herald-Leader* to see when the next time Nine Pound Hammer was playing an all-ages show.

Knowing my parents would never let me go to a bar at 16 years old, one friend (30 years later, I'll still protect my accomplice's identity) and I pulled the "I'm going over to so-and-so's house to work on this project I forgot about" ruse with our parents.

Given a 10 o'clock curfew, very begrudgingly, my friend and I left quaint Paris for the mean streets of Lexington 18 miles away. We knew full well that getting caught would mean we'd both be serving time in parental jail until our mid-30s.

After parking in a sketchy lot, we walked toward The Wrocklage, where it became instantly apparent just how much of a difference those 18 miles make. In Paris, the sidewalks were rolled up and Sunday afternoon football was wrapping up, but inside The Wrocklage, it was a mob scene. Anarchy and lunacy. The air was full of the smell of sweat, cigarette smoke and Saturday night's beer souring between the cracks and crevices in the floor.

Then there were the people. Kids our age were wearing JNCO Jeans, lip rings and hair the color of road construction vests – that wasn't happening in Paris, all we had were a few goth kids and mulleted metalheads. There were college kids and pseudo adults in flannel shirts and combat boots. And dudes dressed in black leather jackets like *Escape from New York* extras.

This was nothing like the only other concert I'd been to – which was with my parents – a 3 PM set by The Charlie Daniels Band in Opryland on a Thursday.

I don't remember much about the other bands that played that night at The Wrocklage. I don't remember Nine Pound Hammer's setlist or how many holes were in Scott's or Blaine's jeans, but I sure as hell remember when their mosh pit started. It was like being in a music video and a blender at the same time.

At 6' 2" and 135 pounds, I was fresh meat. Five steps into the pit, I was leveled by a 250-pound college student, who then politely picked me up off the floor. There was a sense of, "Am I going to make it home with all my teeth, much less make curfew?" mixed with "When can I do this again?"

That show, or getting leveled by somebody almost twice my size, was a wake-up call and a moment of confirmation. There was nothing like this in Paris, and I didn't want to stay there for the rest of my life and end up painting swimming pools, selling cars down at the Chevy dealership or building fences with the quarterback of our high school football team. Those jobs are all important, but they weren't for me.

I knew I wanted to do something creative, but music wasn't going to be it – there weren't many bands looking for high school trombone players. I decided I wanted to write. I thought if this band from Owensboro, Kentucky, could write songs that made me laugh, I could surely find a way to write things that made people laugh – like commercials or newspaper columns.

By the time I reached college at the University of Kentucky in the fall of 1995, Nine Pound Hammer had all but disappeared. No more all-ages shows. No band news. No website to see when or where they were playing next. So, I moved on to thousands of other bands. I visited Cut Corner – now across the street from my dorm – most weeks looking for "alternative rock," hip-hop and rock albums that hadn't been ruined by local rock radio. Things like Neil Young's *After The Gold Rush,* Jimi Hendrix's *Band of Gypsys* and something by the Rolling Stones called *Exile on Main Street.*

When Nashville Pussy started touring in 1996, I had no idea Blaine was in it. I didn't know that until a friend mentioned it to me in 1999 when I was living in Chicago writing ads for M&M's, Snicker's, Burger King and Visa. So, the next time Nashville Pussy came through Chicago, my friends and I went.

Seeing Blaine on stage for the first time in a completely different role was jarring. Even more jarring was seeing Ruyter Suys climb the scaffolding at the Metro and play face-melting solos in a leopard print bra and not much else. The music was a lot louder than Nine Pound Hammer, but I still connected with the writing, and their first couple of albums got me through more than a few cold January night jogs in Chicago.

After a few more Nashville Pussy shows, I somehow learned about the fan site NinePoundHammer.homestead.com, the band's reunion shows and *Kentucky Breakdown.* With Hammer playing shows again, I would routinely come home for shows and even managed to catch them at the Double Door in Chicago – that concert is still in my top five.

After nearly a decade in the Windy City, I'd grown tired of the pace, the taxes and having my groceries stolen every other week in the Jewel parking lot on Milwaukee Avenue. So, I moved to Louisville, Kentucky, which made life a little less stressful and afforded me the time and space to dive into projects that interested me, like woodworking, rebuilding vintage bicycles and recording music – I ditched the trombone. It also allowed me to write more for personal joy, which is how this book came about – that and a little help from my co-worker Christian Walsh who is a hell of a guy, writer and Scott Luallen's relative by marriage.

Struggling to find the right voice for a :15 TV spot for our local gas and electric company, Christian put me in touch with Scott for the role of a singing shrub that was dying from a gas leak. Real high-concept stuff.

Scott nailed the spot and made me wonder, "Why has nobody written a book about Nine Pound Hammer? They're one of the few cowpunk bands still standing. And why the hell aren't they bigger?"

After talking to Scott and Blaine, they both opened up their list of contacts and put me in touch with fans, friends, former drummers and bass players, members of other bands, booking agents, TV show creators and countless other individuals.

I initially expected countless tales of debauchery from years on the road. Sure, there are a few stories, but that's not this book. That's been done to death. This book is about their writing, their music, their observations on the world and the stories behind the songs – which are the things that made the bootleg cassette my friend gave me one of my favorite possessions as a teenager and still why I'm a fan of this band.

Okay. Enough of the opening act. It's time to "Put Some Gravy On It" and get this thing rolling.

AUTHOR'S NOTE

Writing a book in this style is a little like going to a party where you don't know anybody.

Usually, you're introduced to a lot of people. At first, their names might be a little challenging to remember, but once you've been there a little bit, you get in the flow of things. Next thing you know, that guy you met named Moses is sending you fun pieces of mail, Kelly and Shawn have invited you over to their house for a bourbon, and you're hanging out with Mike at his bar two days before Christmas at 10 in the morning.

So, go ahead, mingle and meet some new people.

CHAPTER 1
LAUGH AT THOSE WHO DON'T BELONG

If you're reading this, I'm assuming you know a little bit about the band Nine Pound Hammer. If you don't, well, you've stumbled into quite a book. (Are you sure you're not looking for the new Danielle Steel novel?)

Since Nine Pound Hammer formed in 1985, Blaine Cartwright and Scott Luallen have kept this seminal cowpunk band rolling along with the help of a Spinal Tapping level of bassists and drummers – eight each by my count.

Throughout this book Scott and Blaine are obviously your two main characters, but there's one more character that helped shape who they are, their personalities and their songs – the city of Owensboro, Kentucky.

In the '70s and '80s, Owensboro was your classic, mid-sized Southern river town. Kind of sleepy, not a lot of industry, plenty of farmland, very blue collar and very religious.

Owensboro, I love you, and I think everybody in this book loves you, but growing up there when Scott and Blaine did left a few marks.

Blaine: Growing up in Owensboro definitely influenced us. It made us determined to do something to get the fuck out of there. It was like a second-class city or whatever you call it. There were like 50,000 people, but it was pretty insular because there was no interstate.

Scott: I call us suburban rednecks. When I was a kid, I remember there was nothing behind our house, just corn and soybean fields. I would literally look out my window, and it was kind of like that line in "American Girl" – "Couldn't help thinkin' that there was a little more to life somewhere else." I thought, "God, is this little suburban thing it?"

Blaine: It was the kind of town you pretty much stayed in, drove around and saw the same people your whole life.

David Epperson (Former Nine Pound Hammer Guitarist): I just remember a lot of driving around, being bored and thinking Owensboro was a pretty sad place to grow up in. It seemed like it was the land that time had forgotten. Nobody ever came to play there musically. We were always trying to find beer. Never could. None of us had girlfriends except Scott and maybe Blaine. Hell, Blaine and I rode the bus home our last day of the senior year – that's how cool we were.

Mike Grimes (Friend and Classmate of Blaine and Scott. Owner of Grimey's New & Preloved Music, The Basement, and The Basement East in Nashville, TN): We were the guys who actually realized there has to be a fucking better way to live your life and do something without living in that motherfucking town. Any city that begins with a zero and ends with a zero, you should get the fuck out of.

Blaine: Owensboro was an okay town when I was riding my bike. Once we started driving cars, I wanted to start going other places. I had to get out and move somewhere. My nightmare was to be stuck there. In all honesty, it was awful, but that was my own personal, intense frustration, too, and my animosity towards the place ended a few years after I left.

If I'd stayed there, I would've been a dangerous person. Every time I had to come home and stay there for a few months, I felt like the biggest loser in the world and thought everyone was looking at me like that. I don't blame them. What was I supposed to say, "Hey, one of these days I'm going to be really cool, and you're going to be sorry." I wanted to leave because people that stayed there, their lives

9

went to crap. It was boring, and a lot of them were fucked up.

Sara Riney (Former Owensboroan, Friend of the Band): It just seemed like everybody in my hometown who a drank or got fucked up got stuck there for life. We knew people that would move away. "Oh yeah, John got out. He joined the Army, and now he's living in Arizona." But sooner or later, they'd be done in the military, come home, and they'd never get away again. People would get into college, and something fucked up would happen with their family, and they'd have to come home.

So there's the Sportscenter in Owensboro. It's like a 5,000-seat arena. It started falling into decline in the early '80s and they were talking about tearing it down, but it was going to cost too much to rebuild it. So they decided to renovate it. I was convinced that there was a giant magnet buried under it, and that's why they didn't tear it down – almost like a spaceship with some kind of magnetic field.

It was almost like you couldn't get away from it, and if you did, it just pulled you back. We called it the Curse of Owensboro.

One time my friend Todd had a job interview in Evansville. He got halfway across the bridge to Indiana, just outside of Owensboro, and his motorcycle broke down. It also seemed like when we'd try to leave town to go see a concert, we'd get outside the city limits, the car would break down.

I felt squished and claustrophobic all the time. It just felt oppressive and depressive. It was just boring, real churchy and judgy with lots of small-town bullshit where everybody's up your ass all the time.

Scott: It was conservative. I did have a song one time called "Churches and Liquor Stores," because there were as many liquor stores as there were churches – it was a bit of a Bible Belt paradox. On one side there was conservatism and religion, and on the other side all the Catholic girls were wild and people were drinking and partying.

Toby Myrick (Former Nine Pound Hammer Drummer): It all came from Owensboro – the words, the delivery, the stories.

Brian Pulito (Former Nine Pound Hammer Drummer, Engineer and Producer): You can't fake what they do. It comes from the heartland and from the gut. Yeah, it looks different, it feels different, but I think people get it. I think they feel it and love it because you've got rednecks in Europe, just like you do in the U.S. And they identify with that culture and see this band that represents that, even though they're from another country or halfway around the world. There's no substitute for it. That's why they've been able to do this for so long.

Mike Grimes: Their songs were written about life in a small town – "The Cadillac Inn," "Run Fat Boy Run," all these songs basically had the context of living in redneck, fucking Owensboro, Kentucky, with this satirical fucking take on it all. I think about it, and I'm like, that's why I still call them my fucking heroes.

Blaine: Before my mom died, when she was in the hospital, I went down to the river and got a drink. I started looking around, and I thought, "This might be it for me in Owensboro." I felt really sad because Owensboro definitely made us, even though I hated it. That was my personal thing, but my ghosts didn't live there for long. I'd proved everyone wrong decades ago, so after I started doing really well, I didn't think anything negative about it at all.

CHAPTER 2
THE WAY IT IS AND THE WAY IT OUGHTA BE

Scott: Both my parents were going to Transylvania University in Lexington, Kentucky, in 1960-61. My mom grew up in Columbia, Tennessee. She was a really good athlete and was Miss Transylvania in 1962. My dad was a bit older than her. He grew up in Paris, Kentucky. When my dad was a kid, his mom abandoned him, so my granddad and one of his girlfriends, Willie Soper, helped raise him. We called her Aunt Willie. I thought she was my aunt – I didn't know any different.

I was born on October 15, 1963, in Lexington. We were there for a bit, then we moved to Louisville and eventually made our way to Owensboro when I was about two. My parents moved into a subdivision called Thoroughbred Acres.

Blaine: Scott actually grew up in the subdivision where my mom grew up. When my mom was a kid, it was a brand-new place called Thoroughbred Acres, and every street was named after a Kentucky Derby winner. Everybody had those big gas lamps at the end of their driveways with little gold horse heads, and every house had their address stenciled on the curb.

Scott: My dad got a job at Western Kentucky Gas, and my mom became a teacher at Daviess County High School. She was the women's high school basketball coach. I was a gym rat. I loved basketball. My sister played, too.

My dad wasn't cut out for Owensboro – he was like from *Mad Men*. My parents split up when I was eight. That was not great, but it did open up the world to me. My dad took me to Gettysburg, Toronto, and a bunch of other places. It really educated me and showed me there was a bigger world out there. It was cool, but it came with a price.

My grandad was in WW2 and had a scrapbook from Iwo Jima with pictures of dead Japanese soldiers in it. He lived in a trailer park, and I remember my dad taking *The Outlaws* cassette over to him – that's all he listened to.

He died of the DTs from alcohol withdrawal in the Veterans Affairs (VA) hospital. My grandad moved around a lot and worked on farms. He was actually a very successful thoroughbred trainer. I didn't know him that well. His nickname was Hoss Doc or Doc. I look just like him.

His family was from Coal Creek, Tennessee, which is now Rocky Top, Tennessee, which is right off I-75. Doc's grandad wrote a song about the Coal Creek mine disaster. Doc had two brothers – Brooks and Joe Bill. All three of them were from Paris, Kentucky. All alcoholics – Joe Bill did have 24 years of sobriety. Doc and Brooks were the basis for the song "Feelin' Kinda Froggy."

My mom's dad, "Peepaw," owned the first Ace Hardware in Tennessee. He was your classic hunter/fisherman and racist as hell. He was funny, but not real sweet. My meemaw was a saint who visited me in a dream while she was dying in a nursing home. She was the sweetest.

Blaine: My grandfather Pat Patterson, my mom's dad, was one of the four Fighting Pattersons of World War II from Princeton, Kentucky. My grandfather's brothers, Homer Ray and Claude, worked at the Kentucky State Penitentiary in Eddyville. Homer Ray was an accountant, and Claude worked in the guard tower. When I was a kid, my grandfather would take us there to visit them at the penitentiary. We'd have to walk past jail cells, and my grandfather would say, "Don't listen to these guys. Don't talk to them."

Uncle Homer Ray had a trustee who cooked for him – trustees were like servants. You were still in jail, but you had your own little house. You usually became a trustee when you were on your way out. Uncle Homer Ray's trustee played games with us when we were kids.

One time, I asked his trustee how come he didn't quit, and the trustee thought it was funny. He told my uncle and my aunt – they all laughed.

Making no money, my grandfather came to Owensboro, which was kind of a burgeoning city at the time. He got a job at the Dr. Pepper plant for $12 a day, which was a fortune then.

His brothers stayed on the farm – that side of the family ended up in jail, or they ended up just fucked-up or dead. I am so glad my grandfather got the hell off the farm.

He had two kids and four grandkids – a doctor; a lawyer; my sister, who was a star athlete, a valedictorian, a prom queen, she also got a master's degree and is a teacher in Louisville, Kentucky; and [me] a Grammy-nominated musician. That's pretty good. That's the educated side of the family.

My dad was from Henderson, Kentucky. He was in college at Western Kentucky University (WKU) in Bowling Green when he met my mom – she was a 16-year-old high school cheerleader. She got pregnant with me. It was 1963, so they had to keep it. She married my father, and they lived in Bowling Green for the first couple years of my life – the only memory I have of living there is when my dad was going for his master's. Me, him and my mom were sitting around the trailer watching *The Everly Brothers Show.*

We lived in Henderson for a while and moved to Owensboro when I was three. We lived kind of in a redneck neighborhood before we moved to a suburban house on a very busy corner. That was a big step. My mom would always try to get us out of these redneck neighborhoods. Eventually she became a kindergarten teacher, and Dad became a high school math teacher. He coached every possible sport – cross country, track, swimming.

They even would lifeguard in the summer to make extra money. My parents worked their asses off. They were gone all the time because they were always working, and they were both trying to get their master's degrees while raising two kids.

The subdivisions that Scott and I grew up in were almost connected. If you wanted to go from his neighborhood to my neighborhood, there was a huge cornfield that never had any corn in it. Between us was a Catholic school where my mom was a teacher's assistant there for a while. I'd go there and just sit. I was real quiet, man.

The church attached to the Catholic school was always open. Once, my friend Jeff, his brother Eddie and I were playing *Encyclopedia Brown* there, and we were thirsty. Now there was a water fountain outside that was basically the equivalent of drinking out of a hot hose.

So, Jeff and Eddie said, "Hey, we found some water inside." It was really cold, so we drank a bunch of it. Then we looked at the cooler it came out of. Inscribed on it was a sign that said, "Holy Water." We start freaking out and saying, "What's going to happen to us? God's mad at us." We rode our bikes home so fucking fast. I ran into the house and said, "Mom, I drank holy water!" She said, "It's okay, just don't do that again."

Scott: Blaine and I first met when we were 10 years old. I was at Immaculate Parish's summer program. We were getting ready for a bike race, and I had a brand-new bike.

Blaine: We met because my friend came across the street and said, "Hey, they're having a race down by the T-ball fields at the school, and they're giving away prizes to the first three finishers. Everyone's going." I had just gotten a new bike from Western Auto with a banana seat. It was the coolest bike in the store. It had streamers and it was fast, but I couldn't touch the pedals on it 100%. My parents said, "Eh, he'll grow into it, he'll wreck a few times, he'll be fine. It'll be good for him."

So, I went to the race and wound up next to Scott. I got on my bike, I fell over, and my pedals went right through Scott's spokes. After everyone took off, it took us about 20 seconds before we could get untangled. Even with all that, he almost caught up to everybody – he came in fourth. I said, "Whoa, I just screwed up." When I finally got to the finish line, I just heard someone say, "There he is!" So, I rode all the way home. I just rode off – yeah, that was our first meeting.

Scott: I was real mad at him.

Blaine: I didn't know Scott because he went to one of the county schools, and I was at the city school.

When I was in sixth grade, my parents pulled me out in the middle of the fucking school year, which was not a smart thing to do. I had my shit down in my working-class neighborhood. But my mom was like, "We have to move to a different school district so we can get you out of the Owensboro city schools. You don't want to go to high school there. You can drink Coca-Cola in the classrooms, and the girls don't wear bras."

So, I got moved to Scott's school, which was Burns Middle School.

CHAPTER 3
LOOKIN' FOR SOMEBODY

Scott: Blaine and I knew each other in middle school a little bit, but we kind of became friends in high school on a trip to Louisville when I was on the basketball team. At first I thought, "Man, he's quiet." The thing about Blaine, he's naturally introverted.

Blaine: One of my dad's best friends coached the basketball team, and he talked me into keeping stats, which meant I got out of class and got to ride the team bus to games. One of the trips, they took the junior varsity team. Scott was there, and we talked about music a bunch.

Scott: Music became an escape for Blaine and me.

I still remember my first concert. My dad took me and my sister to see Jerry Lee Lewis at the Executive Inn in Evansville in 1974. I was 12 years old, and that concert made a big impression on me. It was in this smoky bar, and I was drinking kiddie cocktails. It was like, "This is what you do, dude! You get drunk in a honky-tonk on Coke and Sprite with a bunch of cherries in it."

Around that time, maybe freshman year, me and my friend Hillbilly John Hill went down the street in my neighborhood and met up with these guys Johnny and Nicky Clark. Nicky showed me how to play "Train Kept A Rollin.'" They also had weed, and I reallllly liked it.

I had these hot, crazy babysitters that would flash their boobs at me and hang out in the backyard getting high. One of them gave me a shotgun hit.[1] Nothing happened. I remember Foghat was playing.

Blaine: Yeah, he started early. He started everything early. I'm sure he regrets it now, but he definitely was a pioneer. He would smoke before he went to school.

Scott: Steve Roberts and Glen Lott lived in the neighborhood, too, and they had a garage band. They were doing "Ain't Talkin' 'bout Love" by Van Halen. I don't know how, but I ended up behind the mic. I was eating a popsicle and stoned and started singing. That was the first time I ever did that, and I thought, "Okay, that was cool. This is something I like."

I went and saw a local band called TF Much (Too Fucking Much) at a concert down at the river during the hydro races. I loved those – still do! My mom told me to cover my cup with my hand so no one would drop acid in it.

Blaine: I think Scott was impressed that I had gone to all these concerts, too. The big one was KISS. I saw them in 1976 on the Destroyer Tour in Evansville, Indiana. Bob Seger opened up. I was 12, and KISS was really controversial at the time.

I had a friend, David Epperson, he called me up and said, "Do you want to go to see KISS?" I thought for sure my parents would say no way, but they had no idea who they were.

My parents always were like, "You've got to make friends. If anyone asks you to do anything, go play. You gotta get out there." My parents were always pushing socialization instead of letting me be myself. They made me go to KISS, seriously.

David Epperson: The real life-changing moment, I thought, for Blaine was when we conned my mom into taking us to go see KISS at Roberts Stadium back in '76. That to me was instrumental in Blaine becoming totally obsessed with music.

---

[1] When one individual blows pot smoke into somebody else's mouth.

18

Blaine: I was scared. I heard they might kill a goat or something, and we didn't have any way to really dispel those rumors back then. I also had a fear – like most kids – I thought they were going to make me dance because my parents had gone to see the Four Seasons a month before. They said everybody dressed nice and danced a little. They thought that's what KISS was going to be like. They did give me one piece of advice, "Keep your hand over your Coca-Cola because hippies will drop acid[2] in it."

David Epperson: I do remember there were guys in the row right in front of us smoking pot. That was the first time we'd ever smelled it. My mom tapped me on the shoulder, pointed and said, "Look, potheads."

Blaine: Some guy passed out. I thought he was dead, turns out he was just really high. Bob Seger closed with "Katmandu," and these young cougar chicks in front of me started bumping. You know, kind of dancing? That scared the shit out of me.

Then KISS came out, and that was definitely geared more towards me. It was like a circus. I barely remember anything. All my senses were overwhelmed. It was loud. It was chaotic. I just remember my mind being blown. I was changed. After that, I got an acoustic guitar and started taking lessons from some guy that was trying to teach me how to play "Desperado" by The Eagles, which I'd never even heard. It didn't go well, so I gave that up and said, "Well, that's not going to happen. I'm not going to be a musician."

Sophomore and junior year were turning points for Scott and Blaine. They started hanging out more, going to more concerts and visiting the local record stores. They also quit sports – real shame, they probably could have taken district, who knows, maybe even regionals.

Scott: By junior year I was quitting basketball, and we had a little clique of jocks and ex-jocks. I became the stoner of the group. Blaine

---

[2] There must have been a lot of free acid back then. Where is all this free acid now?

was kind of the head honcho. He would write things in the high school newspaper, like "Springsteen kicks AC/DC's ass" and "Listening to AC/DC is like banging on a brass bed with a hammer." He did that stuff just to piss off the jocks, and that caused some tensions.

Blaine: Scott and I were both okay athletes. He was better than I was. I ran cross country and track. I finally quit that – it was a waste of time. It's like we did sports all the time when we were kids, but then all of a sudden we were interested in music.

Scott: There were about 10 or 12 of us, kind of John Hughes nerds and ex-jocks. Girls liked us, and other guys didn't like that because we were cool. We were smart, and we made fun of people. I mean, we thought we were cool. We were cool – but thought we were cool, too.

Blaine: Scott was a popular, very confident dude. He was friends with everybody. He didn't really run with the popular clique. He kind of did his own thing. He was a good friend for hanging out with. We would just smart off about everything. I think he had more fun hanging around us than he did the jocks.

Speaking of hanging out, what were the guys hanging out and listening to music-wise around this time?

Scott: Blaine and I talk about this a lot – both our dads were playing country music in the background all the time.

Blaine: My dad listened to cool music. Both of our dads did.

Scott: It seemed like my dad always had that Willie Nelson and Waylon Jennings *The Outlaws* record on in the background. And when we'd go stay at his house and sleep on an air mattress in the living room, it was *Johnny Cash's Greatest Hits*. I remember falling asleep to "Big River."

Blaine: My dad had a couple of Johnny Cash and Elvis records and stuff like Johnny Preston's "Running Bear." He also had a lot of Everly Brothers. He listened to the Four Seasons and a lot of oldies.

'50s music would ring out all the time – Young Belmont and a lot of Buddy Holly.

I liked all his '50s stuff because my Great Aunt Lela and Great Uncle Bub had a record store, The Record Shop in Henderson. When I was a kid, my parents would drop me off, and I'd spend all day there. I would walk around, and they would give me records, bubblegum stuff from the mid-60s – "Yummy Yummy Yummy," "Wooly Bully" and "Gitarzan."

I'd go there and play records on my aunt's record player. I remember "Great Balls Of Fire" being under two minutes. I was obsessed with numbers and times. It was the shortest record I'd ever seen. I was like, "This can't be any good, it's too short." I put it on, and the way it blasted out of that speaker – it had this little edge to it, and I just freaked out. I played it over and over and over and over again. I'd flip it over and play "You Win Again" and flip it over to get a break from "Great Balls Of Fire."

When I was in third grade, I had this vision – I saw myself doing something where everyone in my class was dancing to that song. But I wasn't dancing. I was in charge of something. Maybe I was like a DJ? I didn't think about playing music myself, but I liked the idea of me being in charge of it.

At some point my dad started listening to Merle Haggard, and we made so much fun of him, but then we started liking it. For Christmas he wanted a copy of *Willie Nelson Live.* I didn't know what he was talking about, but I did know you could order these 8-track tapes – eight of them for a penny – I did that all the time. That was how I got everyone's Christmas presents and then a couple months later, I'd get in trouble for not paying the bill.

On that Willie Nelson record, the first song is "I Gotta Get Drunk." Me, my sister and my mom listened to it and thought, "This is terrible. This is the dumbest thing we've ever heard." But after a little bit, I started liking it. I started playing it for my friends as a joke at first, and then they'd go, "It's pretty good."

One of my friends, an actual farmer, was into George Jones, and that's when the country stuff started kicking in. Everybody loved Johnny Cash – it's so close to rock and roll. We started liking all this country music because you could hear what great musicians they were, and there was something about the storytelling. Punk lends itself to that.

Scott: First real record I bought was one of those K-Tel compilations, and it had "Sweet Home Alabama" and "Radar Love" on it. That really moved me.

We also had a dance at Burns Middle School in sixth grade with a band called Freedom Jam. The first song they played was "Razamanaz" by Nazareth, and then they played "Rock and Roll All Nite." That made a huge impression on me, too. I floated out of the gym that night.

Fast forward and here comes the KISS records and Aerosmith and Ted Nugent. We were in Owensboro – there wasn't anything to do except sit up in your room and listen to music or get in trouble sneaking out and sneaking alcohol.

Blaine: I wasn't drinking or anything back then but, my dad, yeah, he was known for drinking. He was just a sloppy beer drunk. I had to get my dad out of the bars a lot. One time he was driving home and was going into the guardrail, and I had to grab the wheel. Yeah, I had to drive him home when I was 14.

Sometimes my mom would drive to the bar where my dad was and say, "Go get your father." I'd go in and Dad's like, "Want a pizza? Why don't you sit down and have a pizza?" Meanwhile my mom would just be out there sitting and waiting.

He wasn't happy. After he got my mother pregnant, that ended his life basically. Back when I was just starting to fool around with girls a little bit, he was just like, "You want some condoms?" He was offering condoms when I was 12, and I hadn't even kissed a girl yet. I said, "No." He was like, "Are you sure?"

We had parties at my house a lot. I saw my teachers drunk a lot, because my parents were teachers and they'd throw parties. I

22

remember coming home from work one time in high school, and there were all my teachers and the mayor – they were drunk and dancing in my front room. They got a hold of my 8-track collection, and they were dancing to Chuck Berry.

We had a very casual house. Yeah, it was pretty loose. My dad could be intense at times, and they were hard on me, but if you wanted to come over to someone's house, read rock magazines, listen to music and just chill out – that was the place.

Scott: We had a record store in Owensboro, a really cool one, Wax Works. The owner went to my church. They had all the singles, all the Top 40 stuff. I remember I bought Van Halen's *Women & Children First* the first day it came out there. That was my main love, Van Halen. I drove to Louisville with Jack Hicks and Jimmy Crisp in 1980 to see the Women & Children Tour. That was mind-blowing!

We also had this head shop in a record store called New Attitude Records. Carl Graham was the guy who owned that. That's where Blaine and I really kind of started hanging out together.

Blaine: We'd ride our bikes there as soon as it would open. I would just sit there and ask Carl about a million bands.

Scott: That's where Blaine got all his punk stuff. I was a metalhead, but he was diving into Lou Reed and stuff like that. So, we would hang out at New Attitude Records, and that's when the new wave of British heavy metal was coming out, like '80, '81. All the UFO, Tygers of Pan Tang and Def Leppard – all that was hitting. Carl would push all that on me, because that's what he was into.

Blaine: Carl always steered me towards the punk stuff, and we'd ask him to play certain albums he had open. We'd just listen and hang out and read magazines. We knew to stay out of his way if someone asked for something.

Back then you had to seek stuff out, too. I'd buy albums from the import section without listening to them. He was trying to introduce something new to the town and to us. He was a big deal.

David Epperson: Blaine's record collection, even then, went from the Ramones to Sex Pistols, Aretha Franklin to Martha and the Vandellas and all the Sun Records stuff. He was into Ted Nugent for a long time, too. He was listening to stuff nonstop. We'd go to Pizza Hut after a ball game or something in high school. He'd get $10 worth of quarters and just play every song on the jukebox until his money ran out.

Blaine: I was 14. Mowing yards and spending all my money on vinyl. That's when my record collection started getting out of hand. That's also when I found out my great-grandmother lived across the street from a used comic book place in Owensboro. They started having records that were cheap, like a dollar. They had a lot of classic stuff – Neil Young's *After the Gold Rush*, Jimi Hendrix's *Are You Experienced?*

I would get in trouble for buying so many records. So, what I would do is, I'd leave my window open, go to the record store, buy a bunch and toss them in my window. Then I'd walk in the front of the house with one record. My parents would say, "Oh you got a record? Let me see."

That's when I started getting *Rolling Stone* and going to the library and looking up albums.

That's another thing we had in Owensboro, a Carnegie Library – they were the biggest. Thank God.

Because my mom was a teacher, she had an audio-visual card, so there was no limit to how many records I could get and keep for a month. I would basically go to the library, get a bunch of records, and they'd eventually call up our house and say they needed them back. I was listening to Springsteen, the Rolling Stones, Muddy Waters, Blind Lemon Jefferson, B.B. King and Johnny Cash.

It seemed like there was new music every day, and if there was something new, you wanted to be the first to hear it, like the Sex Pistols. They got a bad rep in America. They were so notorious. I remember there was an AP News story about them.

Then, I heard they were going to play "Pretty Vacant" on the local AM Radio. After they played it, I was like, "That's it? That sounds like 'Wooly Bully.'" Then the DJ said, "Well, there it is. That's what all the fuss is about. That's the Sex Pistols." I liked it and started thinking to myself, "Oh no, I like the Sex Pistols. I'm a punk. What am I going to do? I already stand out enough."

Scott: Sophomore year we did this thing in the talent contest. We were called The Clappers. It was this thing Blaine put together. He had a live mic and sang over "God Save the Queen," and we were in the background pantomiming on guitars. We came out to "Pilot of the Airways," by Juice Newton, which I had recorded on my tape recorder, and then there was the sound of a needle going across a record. Then the Sex Pistols kicked in.

Blaine: We played all this over a PA, and I sang lyrics like, "I want to rape your mom and kill your dog." We dressed like what we thought was punk. I think I was wearing an athletic shirt and blue jeans with holes in them. When we got on stage and had this powerful music behind us, that's one thing that kind of got us thinking, "That'd be cool to learn how to play."

Scott: He had his Lou Reed sunglasses on, and we had these crappy guitars not plugged into anything. There were two other guys, David Epperson and Mark Ralph. Mark was a senior, and he was just back there banging on metal trash cans that I stole from my mom. He's smashing them with croquet mallets and baseball bats. And Blaine had a fire extinguisher.

Blaine: I stole a fire extinguisher, which was really easy to do. You just took them off the wall. It was a powder one, and those things go everywhere.

Scott: People said the first 30 seconds were the greatest thing they'd ever seen. But it went on too long. We were breaking disco records and throwing them out in the crowd. It was mayhem. The judges said, "If you would've stopped after the first thing, you would've won." But then we did "Blitzkrieg Bop" and almost got kicked out of school.

Blaine: It was great. I think for talent, we scored straight zeroes. My dad actually saw it and said, "If you had gone off after the first thing, y'all would have won." He was impressed. He thought it was funny.

Scott: For the first time, we got that crowd thing. It was like, "Oh yeah! There's something to this."

Now nothing's really being said about getting a band together yet, but we started going to concerts more.

Blaine: Scott was a few months older than the rest of the class. He got his license before me, and we'd drive around and go to shows. We went and saw Chuck Berry down on the river. I think there were four or five hundred people down there – it was great.

Scott: We all went, hung out, drank Boone's Farm and watched Chuck Berry.

Blaine didn't go to this show, but I went to see Ozzy Osbourne like a month after Randy Rhoads had died. I drove Carl Graham from New Attitude Records and a couple members of this local metal band called Struggling.

The big rumor was, Randy Rhoads wasn't really dead and he was going to come out of a casket and start playing guitar. He didn't. I dropped acid and had to drive everybody home. I was 16 or 17, and it was raining. I'm in my mom's car with a heavy metal band in the backseat driving through a thunderstorm. It was crazy as shit.

Blaine: His dad left home, and that fucked him up a little, I think. Divorce was a big deal in the '70s. It was a social stigma, and he was a popular dude. He ended up taking care of his brother and sister a lot. He was confident, and he handled it, but I think it's one reason he's always wanted a normal life.

His dad and mom, they let him get away with murder. His dad couldn't say anything to him because he had left home.

He had a party one time and had to clean up before his mom got home – the house was ankle deep in beer cans. I went over there, saw how huge the party was and just said, "Screw this." So I went back the next morning and kind of helped him clean up. He got it done in time, but it was insane.

He had his own room – it was actually two rooms. He got to play music loud, or he'd tell his mom, "I got a headache, I'm going to bed." Then he'd sneak out.

Scott: I was smoking pot at Carl Graham's house one night, and he showed me a copy of *Cosmos*, and I started tripping out about the universe. It left a big impression on me. This is when I was having an affair with my English teacher. The pursuit was mutual, but it wasn't really healthy, and it kind of fucked me up.

Anyway, she was really mad that I was out smoking weed with Carl – and I got in trouble.

People knew about the affair. I remember one time, I went to WKU to see David Epperson and my friend Steve Terrell. When I walked in their dorm room, there were a bunch of guys just sitting around drinking Busch Light. I didn't know these guys, but one of them said to me, "Oh wait! Are you the teacher fucker?"

Blaine: Scott and I mostly got in mild trouble for being smart-asses and trying to entertain ourselves. Every day seemed like a challenge. I knew I was going to get out someday, but it seemed like it was taking forever, and there was nothing I could do about it. School was very frustrating, and there really wasn't a creative outlet.

I was kind of wandering aimlessly. We got shit at home. We got shit at school. We got shit from our old coaches because we quit. We got shit all around. We didn't have anyone. We had ourselves. That was it. We didn't have instruments. We were just trying to survive. We probably bullied as many people as bullied us. We burned bridges – a lot of them.

I think Scott and I both graduated in the top third of the class. We should have been in the top 10. We had a couple subjects pull us down, and we just had shitty attitudes.

We had typing together our senior year, and we were going to get F's. We talked all the time and got way far behind. We were both already going to college anyway, so this class did not matter other than actually learning to type, which we had total disdain for. "We're not going to learn to type. What for? You're never going to have a typewriter in front of you all the time. When's that ever going to happen?" So we just read rock magazines and put our feet up on the table right in front of the teacher.

We were both smart, and everyone knew it, too.

I wanted to write for TV shows, and that wasn't a farfetched thing. I had my parents and everyone saying, "You should be a writer. Go to school for that."

I thought, maybe I can do something creative and use music like Scorsese does. You know, make a movie and throw in obscure songs. I thought, "That's what I'm going to do." Then I saw Bruce Springsteen on The River tour, 1981 in Cincinnati. It was the last stop on a year-and-a-half tour, and that's still the best concert I've ever seen – I know most people wouldn't guess that about me. I was like, "This guy's got it figured out. He's got music. He's kind of acting. He's got this Al Pacino thing going on." I envied the guy, and I didn't want to envy anything or anybody. I was like, "Man, I have to try to do that somehow, but I can't even play guitar."

I knew I'd be starting at square one, but I got a cheap electric guitar when I was 18 and actually went and took some good lessons. I had a teacher who taught me how to play the Ramones and Chuck Berry. That was it. Seriously, that was it. He taught me how to play bar chords. I was like, "That's it?" That made the Ramones and Chuck Berry worth practicing. Also, electric guitars are way easier to play, and you tend to make noise with them, too, which makes you start wanting to play.

Before we graduated high school, our clique started talking about forming a band, but we all just went to college. I didn't want to go to college. I went kicking and screaming because back then when you

28

were 18, you were either in the army, in college, or your parents kicked you out. I shouldn't have gone. Scott and I both flunked out pretty fast.

Scott: I went to the University of Kentucky, but man, I just wasn't cut out for it. I liked partying.

CHAPTER 4
HEY! HO! LET'S GO!

If I've learned anything from interviewing Scott and Blaine and their friends, it's this – know your damn Ramones. After our first interview, Scott sent me his four-hour-and-26-minute Ramones Spotify playlist.

Growing up, I never gave the Ramones much pause because classic rock radio in Lexington, Kentucky, in the '90s ruined them for me. There were no deep cuts, and the songs we did hear didn't seem like they had any depth to them. All we got served was "Blitzkrieg Bop" and maybe "I Wanna Be Sedated" once a week. Compared to grunge and the sonics of classic rock, those Ramones songs just sounded tired and flat.

But after digging into Scott's playlist, I was wrong. There's humor, there's insanity, there's heartbreak, there's vulnerability and there's pretty much a Ramones record for everybody.

Without the Ramones, there is no Nine Pound Hammer, so here's how four New York legends influenced some punks from Owensboro – 1, 2, 3, 4!

Blaine: I got the Sex Pistols record, and it grew on me so fucking fast. I was like, "What do I get now?" When I went to visit my grandmother in Henderson, there was a place called Matt's Newsstand where I could get *Cream* magazine and check out other punk bands, and I was like, "Oh, the Ramones."

I got *Rocket to Russia* and did not like it at first because it didn't sound near as heavy as the Sex Pistols. I didn't get it. I got the Beach Boys factor of it, but I didn't *want* the Beach Boys. I *wanted* the Sex Pistols again. I *wanted* anger and heavy guitars. Sonically, it just wasn't there for me like the fucking Pistols record – that thing was huge. *Rocket to Russia* grew on me, but the Ramones' live record, *It's Alive*, was what really did it for me. That album converted people, because everyone who listened to Judas Priest and other heavy stuff would hear that and realize this stuff was just as cool.

The Ramones were a big, big deal, and we definitely copied their style. Also, I was not a good guitar player back then, but I knew how to make a bar chord. I fooled around on an amp one day. I put all this distortion on it and figured out "Blitzkrieg Bop." That's how we started writing songs – for our first couple records, that's pretty much it. There are a couple other chords and a couple of riffs, but it's pretty much just bar chords like the Ramones.

Scott: They are what makes "this" Nine Pound Hammer. We had a vision of what we wanted to create. I wanted to recreate the intensity of going to see the Ramones and that honky tonk show I saw with Jerry Lee Lewis – that and Johnny Cash and Jason & The Scorchers all mashed up together. Granted, the Scorchers were doing this in Nashville, but ours was the Kentucky version of that.

We wanted this symbiotic thing between us and the crowd like the Ramones had. It's like, "Are you here to get fucking wild and to really have fun and laugh?" It's that interchange and recreating that in a small, intimate setting – a sweaty, hot, intense experience where we get something from you and you're getting something from us.

I also loved that the Ramones mainly wrote about shit they did in everyday life. I connected with it, and that's kind of what we started to do. It's like, I've baled hay, I've been frog gigging and I've shot weapons – but I've never been deer hunting. I can't tell you how much the Ramones were at the foundation of this – everything came out of that. All the other punk came out of that. Everything.

Blaine: If the Ramones hadn't happened, we wouldn't have known how to do anything. They were something we could do immediately. It sounded cool, it was fun, and I can still do it as good as anyone.

31

Scott: It's simple, but it ain't easy. The arrangements, they really stuck to that pop song blueprint. I remember sitting in David Epperson's bedroom listening to the Ramones' cover of "Surfin' Bird." It was just crazy – the humor, the intensity of the music was like, this is how you do it.

When *Rock 'n' Roll High School* came out, we snuck out of the house to go see it at the Rio Drive-In Theatre across the river in Indiana.

Blaine: No one knew who the Ramones were, and no one knew that movie. But Scott convinced this dude, Allen Waltrip, to take us. Scott actually put pillows in his bed to make it look like he was asleep. He climbed over the fence, met us on a dead-end street and jumped in the car.

We got to the drive-in, and we had one of those crappy speakers you put on your window. We were blasting it and then, holy shit! It was like the first time I heard "Great Balls of Fire." It had this edge to it, and I just freaked out.

We were convinced that Johnny Ramone was the best guitar player ever because he was so fast. I thought it sounded great. His guitar was really loud, especially through that little speaker. It was like seeing them live. They were playing right there on a big screen above a grassy field, and people were eating corn dogs and drinking Coke and Dr. Pepper.

Scott: In '84, Blaine shows up at my mom's house in his dad's Thunderbird with the new *Too Tough to Die* cassette. He's like, "Oh my God! You got to listen to this!" So we went out driving and listening to it.

Blaine: Oh God, we played the Ramones on a jambox[3] and drove through some poor farmer's field. I don't know what we really did to the field, but it wasn't good.

---

[3] Jambox/boombox is a pop/soda situation.

Scott: *Too Tough to Die* was like the best-produced Ramones record to that date. It was super intense – "Mama's Boy," "Too Tough to Die," "Endless Vacation." Again, it's an acquired taste. Either you get it or you don't. You can handle it or you can't.

Blaine: Scott and I saw them tons of times. The first time I saw them live was in '84 in Houston, Texas, on the *Too Tough to Die* tour, with my friend Randy Ratliff. Instead of pogoing, everyone started stage diving. I didn't know what was going on. People were slam dancing, and I was ready to dance up front, but I kept getting knocked away by these dudes.

In '86 or '87, the Ramones were playing Bogarts in Cincinnati, and all the local punks would say, "They should have retired a long time ago. They're terrible." And then 10 years later, those same people were saying, "Oh my God, the Ramones are the greatest!!!" So when we started playing, we were filling a void. I still think we are.

Scott: Blaine and I saw the Ramones at the Jockey Club in '87 in Newport, Kentucky. It was this rundown-ass club that was packed, and people were slamming. It was hot chaos, and nobody was really in charge. You have to remember, the Ramones weren't these icons, and they still weren't really revered. If they somehow survived and were back out there touring right now, it would look like all these other legacy tours – it would be huge. But back then it was maybe 350, 400 people at shows.

Blaine: The really good show was at Kings Island[4] on the *Escape from New York* tour. It was Blondie, The Tom Tom Club, and the Ramones. They would rotate who was headlining. The Ramones were headlining that night, and there were probably 6,000 people.

---

[4]If you're from the Kentucky area, you know Kings Island is a giant theme and water park just north of Cincinnati where kids run free on cotton candy highs and parents' wallets run low. If you're not from around here, go watch the 1973 cinematic gem "The Cincinnati Kids" starring the world-renowned comedy troupe, *The Brady Bunch*. Pure gold.

Scott: I met them when they played Kings Island. I weaseled my way backstage with a friend, Kelli, who was a DJ. We were sitting right by Joey. He had an ankle brace, and he was lacing it up.

They had a Chinese buffet backstage, and I was standing there eating broccoli when this security guy came up to me and said, "What are y'all doing back here?" I said, "Eating broccoli." He went, "Oh, okay." I Jedi mind-tricked him. He left us alone, and I gave CJ Ramone, who was playing bass for them, a Nine Pound Hammer cassette.

CHAPTER 5
FROM HELL TO TEXAS
(Yeah, it's a Nashville Pussy song, just go with it.)

Blaine: After high school, I went to WKU for two semesters, but the second semester, I didn't go to class. I had a 0.0 GPA. My mom went to her grave not knowing that. Back then they mailed you your grades. I just tore up the envelope.

I went to WKU to study communications, but after I saw Springsteen I was like, I have to do this or I'm going to die. David Epperson and I were going to form a band, and basically I said, "I've got to quit college because I want to learn how to play guitar, which is going to take a year or two. You guys go to college. I'm just going to write songs and play guitar. I can't do both."

I decided I wanted to be a rock star, and my family said, "What are you even talking about?"

I was like, "I'll repay you one day, you'll see. I'll figure it out." They said, "You don't even know how to play guitar." They thought I was too much of a dreamer and had very unrealistic expectations based on nothing real at all.

This was '84. I was back in Owensboro, living with my parents. I was working at Hardee's, and I had a girlfriend. Then I just ran away to Texas with Randy.

Randy Ratliff (Friend of Blaine and Scott): My sophomore year of college, I put all my tuition money up my nose, and, well, mostly little girls' noses around me because of what they would do for cocaine.

So, one day I called Blaine, and I said, "Man, what are you doing? This school shit's bullshit. Let's go on the road, man. Let's go be rock stars." Now I can't sing and at that time, I couldn't play a musical instrument, but I'm arrogant – so that didn't matter.

I came home from college and was dating a Black girl named Ava. That did not go over well with my family, and one day everything kind of came to a head. I lived on a farm, and my mom was mad, so she bought me out of my tobacco crop. I called Blaine and said, "I've got money. Do you want to go?" He said, "Yes."[5]

Blaine: My parents found out I was going right before I left. My father thought it was a good idea. He thought I should go out there and sow some oats. He didn't want to spend any money sending me back to school unless I wanted to go. So he thought the best thing was to scare me with real life.

My mom asked if it was something they did. I'm like, "No, I hate this place. I want to go somewhere." I wanted to go to L.A. and play music, but we ended up in Texas. My mom cried, and my dad just thought I was going to get bored and come back.

Randy Ratliff: I go over with Ava and pick up Blaine, and our friend Brent Ford[6] went with us, too.

Blaine: Brent tagged along just for the hell of it.

Randy Ratliff: We hit the road and went to New Orleans first. Then we wound up in Galveston, Texas. The day after we got there, I had to send Ava back because the cops were looking for us. She told me

---

[5] At the time in Kentucky, tobacco was the same price as gold. It wasn't uncommon in my high school for kids to show up with flatbeds of it and mid-day take off down to the tobacco barns to sell what they had worked all summer for.

[6] Brent Ford is Suzanne Ford's dead name. Suzanne Ford is currently the first openly Trans Executive Director of San Francisco Pride. She's amazing and a great interviewee. For the purpose of this chapter, Blaine and Randy refer to Suzanne as Brent to align with the timing of the story and to avoid reader confusion.

that her mom said it was okay if she went, but that turned out to be a lie. Turns out, too, she was only 17.

We went to a friend of my mom's, Monde Wiggins. We stayed there for a little bit, and then we moved to downtown Galveston on the fourth floor of a six-story building above a Korean strip club. I think the strippers felt sorry for us. I started dating one of them, and that got us entry to the club and some free beers here and there.

Blaine: Randy had traveler's checks from his tobacco crops. I didn't have any money at all. One night we went down to the strip club, and the girls started rubbing on us and making out with us. We thought, "Oh, the girls like us." It was stupid, but he kept on signing over these traveler's checks. It was funny that night when we were drunk – the next morning it was not funny. We were broke, so we had to live on like two or three hot dogs a day.

The story you're about to read has been told to me three different ways. I've stitched it together in the most linear fashion I can come up with. Turns out fireworks, alcohol and Korean strippers can cloud memories.

Randy Ratliff: Around the 4th of July, me and Blaine sent Brent downstairs to get some more beer. It was probably three o'clock in the afternoon, and we had fireworks. So, I threw some out the window trying to hit Brent. Well, there was this monster of a dude hanging out outside.

The firecrackers go off before they hit that guy, and he yells up at me. When he does, Brent, who's on the street now, yells at him, and they kind of square off. This dude shoves him, and three unmarked police cars pull up. That guy turns and runs away. The cops grab Brent and throw him up against the wall. I'm yelling, "That guy shoved him!" I go downstairs. The cops are gone, but Brent's there and I'm like, "What the fuck was that?"

Later that night, we're in this bar across the street shooting some pool. In walk two cops. We're all the way in the back, but they make a beeline for all three of us and start pressing us to see our IDs. I've got mine. Blaine has his.

Suzanne Ford: I didn't have my ID on me, but I was old enough. Well, one of the cops said, "Doesn't matter. You're drunk. You're going to jail."

Randy Ratliff: We turned to the guys we were playing pool with and said, "Did you see that?" One of them said to us, "Shut your fucking mouth. Drink your beer and get out of here."

Whole bar is just totally quiet. The vibe changed completely. So, we left, and I said, "Well, we gotta go get Brent out of jail." We spent all night trying to find a place to cash Brent's money orders. We get him out of jail and a couple of days later, maybe a week, Blaine takes my car to pick up Brent at work.

Suzanne Ford: I found a job at a Dairy Queen.

Blaine: When I picked Brent up, he had this big, huge milkshake that he'd made himself. He starts telling me, "I need to go back to Miami, Ohio. I want to go back to school and get my life together."

Randy Ratliff: Well, I noticed they'd been gone a long time. I look out the window, and down the street here comes Blaine driving my car. Blaine pulls up and rolls his window down. He looks up and goes, "Brent got arrested again!" I said, "What the fuck happened?"

Blaine said, "Okay, so we're driving and this cop pulls up next to us. The light changes, and we both start making a left turn and Brent says, 'Fucking cop!' and throws his milkshake."

Blaine: It starts flying, and the top comes off in midair like it was designed by NASA. The cop had his driver side window rolled down, maybe halfway. The milkshake hits the window, splashes and goes all over the cop's face. That's when the cop turns his siren on, and Brent says, "He's pulling us over for that?"

Suzanne Ford: That Texas cop, he must've been a good man. He wanted to beat the hell out of me. He didn't, but I went to jail.

Randy Ratliff: And that's when Blaine and I just up and moved to Houston.

Blaine: I got a job at a donut shop in Humble, Texas. It was easy, but depressing. You could eat all the donuts you wanted, and I was trying to live off that, which was not good. That job was like three hours worth of work spread over eight hours.

I had no money to buy music, so I'd go to the donut shop, work the graveyard shift and crank up the radio station from Rice University in the back. I mean, I was 19. It was an adventure to get out of the whole little suburban track of Owensboro, but I was broke. It was horrible. I was dating this girl down there for a while. When she left, it was just instinct to come back to Kentucky.

Randy Ratliff: Blaine left before me. I stayed.

Blaine: When I moved back to Owensboro, that's when I started hanging around Scott again, and we started thinking about getting a band together. We were talking to all of our friends about playing, and they said, "You've got to do this. You've really got to do this."

CHAPTER 6
BEFORE I COULD KICK MYSELF FOR COMIN' HERE, I WAS ALREADY BACK FOR MORE

Scott: I flunked out of the University of Kentucky and Transylvania University.

Blaine: Scott was there when his mom got his grades. He was like, "Chill out, Mom. It'll be fine." That night, me, him and our friend Lance decided to get drunk on tequila. When his mom got home and saw what we were doing, she said, "This is not good." Probably wasn't. We thought, "What's the big deal? We're just drinking tequila."

Scott: We're back in Owensboro. This is '84, and Blaine's taken a few lessons and is just banging out stuff. Then, it just happens organically – Blaine and I run into Toby Myrick at a keg party. We knew he played drums. I had a cheap Indian necklace on and jokingly said, "Chiefy Weefy says, 'Start a band.'"

Toby Myrick: Scott's mom was my 10th grade health teacher. I was very close to her. When I was having a hard time with my mom, sometimes I would go and live with them for a few days.

Scott: We're talking, and we say, "Let's try it." Then we found this bass player named Brian Payne who was this smart, new-waver dude. He passed away like 15 years ago – gone too young.

Toby Myrick: My friend said, "Hey man, I got this drum set. 150 bucks, it's yours." So Brian Payne took me to Knoxville to get it. I brought it back and set it up in Scott's mom's living room.

Scott: My mom was out of town, so we set everything up in her living room. I taped a microphone to a rake. It sounded like total shit because there was a bunch of feedback.

Blaine: Scott started singing, and I mean he could sing. When we hooked up a microphone to an amplifier, that's when I thought, "Yeah, we can do this." His voice lends itself to the country stuff for sure.

Scott: We started doing covers, just basic three-chord stuff we could get through – "Wild Thing," "Hang On, Sloopy," "Louie Louie," a lot of the Ramones, "Police on My Back" by the Clash, "I Fought the Law," Sex Pistols stuff and Jason & The Scorchers.

Blaine: We were big fans of Jason & The Scorchers to the point we wanted to be just like them with a mix of the Ramones.

Scott: We knew we were going to do cowpunk. We loved doing "Folsom Prison Blues" and all that stuff. When we heard Jason & The Scorchers, we were like, "Oh, that's how. That's the template."

So, it was Toby, Brian, Blaine and myself, and we had another guitar player, too – David Epperson.

David Epperson: We would just go over to either Scott's mom's house or Blaine's house until they basically said, "Oh my God! Stop!" We would play ungodly loud, all hours of the night. I thought we were terrible. They thought they were great.

Blaine: We'd practice anywhere. If I knew a place where there was an outlet to plug into, we'd go there. I found out there were outlets in the picnic shelters at Yellow Creek Park where I used to run cross country. We went out there, set up drums and a guitar and practiced. Finally some kid came over, and he said it was echoing through the suburbs, so we had to stop.

Scott tried to get us into his church's basement so we could practice, but Toby was like, "Mannnn, I don't want to do that because I might get mad and cuss, and God'll get mad at me."

Toby Myrick: We practiced in this house I knew about.

Scott: It might have been abandoned, but it had power. We used that place for a while, and that's where we wrote some of the stuff that made the first record. Some of the other stuff we were doing was hardcore. We were just jamming. We had a hardcore song called "Protestant Jihad" and another one called "Sorority Dress." Toby liked doing that hardcore shit, but we also had "Redneck Romance" kind of brewing. It was originally called "Daviess County Romance."

Blaine: Scott called me up when he wrote this song called "Gearheads of Daviess County." It ended up being "Gearhead Blues." He read me the lyrics over the phone, and I was like, "You're writing songs about these fucking people? The ones we're trying to get away from?" I didn't want to do that at all. I wanted to write about people in New Jersey or outer space or some shit – anything but the people in that town.

Scott set the pace for what we wrote about, and he was just making fun of people in Owensboro.

Scott: We were trying to capture that type of working class of people that we went to high school with, just lyrics about everyday life and the lives of quiet desperation.

Blaine: My dad was not against me playing music or anything – ironically my dad is the one person of all of our relatives who actually listens to our music. At the time, I think he just thought I was going to approach it with the same laziness I did everything else. Scott's mom was horrified when we formed the band. She thought it was going to be a waste of time and was going to fuck his life up further.

But, we were playing gigs soon, like two weeks after getting a band together.

CHAPTER 7
DON'T GET NO BETTER THAN THIS

Scott: We're building this thing. It's not bad, and we get a show at the Ross Theater in Evansville, Indiana.

40 years is a long time, and everybody remembers things their own way. Who booked their first show and how it got booked are slightly different depending on who you ask.

Blaine: One night, my friend Lance and I were killing time in Owensboro – I always looked at the midnight movies in the paper. That's when I saw an advertisement for the Ross Theater in Evansville and said, "What the fuck is this? I think this is an ad for a band. That's weird. I think they're having bands play."

Lance and I drove to Evansville to check it out. We got there, went in and there was a band called The Big Employees. They were a trio, and we thought they were terrible.

Rick Lynch (Booking Agent): I was in high school and working with bands, and I was also a DJ for the local high school radio station. I just started putting together shows, like free shows in parks and places like that.

We didn't really have a lot of venues or anything for these bands to play, so a lot of kids were getting in trouble. That's one of the reasons I started working with bands more and more to get kids off the street, give them some place to go and feel welcome, like part of the family.

Evansville was a very small town with a small punk rock scene. But, all my friends were musicians, and they were all writing original material and the scene kept getting bigger and bigger. Eventually we started doing shows at a local movie theater, the Ross Theater. The guy who owned it was kind to us. He let us use his stage, and we split the profits.

Blaine: We're lucky he did that. He was giving people a place to go.

Rick Lynch: I started booking bands, and Blaine and Scott came along. They wanted to try their band they had just formed. They really didn't have a name yet.

Scott: We were Nine Pound Hammer, the very first gig.

Blaine: Scott wanted it to be called Nine Pound Hammer off the bat. Which is a great name, but other people were like, "What's that mean?" I'm like, "It's a song written by Merle Travis." We went to school with his great nephew – he was from Libya, Kentucky. He was part of our clique, and he really liked Lou Reed and punk.

Rick Lynch: From what I remember, Blaine and Scott were the two that approached me.

Blaine: I think I talked to the manager. I knocked on his door and said, "Hey, I'm in a band. Can we play next week?" He said, "Well, we've got another band, but maybe you can open up."

I said, "Okay, alright."

The next week, I probably showed up six hours early before the show.

David Epperson: One of us heard about them having bands at the Ross Theater, and we went there one night to check it out. Then we couldn't find Toby. Suddenly here he comes wandering out, and he says, "Man, what'd you think of all that?" We were like, "Yeah, it's cool." He was like, "Well, good. We're playing here next Friday." We freaked out. We were like, "What are you doing?" So that week we tried to learn some actual songs.

Toby Myrick: I think I called the Ross Theater and said, "Can we come play? What's the deal, and what do we have to do?" They didn't have anybody, so they let us do it.

Scott: We got a slot opening up for this other local band – that's the most nervous I've ever been. I was pacing around out in the lobby almost to the point of… I mean, I get it when people say they throw up.

I was wearing some ridiculous purple coat, and Blaine was wearing a skid lid. You know those Harley Davidson hats? He was a big-time Springsteen acolyte and played a Telecaster, which just fed back like crazy. David Epperson was playing a Gretsch. He was a big Brian Setzer, Stray Cats guy.

David Epperson: Our guitars were really bad. They would fall out of tune really easily, and we didn't know anything about foot pedal tuners. We'd play a song, and then we'd spend two minutes going, "Ding, ding, ding, ding, ding," trying to get our guitars in tune again. Every single song was like that. I think at one point I was playing in the wrong key, and Blaine realized it and kept staring at me.

Blaine: We had to bring our own PA – that sucked.

David Epperson: We couldn't really get it working. It just sounded like crap. Toby, I could hear, but I had my amp turned up all the way, and it just didn't sound like anything.

Blaine: I threw a tantrum because it was not going good. During "Wild Thing," I threw my guitar, and these local punks with mohawks started cheering us on.

We did 15 minutes and just blitzed through our entire set. I thought we were going to quit because it was horrible. It was like, "That didn't work out. Let's go back to our lives. We tried it. It was a nightmare."

Scott: We went up there, and it was what it was, but people were kind of into it. I was jumping around, and a buddy of mine afterwards was like, "Hey, it wasn't that bad. Man, there's something there."

Blaine: Some of the punks came up to us afterwards, and they were in a band called the Disciples of Death and said, "You guys were great." I was shocked. I said, "Really?" They said, "What you're doing is great. Do you want to play with us next week? We'll play first and you'll play second."

Scott: The next week we played again. We were called The Yuppie Mop Dogs. I think Epperson came up with that name.

Blaine: My friend Mike Grimes was there. He was really impressed with Scott. We did "Street Fighting Man," "Police on My Back," "I Fought the Law" and a couple Jason & The Scorchers songs.

Scott: The second show we got a really good response. It was a lot better.

Blaine: I think my parents were there. They didn't know what to think about it. I was always on the wrong track according to them. They just didn't know what we were trying to do.

David Epperson: The second night, it seemed like it went better, and then we didn't play for a while. That's kind of when I said, "Guys, I don't think I want to do this." I just couldn't see it, and I just bowed out.

Blaine: Our split with David was a very big deal. Him, me and Scott were very close friends, and David was a really good guitar player – but Scott and I wanted to go more punk and I think if David stayed, we would have been more like a college rock radio band. It just wasn't a good fit.

Brian Payne did the second show, but that was it for him, too. I think he was a photographer or an art student.

Scott: Again, it can't be overstated how important those two shows were. If they had gone south, we probably wouldn't have done this at all. I can't ever recapture that feeling and sense of like, certainty and euphoria. There was just this sense of contentment.

Rick Lynch: They were so raw back then, but it was pure. It was just so much fun, and the songs that they started writing were just hilarious. Their taste in music blended so well with everybody.

With every show, I saw Blaine getting much better on guitar. I mean, he was just cranking out riffs like Johnny Ramone.

By the end of every show, Scott would be drenched in sweat and lying on his back on the stage screaming out the last few lyrics, trying to make it through the show. He could barely get up and get off the stage afterwards – that's the kind of energy those guys were putting out, and the crowd was the same. Everybody at the end of their shows would be moshed out and so tired from dancing.

With the band starting to roll, they encounter their first major detour. Toby had met a girl the previous spring break and decided to move to Montreal to live with her.

Toby Myrick: I went to Montreal in the fall of 1985. Blaine and Randy Ratliff went to New York City. They were there for maybe an hour, and they saw Ric Ocasek and he just looked at them because they were carrying their guitars and their amps around. Their plan was to find a fucking place to live and play at CBGB in a week. So, not really much of a plan.

Blaine: I tried to move to New York. I went on a Greyhound bus with $400, and I slept in the bus station for one night. I looked enough like a college kid that they didn't run me out.

I quickly realized that New York wasn't happening. I called Toby up and said, "Hey, I want to come to Montreal." He goes, "Yeah, cool. Maybe Scott will come, too."

Toby Myrick: Blaine stayed with me for about two weeks in Montreal. While he was there, immigration came to my girlfriend's apartment and raided us with their guns out. They told me I'd stayed as long as I could on a visitor visa, and I had to split.

Scott: I remember talking to my dad about it. I was getting ready to go up there, and then they got kicked out of the country. I remember

Toby coming back with Nutella – we didn't have that down here.

Blaine: When we got back together, we started playing in Owensboro or Evansville every other weekend – it was me, Toby, Scott and a guy named Bart Altman who was 17 years old. He was the only other person we knew who played bass.

Scott: We played a party for the Kentucky Wesleyan College football team. My buddy, Hillbilly John Hill, asked us to do it. So, there we are at the VFW outside Ben Hawes Park in Owensboro – classic setting. It was like something from the roadhouse scene in *Animal House*. I get on the mic and say, "If you don't like us, just pull the cord. Don't throw anything and don't beat us up."

Anyway man, that show, we started off with a revved-up version of "Folsom Prison Blues," and they fucking loved it. My sister, Mary Lynn, and Steve Terrell were the first ones to get out and dance around. They set the tone, thank God. Me and Blaine were just looking at each other. I can't describe the bliss. We were both just in awe of what happened, and we're like, "Oh my God! We've got something here." I do what I do – I'm Joey, Blaine was Johnny. We both had something the other didn't have. It was like, we've got to do this. It was beyond our wildest expectations.

Then we started playing at The Alhambra Theatre in Evansville. It was this nice little theater.

We were working on more originals. We had "Redneck Romance" and these bad hardcore songs – "Born To Shop" and "Army. Navy." – and a great song called "I Don't Think So," which made it on the first record. "Runaway Train" was getting written around then, and we also had a few of these new-wavy kind of songs. Toby was big into experimenting.

Blaine: We tried to give everyone a voice. Toby would play stuff by Millions of Dead Cops. So, we started writing some hardcore songs because Toby thought it was a good idea. Most of them were terrible. Scott hated doing them. A couple of the good ones are on the first record, "Doomsday Poptarts" and "Bye Bye Glenn Frey." They're kind of rock and roll songs just played real fast. People would come out when we played, and they just wanted that energy. They wanted to slam dance.

We really didn't love hardcore. Me and Scott were more likely to go see George Thorogood, Tom Petty or the Georgia Satellites than we were to go see a hardcore band – we didn't relate to it at all.

What we were doing sounded like Johnny Thunders singing about taters, and it was starting to sound great. People sometimes gave us shit, "You're trying to sound like Jason & The Scorchers." In my mind, I thought there needed to be a band like us. Why wouldn't you play country revved up? It's really cool when you play old rock and roll sped up, and that's what most other punk bands would do.

When we started playing, I could get a country song book and take a song like, "Is Anybody Going to San Antonio?" and then just play the chords like the Ramones. When we started writing our own songs, it mostly came from country songs instead of rock songs. We were definitely more singer oriented because of Scott's vocals.

CHAPTER 8
HE'S GONE, AIN'T COMIN' HOME

Toby Myrick: Why did we leave Owensboro? Because there was nowhere to play and we figured that if we went to Lexington, we'd be closer to Louisville, Cincinnati, Chicago and Indianapolis.

Scott: We had kind of done all we could in Evansville, and this is '86. We could tell it was starting to be the same old thing. We're like, "Oh yeah, we're ready for the big city. Let's go to Lexington." The fact that I'd lived there before and had gone to college there helped.

Blaine: We were all in Kentucky, and they were talking about going back to school again. I go, "Man, let's just go to Lexington." I didn't know if there was a scene. I didn't know anything about scenes – there was no way to look them up.

We decided to move there because if you're going to go to school or whatever, it's there. I said, "I'm not going to school, but I'll write songs." When we got to Lexington, we really liked it, and we got to play a lot. There weren't a lot of bands, but there was a punk scene.

Scott: Toby, Bart, me and Blaine found this house, 380 Bassett Avenue. The landlord was this guy named Boris Chang. Oh my God, it was a dump. When we finally left, it got condemned. That's how bad it was. There was a big hole in the floor that we would just throw trash into.

I lived in the basement for a minute, but it was nasty, man. Just a nasty place. We did have a hilarious neighbor named Rocky who would come over and get drunk with us.

David Epperson: We went there one winter, and they had absolutely no heat and no food. Steve Terrell and I had to buy their beer and their food. I remember Blaine was eating a bag of potato chips – that's all he had to eat. Those were some lean times for those guys. They never had any money. I don't think they were working regular jobs most of the time.

Scott: Blaine made the call, "I'm not going to work." It wasn't, "I'm going to be a writer." It was, "I'm going to be a rock star."

Blaine: I didn't have a room. I slept on the couch. There were only so many rooms, and I was just eager to keep the peace. I didn't have any money to eat. I lived on oranges for two weeks once. I had nothing. I walked everywhere. Ironically, I was in amazing shape.

I was writing songs, so I didn't work for a bit, but after a while I started working crappy jobs, too – Long John Silver's, Billy's Bar-B-Q, temp stuff. At Long John Silver's, I was getting burned. My face broke out all over again because there was so much grease. We were doing whatever we had to do.

Kelly (Holt) Chambers (Blaine's Former Girlfriend): Blaine was an intense little fellow with a chip on his shoulder who escaped from Western Kentucky.

He was working at Long John Silver's, and he hated it. I remember there was one point where he thought he was in danger of becoming employee of the month, and he sabotaged that big-time. I was like, "You're so crazy." Just having his picture or his name up there would have been soul crushing to him.

Blaine: My parents came to the Bassett Avenue house after I'd gotten attacked by a couple of dudes walking down the street. They came up behind me and hit me with some nunchucks. So my parents came up to check on me. They saw how I was living, and they weren't happy. It was a mess, but we were barely there.

Toby Myrick: It was a miserable existence.

Kelly Chambers: That Bassett Avenue house was fucking disgusting. I think Blaine and I spent our first night together on a mattress on the floor in the basement, and roaches were dropping from the ceiling on us. Yeah, it was lovely.

There would always be a giant pile of garbage in the middle of the kitchen. You'd come in and you were just like, "What the fuck, dude?" It was the worst place I've ever seen. Yeah. I'd never seen or smelled anything like that.

Besides trash and bad diet, The Black Sheep – yeah, more on that band name in a bit – were starting to make some inroads at a local college bar.

Blaine: When we got to Lexington, Toby went and talked to a guy at a bar called Great Scott's Depot. Toby was really good about networking. He was always very, very confident.

We got to where we were playing twice a week. It gave us a chance to get good. We basically learned how to play while we were on stage. We had a lot of friends from Owensboro that went to college in Lexington, and they all came out because Toby and Scott were pretty popular guys.

Kelly Chambers: Great Scott's was very minimal. It had pitchers of the shittiest beer. Very plain, very punk rock. I think it was painted black all the way through, and it was right next to a strip club. Whenever we would come out, the strippers would hit on Blaine and all the guys – there was always just weirdness.

Scott: We were playing Monday nights and Tuesday nights, kind of as a house band. We were getting some weekend gigs here and there, just slogging it out. We're playing covers, we're writing originals – "I Don't Think So," "Runaway Train," "Crawdaddy" – all the first record is starting to be written.

When we first moved to Lexington, we got some pushback from the locals for stepping on their turf. Thank God for Lawrence Tarpey. He was in a band called Active Ingredients. He was the godfather of Lexington punks – he and this little fanzine said that he liked us.

That took a lot of heat off and allowed people to come see us.

Lawrence Tarpey: I remember seeing those guys and saying, "Oh man! These guys, they've got something going on. These guys are fucking legit." Blaine was just a little fireplug of a guitar player, just a buzzsaw. Scott had that great baritone voice, and they wrote great cowpunk songs that were hilarious – two, three minute songs. They were right up my alley. They had great songs, great stage presence, great showmanship – they had the whole package basically. They were very tenacious.

Kelly Chambers: When Lawrence Tarpey said, "Hey, they're cool, man," it was sort of like the king had spoken.

Scott: Great Scott's was so cool, man. One of the greatest nights we ever played there was after Iggy Pop and The Pretenders had played at Memorial Coliseum. There were all these college girls and Christ, there were high school girls up on the roof. Nobody was checking IDs, and I remember everybody drinking Black Label beer.

Matt Bartholomy (Future Nine Pound Hammer Bassist/Owensboroan): I went to see Iggy Pop and The Pretenders, and then I went to Great Scott's after the show. I didn't know Nine Pound Hammer was playing there, but as soon as I heard them, I said, "I know who this is." People were going crazy and dancing. I was really into punk rock then and to hear it with that Southern flair, I thought it was a perfect fit.

Scott: One night we were playing at Great Scott's and this dude tried to steal Blaine's guitar, and there was a straight-up barroom brawl. I literally cracked a chair over this guy. It was a Burt Reynolds' *Smokey and the Bandit* barroom brawl.

Another night, a stripper from Coomers next door came in with a gun. She pointed it at me and other people in the bar. She was mad about something. I still don't know what that was about. Great Scott's was wilder than hell, and we cut our teeth there.

The guy who ran that bar, his name was Court Bradberry. He was this real middle-class dude. I don't know what he thought he was getting into. He tried to fix it up and make it nice. It was like, "Do you know where you're at? These are old rundown honky-tonks and strip clubs." He wanted a nice club in the beginning, and finally he just capitulated and just started catering to local bands.

One show there, Blaine and I electrocuted one another. I had a microphone, and he wasn't grounded, I guess. I touched his guitar, the lights went down, and they said you could see a blue flame between us.

While the band was taking off, things with Toby were nosediving.

Blaine: When we moved to Lexington, we were called The Black Sheep. There were 20 million bands called The Black Sheep. Toby wanted to call us "Les Black Sheep" because he said, "Man, we can't be The Black Sheep – people will think we're a bunch of hicks." He'd been to Montreal and would walk around with a beret saying "Les" all the time. So, we put up our first flyer, and everyone in town laughed at us saying, "Your drummer's an idiot."

Toby Myrick: I worked at a Little Caesars way out on Alexandria Drive. I rode Bart's motorcycle out there and would drink whiskey and drive home.

Blaine: I remember Toby pulling into Bassett Avenue on Bart's motorcycle. It was the same feeling I got when my dad came home drunk.

Toby Myrick: My mom died in '86, and that was right when we were doing all this shit. I had hair down to my ass, and we were playing gigs every night. I thought it was cool – and then they kicked me out.

Blaine: Toby left because he was a jerk. We didn't kick him out. Toby quit.

I had some great fucking songs. We were learning "Drive-In" and "He's Gone," and Toby would say, "These songs are dumb." Scott would take up for my songs, and Toby would say that Scott and I agreed on everything. Which was fuccccking far from true! We don't agree all the time, but when we do agree on something, then that's set in stone.

When we first reformed the band after we got back from Canada, we went to see R.E.M. in Nashville. Toby had seen them in the early days at WKU on their very first EP. He was really into them. We all liked them – it was something new, and we were open-minded. Anyway, I'm driving to the concert, and Scott and Toby get wasted on tequila on the way there.

We had seats in the balcony, and 10,000 Maniacs opened up. Before R.E.M. came on, we weasled our way down front. We ended up right in front, and Toby just started yelling at Michael Stipe, "Play the old stuff! Michael! Play the old stuff!" between every fucking song.

Toby didn't know anything past that first fucking EP. They'd play the old stuff like "Gardening at Night," and then they'd play a new song. So, Toby starts booing Michael Stipe.

Well, Michael heard him.

Michael Stipe goes, "I don't know who you are, but I wish you'd shut the fuck up." Then the whole place, fucking 2,000 people, started cheering, and Toby was like, "Oh, cool man, he noticed me." That was what we were dealing with.

We went to see The Replacements on the Tim tour at Bogart's in Cincinnati. They were playing "Doctor Love" and goddammit, he jumped on stage to try to sing. Everybody from Lexington was there, and they kept saying, "That's your dumbass drummer." He was a fucking embarrassment.

Back in the early days, when we were in Evansville, Toby stole some guy's drum. He said he borrowed it. Toby took it to Lexington with him, and then when we came back and played Evansville, he was dumb enough to take that fucking drum. The guy Toby stole it from saw him coming into the show, and then he sees his fucking drum on stage and loses it.

Toby's like, "Y'all wanna fight?" I was like, "I'm not coming to your fucking defense, Toby."

Kelly Chambers: I remember them getting mad at Toby because he stole some equipment from some band. Blaine was very incensed. It was like a fucking community of people and a "We're all in this together" attitude, and Toby was just in it for himself.

Scott: We played Cincinnati a lot back then, and we played a show at a bar called Bash Riprock's. Somehow these punks were running it, and they were giving us free Heineken. We killed it. I think we played all our songs twice – people were losing their minds.

On the trip back from Cincinnati, we pulled off to get gas, and we're getting ready to fight because Toby wouldn't come off a dollar. We needed him to pitch in a dollar for gas to get home, and he just wouldn't do it.

Blaine: We'd played a good gig in Cincinnati. We were coming back, and Scott and Toby got into a fight in Grant County in front of this all-night diner. Toby wouldn't give us any fucking gas money, and we'd paid for everything. When me and Scott were being the responsible ones – that was fucked up, because we were not responsible.

Scott: I was going to kill him. I was kind of buzzed, and we'd all just had it.

Blaine: Toby said some smart-ass thing. Whatever it was, it was the wrong thing. Scott and Toby were both big guys, bigger than me. They could do some damage. I jumped in between them, and I don't think they even noticed. There was a constable eating at the diner. He came out there and threatened to throw everybody in jail.

Scott: Here comes this constable, this old dude, "Cooter" or whoever. He had a gun in his hand and said, "You the boys who've been raising hell?" I'm like, "No, man!" He says to me, "Quit calling me man, man." So we got out of there.

Blaine: All this is less than one year after we reconvened the band. It was going good, but it was not fun. I was ready to quit. I couldn't play with Toby anymore. When he quit, I just remember people hugging us saying, "Congratulations, Toby quit."

Steve Terrell: They had just gotten their first writeup in the *Kentucky Kernel*, the University of Kentucky's student newspaper. Scott read it out loud – it was talking about their band, and it said "Scott Luallen, Blaine Cartwright, Bart Altman and Toby MyCrack." We didn't let that slide.

Toby Myrick: I loved it so much, but it's just like if you date some girl who's a prostitute. You love her, but she won't stop being a prostitute, and you don't know what you're doing wrong. I missed it a lot, but I would've never gotten to do any of the things I got to do otherwise. I so love my musical experience, what I've gotten to do, the things I've gotten to play.

CHAPTER 9
ROLLIN' RHYTHM, EASE MY MIND

With Toby 86'd in '86, Nine Pound Hammer found a new drummer.

Darren Howard (Former Nine Pound Hammer Drummer): I moved up to Lexington from Nashville, probably around '85, and I didn't know anybody. I was working little odd jobs here and there and one night, I had an idea. I was just kind of like, "What do I want to do? I want to play music, but I don't know how to get into any bands up here." I'd played drums growing up in Nashville, so I wrote out this list of bands I was into and put it up on a bulletin board in a store called Carl's Music. It sat there for months, maybe even a year.

One day I was getting off work from this shit job. I remember getting in my car, and I was at the lowest point in my life. I sat there for 20 minutes, and everything just came crashing down on me. I go home and low and behold, my mom says, "Well, some guy called here for you. I guess he read your ad in the music store or whatever." It was Blaine.

Now, I had seen this band called The Black Sheep in newspapers and I'm like, "These guys play out a lot, almost every weekend." I wanted to go see them, but I'm shy, man.

I called Blaine, and we talked. It was weird – he worked right across the street from me at a Long John Silver's. Blaine goes, "I'll have a demo tape here when you get off work. Just come pick it up."

I go into Long John Silver's, and Blaine's in there with other workers, throwing food on a tray in his little outfit. I was in jeans and a white t-shirt and a pair of Ray-Bans. He handed me the demo and said, "You don't look like you'd be into our band."

I got the tape. I popped it in, and I'm going down I-64 and it's very new to me, the sound and everything – there was a lot of fast punk rock stuff. When I got to "Redneck Romance," that was the song that made me join the band. When I heard that, I was just like, "Man, this is funny as shit. This is true to life. This is like somebody that's been there." The lyrics were cool, the music was cool, and I said to myself, "I want to give this a shot. At least I'll be getting out and playing and getting to know people." I called Blaine back, and I'm like, "Man, I love it. I'm in."

Blaine: When we got our second drummer, Darren Howard, after being in Lexington for a year, we changed our name to Nine Pound Hammer. Scott wanted it to be called Nine Pound Hammer off the bat. It just fit. Perfect name.

Darren Howard: I always say, I was the "first drummer in Nine Pound Hammer." We started playing open mics just to kind of break me in. I was nervous as hell – anxiety and shit. But I got through it, and we started playing bigger venues, bigger shows, opening up for some pretty good bands, upper-tier bands that had records and had toured. We were just openers, but everybody seemed to like us.

Then we started playing a lot – Monday, Tuesday, Wednesday, Thursday and then we'd have a two-week mini tour around the state. It was every night almost. Man, they were wearing me out. I was still working a day job.

Playing constant gigs got them in shape to try their hand at recording.[7] They recorded a set of demos February 24, 1987, at Sound on Sound studio in Louisville, Kentucky. Their engineer and producer was Howie Gano, who had recorded albums for Squirrel Bait, Bodeco and Kinghorse.

---

[7] The band did record a three-song demo with a blind Lexington musician named Harley Cannon. It didn't turn out that well.

Thirty-eight years after they recorded those demos and who knows how long since hearing them, Scott, Blaine and Darren had this to say about the recording session:

Scott: I forgot about that demo – that was the very first thing we officially recorded. It got us into the local rock radio station WKQQ's battle of the bands. But we got disqualified because the club hosting the event didn't want green-hair punks in his bar and accused us of stealing mics from a previous show.

Blaine: Recording that was like a lesson in what not to do. It was pretty good. It probably sounds better now. I thought Scott sounded better because of the way he was recorded, but you couldn't pick out the guitar, so the producer said, "I'm going to push a button and double it." He did, and it duplicated it – it's not as raw.

The stuff we were competing with was nuts, like Black Flag and all the hardcore bands. We wanted it to sound really aggressive. I thought everyone sounded good except for the guitar.

Darren Howard: I do remember it was a well-produced demo, but Blaine was looking for something dirtier, a little bit noisier, more punk rock, so it never saw the light of day. I loved it.

Talking to Scott in February 2025, he asked me, "Do you want those?" A couple weeks later he handed me two reel-to-reel tape boxes and said, "Run with it." So, I decided to see if I could get the demos digitally transferred.

These demos were recorded on 1/2" Ampex Precision Magnetic Tapes. I soon found 1/2" tape wasn't that common. Big studios used 2" or 1" reel-to-reel machines for recording. Those machines are still pretty easy to find, but the 1/2" machines have mostly been landfilled.

After a few weeks of running around Louisville and talking to sound engineers and studio owners in Cincinnati and Nashville, I not only tracked down a battered 1/2" reel-to-reel machine, but also Howie Gano.

I took the machine to Howie's newest studio, Louisville Recording Arts. After replacing a couple parts, getting covered in black debris and gunk and taping down a broken locking mechanism, Howie reached to rewind the first reel and warned me, "This may come apart."

Essentially, after nearly 40 years the glue wears out, sheds itself onto the tape and causes the tape to stick. As Howie rewound the first reel-to-reel tape for playback, we were both ready for anything – complete failure and a long apology to Scott or maybe it would work. The results were better than expected.

Scott: Beyond my wildest expectations, and the reception has been amazing. Thankfully fate intervened, and we had help getting that thing out.

Blaine: It's better than I remember, that's for sure. It aged really well, so I'm happy about that.

Howie Gano (Producer of Sound on Sound Demos aka *1987 Revisited*): It sounds damn good. They had to have been one of the first bands I recorded at Sound on Sound. I didn't move up there until the beginning of February of that year. The lyrics to me are still what really set them apart from the other bands I'd recorded.

Darren Howard: We had such a fucking blast at Sound on Sound. That was my first time ever in a studio. I was like 19 years old, maybe 20, but I knew what I wanted to do. I only took a few cymbals with me, because Howie said he had a kit. When I got there, he was right. He had a kit. It was probably an $8,000 Yamaha kit, beautiful. So I was like, "Yeah, I think I'll play your drums."

We all set up and played live in the room. There wasn't any building of the rhythm tracks, no, we played it fucking live. Punk rock, man. Roll damn the tape!

Blaine might have done one or two overdubs to fix something, but we got the tracks down. I think we came back a little later to do Scott's vocals because we took these two girls with us. One of them was dating the guy who booked for Tewligans,[8] and the other was a friend of hers. I remember this because they dropped acid, and we couldn't get shit done. I don't know, maybe a couple of us were on acid, too, but the girls freaked the fuck out and were running around giving us fucking nicknames and shit.

Demo in the can and playing nonstop, Nine Pound Hammer started to venture outside of Lexington, Louisville and Cincinnati a little bit more.

Darren Howard: We went to Detroit and played several shows up there.

Kelly Chambers: Detroit was kind of weird because we got up there and realized there were rednecks everywhere.

Darren Howard: After one of the shows, we didn't have a place to stay. This couple comes up to us, "If y'all want a place to stay, you can crash at our place." Huge loft above a business? Yeah, that sounded pretty cool.

Kelly Chambers: Bill and Michele – they were very tall. Too tall. We called them the Twin Towers. They were just the wildest people.

Darren Howard: As soon as we walked into their place, we all just kind of looked at each other. It was weird. There was definitely a vibe going on. First, there was this dude, man – he's on the couch, and he's throwing lighter fluid all over this coffee table and setting it on fire. And the flames are coming up at least four feet.

We're like, "What the fuck?" Well, behind him was this weird fucking painting. It kind of looked satanic. It had this dude, and he'd cut off this other guy's head and was just holding it.

We were not ready to comprehend this, but they seemed cool. So we stuck around. My girlfriend was there, and she drank too much, so I

---

[8] Tewligans was a popular club in Louisville and a place Nine Pound Hammer played quite a bit.

ended up babysitting her. That sucked because I wanted to fucking party and just see how far these people would take it. Well, they took it pretty fucking far.

At one point, me, Kelly and Blaine were in the kitchen, and we noticed these people didn't have any doors on any of their rooms. I look over toward the refrigerator and there's a bedroom beside it, and this dude is orally pleasing his girlfriend right there. There we all are, just staring.

They're butt-ass naked, and he's going down on her, just lapping it up like a dog, and she's fucking writhing and moaning and shit. Then he noticed us and his face turned beet red, and he started laughing.

Later on that night, everybody gets kind of tucked in, and there was a guy, he's dead now – we called him Cool William. He wore those little square '60s sunglasses. They were black, and he never took them off. Not in the club. Not at night. Never. Well, Cool William had this girlfriend, man, and she was like a model.

I get up at one point in the night, and he's in there pounding her. Man, there was a lot gyrating and bodies are coming off the mattress, and he fucking winds up knocking the bed into the wall across the room. That's how hard they were going at it.

In the morning, Kelly gets up and goes to use the bathroom, and Cool William just gets up out of the bed, not a stitch of clothes on. He goes, "Oh! How you doing? Good morning." Even though Scott didn't stay there that night, he started calling it the "House of the Naked."

Kelly Chambers: We were Kentucky kids. I think Darren was really weirded out by it, but I said, "Hell, Darren, just roll with it."

It's been a few pages since we've switched members, but two years into playing with Darren, bassist Bart Altman decided to call it quits.

Blaine: For some reason Bart and Scott stopped getting along. I have no idea why, but Bart was sick of it and was ready to start working. He always wanted to own his own business. He just wasn't like us.

That was a bummer for sure, but I also knew we could get someone else. Bart could be a little bit lethargic sometimes. He would just stand there on stage when we were all jumping around. I don't think he ever played in any other bands, but he lives in Lexington. Whenever I see him, we hang out all night together.

Bart was replaced briefly by Kathy Lewellan. Kathy didn't do too many shows, and the shows she did were with her back to the audience because of her shyness. After about six months with Kathy in the band, she and Darren decided to move on.

Darren Howard: Kathy and I bowed out at the same time. Our last show was at this place called Babylon – Babylon in Lexington. I was ready to do other stuff. I'd done three years with them, and obviously I wished I had known they were going to write more songs. I was just kind of getting burned out on the stuff we'd been doing.

But, I'll be forever grateful to Blaine for calling me up because it just kind of jump-started – I wouldn't really say a career – me being able to play with a lot of really good musicians. So, he kind of catapulted me up some by answering that ad. I gotta thank Scott, too.

With Kathy and Darren gone, Blaine and Scott assembled a new rhythm section.

Brian Moore (Former Bassist for Active Ingredients and Nine Pound Hammer): When Scott asked me to join Nine Pound, I'd just gone through the breakup of my band, Active Ingredients. Actually, I'd decided to quit playing. I thought punk was dead because one of the last big shows I did with Active Ingredients was opening for the Rollins Band at Bogart's in Cincinnati. Henry Rollins had just shaved his head and, as a result, there was this large showing of skinheads. Henry is definitely not a skinhead.

After we played, I was watching the Rollins Band, and I noticed fights breaking out between skinheads and punks and skinheads and metalheads. It was a complete bummer. I was done, but then Scott called.

I knew him, Blaine and Darren from shows around town here in

Lexington, and I really liked their band.

Blaine: Toby's gone. Bart's gone. So is Darren Howard, who was great. We found Rob Hulsman, a fresh-faced kid from Jersey who liked Ronald Reagan and Winger. Those were big no-nos. We made him change that.

Rob Hulsman (Former Drummer for Nine Pound Hammer): It was in '88. I was a percussion major at the University of Kentucky, and Nine Pound Hammer put up a flyer in the music building. I saw it, answered it and auditioned.

Scott: Blaine wrote the ad, "No Neil Pearts!" Well, this guy (Rob) was a Neil Peart, but he wanted to play music – but he'd never played music like this before. He was a really good drummer. Now, the Neil Peart-ness did come back out, but overall Rob did a great job.

Brian Moore: As a rhythm unit, Rob and I bonded pretty quickly, especially because of our mutual love of Black Sabbath and Led Zeppelin. Rob could really play some killer John Bonham stuff.

Rob Hulsman: The first show I played with them was in Evansville, and that was a lot of fun. It was their hometown crowd and a cool venue. We played a lot of punk rock shows around Lexington, and I wasn't even old enough to get into some of the clubs at that point. I wasn't really taking in the big picture. I was just having a really great time.

Scott: We played Tewligans and Uncle Pleasant's in Louisville, Kentucky, every month for a while.

Blaine: One of the big gigs in Louisville we had was with a band called Snake Out.

Scott: Both bands did the "Green Acres" theme song. Len Puch, the singer and guitar player for Snake Out, couldn't believe somebody else was doing that song. That's back when we'd do the "Metal Health" intro and go into "Yummy, Yummy, Yummy. (I Got Love In My Tummy)."

That's how we started talking to Len, and he said, "I got this label. You want to do something?" We're like, "Of course, yeah!"

Len Puch: Snake Out was on tour, and we were in Kentucky. We played a place in Louisville called Tewligans, and Nine Pound Hammer opened up for us. I thought those guys were great. They were the real deal and kind of blew me away.

It was a crazy night. We did this song that made jokes about being a hillbilly redneck, and this one guy in the audience did not take to the humor in it, so he whipped a bottle at my head. This Puerto Rican friend of mine, in his big booming voice, yells out, "Who the fuck did that?" The place goes silent, and my friend runs up to the guy who threw the bottle and says, "I want to bite your fucking nose off! Get the fuck out of here!" He leaves and comes back a few minutes later with a gun. We eventually talked him down.

In three, four years of solid touring, I think we got a motel room once. We would always just ask during shows, "Hey, anyone out there we can stay with?" Then we'd make them breakfast the next day. We always found someone. We ended up staying with Scott and Blaine and watching all these Russ Meyer movies and weird shit like *Texas Chainsaw Massacre 2.*[9] We just hit it off and became friends. I said, "I just started this record label called Wanghead, and I would love for you guys to come do a Detroit show and maybe record."

---

[9] This movie is going to come up a lot.

CHAPTER 10
THE MUD, THE BLOOD, AND THE BEERS
(1988)

What would have happened to Nine Pound Hammer without Len Puch? That's not a knock on the band. His timing and work ethic helped the band take their first step to becoming known in Europe. Without Len there would be no Crypt Records, no European tours, and I'd probably be sitting here writing a book about dust mites in Peru. Thanks, Len, this is way more fun.

Scott: Len Puch. Genius, mad scientist. He's a good man and incredibly hardworking. He lives in New Boston, Michigan, this little hamlet that's maybe 30 miles south of Detroit. There was a cool scene up there of all this independent music.

Len had this farm. He built a drag strip on it, a ferris wheel and a studio called Garageland. Going up there was like going into uncharted territory. Just getting out of Lexington was an adventure, man. Before the album, we did record "Runaway Train" and "Crawdaddy" for a compilation called *It Came from the Garage II*.

Anyway, this is '87. We went up there a couple times and played several shows with Snake Out and Elvis Hitler.

Len Puch: Out of necessity, I started Wanghead because no one would sign my band. I thought, "Fuck it, I'll start my own damn label," and I threw together a little studio – there was a live mixing board, an eight-track recording machine and a reel-to-reel. It was bare freaking bones.

Brian Moore: Len's studio was a classic garage studio. His brother did mechanical work on big-rig diesel trucks in this huge prefab metal garage, and Len had the back room. It was small, but it was filled with old, used recording equipment. He was a master at getting the best sound out of that gear.

Blaine: We drove up to record the album. Elvis Hitler recorded there, and that sounded amazing – big guitar sound. I just remember, I was pretty wide-eyed about the whole thing. I didn't know anything about recording. I didn't know if we were doing something that might last for a while.

Scott: When we went up there, we had the songs down. We'd been playing them so long that it didn't even take a weekend. It was just boom, boom, boom.

Len Puch: It took a couple of times to get it, but we did the album in maybe six to 10 hours.

Rob Hulsman: That was great. I joined, and it happened almost immediately. We went up to Detroit and recorded with Len and stayed at his house.

Len Puch: My mom was around then. I remember she had to feed them all, and she made this big kielbasa. She pulled out the stops and made sure they were all well fed.

Brian Moore: His mom and dad were very supportive of him. It didn't matter that we were these kind of sketchy-looking weirdos from Kentucky. We were welcomed with open arms. His mom cooked the best Polish sausage in the world. Here we are kind of starving, and it's like, "No, boys, eat more, eat more."

Scott: It was hot. We were sleeping on couches in the studio – covered in flies. There were dogs running around. We were drinking and smoking weed, and there was a party while we were there – that's what I remember more than anything. A band called 3-D Invisibles played. It was just wild as hell, and that was one of the worst hangovers I've ever had in my life. Wonderful, though. I danced all night. Salad days.

Blaine: When we heard the playback of the recording, we thought it was amazing.

Scott: I remember the playback sounded so good. It was really punchy, but something got lost in translation between playback and the mastering.

Blaine: We thought we'd done a classic until we listened to it on vinyl. I remember it sounded thinner than we wanted it to. It just sounded like shit. The first mix was way better. I don't know what happened to it. I don't know why they had to remix it, but the first mix sounded amazing, and it was really aggressive and huge. The next time I heard it, it was squashed and sounded way different.

Len Puch: Yeah, I think the mastering was a lot of it. Being a novice, I was kind of at the mercy of who was mastering it. Whoever did it was supposed to fatten it up and make it sound thicker, but what they did was basically compressed it.

Each time you master something, it was a few hundred bucks, and there was just no budget. I wish I knew more at the time. I was pretty ignorant.

Scott: We're like, "What happened?" It sounded so good in the playback. It still rocks, and I think that's because the songs are so good.

Brian Moore: What that record lacks in fidelity, I think it more than makes up for with that just punk rock urgency.

At 27 minutes and 51 seconds, The Mud, The Blood, and The Beers *skewers small-town life, takes us to the magical land of drive-ins and manages to flip off right-wingers and religion. If you have a copy, pull it out or open it up on Spotify and let's go behind the songs. (If you're on Spotify, it's on the back half of* Smokin' Taters.*)*

I DON'T THINK SO
Scott: That's pretty political, and we were at that time. We didn't like the "Age of Reagan" – hated him. You had to hate Reagan. "I Don't Think So" was our protest song.

Blaine: That was the first thing I played with Toby, and he knew exactly what to do with it. We were playing a version of "Six Days on the Road," and I was putting this riff at the beginning of it. Well, I took that riff, made a song out of it and ditched the "Six Days on the Road" part. That was our statement back then. It was defiant and summed up what we didn't like in three verses – GOP, TV, successful people and preachers.

It was about the people we thought were influencing culture too much. Those were the people who were squashing every cool.

CRAWDADDY

Scott: I was in Owensboro, living at my mom's house, and I saw it – a 1975 Pontiac Grand Ville convertible. I talked my mom into helping me buy this thing. It was like two grand. I said, "I've got to have this car, whatever it takes." I just nicknamed it the Crawdaddy out of nowhere. It was a big crawdaddy. One time, Hillbilly John Hill and I did the "cornfield hop" in it – just tearing ass through this guy's dirt fields in the middle of the night drinking Dickel.[10]

Blaine: Yeah, it was huge. You could sleep in there, and we could fit a lot of stuff in it.

Scott: We were practicing at Yellow Creek Park in Owensboro under this picnic shelter out in the middle of nowhere. Me, Toby and Blaine were banging around – Toby went somewhere – I got behind the drums and said, "Let's do something like 'Road Runner' by the Sex Pistols." I just started doing this beat and going, "Go, daddy, go!" That's where the beat and the chorus for Crawdaddy came from.

Later Blaine came back with, well, he ripped off "Cadillac Ranch" by Bruce Springsteen. "There she sits just gleaming in the sun," that's straight off "Cadillac Ranch."

---

[10] Between this instance and the Ramones incident, I'm shocked farmers in the Owensboro area weren't reporting crop circles.

God, we drove that thing to death. It was great. I mean, all those first trips up to Detroit were in that car. I remember one time we were coming back from Detroit on the Fourth of July weekend, and we were lighting bottle rockets out of it driving through Cincinnati.

One night we were getting ready to play Boot's Bar in Lexington. Across the street was Coomers strip club. Everybody called it "Comers." Blaine and I and Jon Quick, our de facto manager, were sitting in the Crawdaddy with the top down drinking Boone's Farm, and this woman comes up and goes, "Oh, y'all want to see the show?" And she puts a matchstick _in_ each nipple, lights them on fire and just gives us a good swing back and forth.[11]

Eventually the Crawdaddy just wouldn't go anymore. I was broke and couldn't fix it. I think I abandoned it in an apartment complex parking lot.

REDNECK ROMANCE
Blaine: One night after I'd come home from Montreal and New York, I was working a graveyard shift at a convenience store and pretty much what I wrote that night is what we do now. I think I jotted down a couple of things that Scott had said and made them rhyme.

Scott: At first we called it "Daviess County Romance." We unveiled it at that party at the VFW in Daviess County. Blaine basically ripped off the music to "Good Hearted Woman" – it's just sped up a little bit.

Yeah, we're making fun of people, but when those same people heard this song, they loved it. It's not based on any singular individual. It's more of an amalgam of Owensboro. It's a slight diss, but it's also paying homage. This was kind of the start of writing about our friends and redneck bar culture – The Brass Ass, The Executive Inn and the stuff that goes down at the Showroom Lounge – just the nightlife of Owensboro.

---

[11] I asked if the nipples were pierced and was told, "No." Scott swears the matches went into the nipples. The human body is a wonderland.

DRIVE-IN

Scott: We had these drive-in theaters around Owensboro. The one downtown was called the Cardinal Drive-In. One night when I was a kid, we were coming home from youth groups at church. When we drove past the Cardinal, I saw a boob on the screen.

Blaine: That's the second really good song I wrote. I had that before the band started. I used to love the drive-in, still do. My parents started taking me to the drive-in when I was old enough to not cry. I'd sit in the backseat, get some candy and pass out. My dad would drink beer and have a grocery bag full of popcorn.

We'd go see stuff like the *Wild Bunch* – my dad saw that so many times, he could talk along to it. We saw *Planet of the Apes.* When I was in kindergarten, we saw *Salt and Pepper* with Peter Lawford and Sammy Davis, Jr. It was terrible. After that, this cartoon came on, *Yellow Submarin*e. I watched it for a few minutes, and my parents started to leave, and I screamed, "Why are we going?!? I wanna watch the cartoon."

My parents had no interest in that movie. My dad did not like the Beatles at all. He thought they were English guys trying to be the Everly Brothers.

Me screaming normally wouldn't work. But my mom said, "Billy Ray, turn the car around. Let's watch the cartoon."

I loved it, man. I didn't know who The Beatles were. I just knew it was a cartoon and the music was awesome. I was five years old, and that was a mind-blowing moment.

In high school we snuck into the drive-in in the trunk half the time. I didn't want to pay the $3 to get in. Usually, two of us would get in the trunk, and they'd ask the driver, "Sure you don't got anybody in that trunk?" We never got in trouble for it or got caught.

One time whoever drove thought they'd be funny by not letting us out and going to the concession stand. I'm claustrophobic and was ready to fucking kill them.

LITTLE HELP

"Self-righteous combination,
Against those who don't share my view.
I picked these targets,
My expert opinion, nothing new."

Scott: I wrote the lyrics on the ceiling of that house on Bassett Avenue when I was in a sleeping bag in the attic. That was about Toby – he was driving us crazy. He wasn't well. Let's just put it that way. Those words just flowed out.

Blaine: I think I might've accidentally written the music, maybe. Scott did a good job. They're really good lyrics.

HE'S GONE

Blaine: When I was in Texas for about a year, I was still learning to play and write songs. I knew that I could eventually start writing good songs, and this was the first good one I wrote.

It's kind of the story of me leaving town and my former girlfriend, even though we weren't quite together when I left. I might have ripped off Bruce Springsteen a little. I liked his live version of "Cadillac Ranch" because there was a call and response thing.

Early on, Scott and I played that together at an open mic night at a place called Goldie's Best Little Opryhouse. It was a super-old redneck, hick bar that people who lived outside of Owensboro would come into town and go to.

I told Scott, "Hey, let's go get drunk and do this. I've done it before, and there were some terrible people there." I told him, "You're not going to be the worst. You're also not going to be the best." He took it really seriously, which was cool.

Backstage was weird. You're back there waiting with a bunch of old women who wanted to be Tammy Wynette and kids from drama classes singing Loretta Lynn.

But we played that song, and the rest of the house band picked it up because it was only three chords.

73

DOOMSDAY POPTARTS

Blaine: Scott came up with the phrase "Doomsday Poptarts." We had all these fast hardcore songs, and they were awful. This was the only good one.

Scott: Well, there was no outlaw country to make fun of back then. We were playing in Evansville a lot and still living in Owensboro. There was this one goth band – they were very pretentious, and all they did was rip off Bauhaus and the Cure. We didn't like that. It was just a little rivalry, and we took a shot at them.

Blaine: We were mad because there were goth bands, and that's what the girls liked. There were also a lot of the cute girls who were goth and some of them liked us, but they'd go crazy for these goth guys. Those guys would paint their faces and talk the most pretentious horseshit.

They were really pompous and nihilistic. And, they're from fucking southern Indiana? Come on! There was one of them that made fun of us, "Oh you're from Kentucky! I bet you like listening to the Police?"

I remember saying, "Kinda."

He said, "Oh, I bet you like Springsteen."

I said, "Yeah, I like Springsteen, too."

When we moved to Lexington, there was still a lot of that goth shit going on – it was all in good fun, but we thought it was stupid.

RUNAWAY TRAIN

Scott: "Runaway Train" is about Owensboro, too. Blaine and I co-wrote that. There were book burnings in Owensboro – record burnings, too. They were burning Kurt Vonnegut and Led Zeppelin up on Mount Pleasant Hill. That's true.

Blaine: They were burning everything. Everything was evil. Even ABBA was evil. Everyone was evil. Everything that didn't take place in church was evil.

Our senior year in high school, they had a lot of record burnings in our town. Every church seemed like they were competing. There had to have been 50 of those fucking things.

It was the Charismatics[12] and the Fundamentalists, not the Baptists. The Baptists, we didn't do that. We'd warn your parents about music here and there, but we didn't have record burnings – that was something rednecks would do.

The Charismatics were huge. They investigated anything that was popular, but they didn't know about punk rock, so they weren't saying anything about that. It was KISS and AC/DC, Deep Purple, Ted Nugent, Zeppelin and the Stones, that was their evil. Of course, Alice Cooper – easy target. I showed my parents some of the records they were talking about and was like, "Man, they're exaggerating. Here's what the lyrics really say."

My parents were teachers. They weren't about standing out and being crazy and burning stuff. I got really upset about the whole thing, and my parents got on me for being that upset about people burning records. They said, "We hate to see you get so upset about something like this. You should get upset about your grades. Get more upset about not taking trash out. You left the Pop-Tarts out the other night. You should be more upset about not getting your driver's license."

There were even people from churches coming to school passing out pamphlets and talking to kids. I had two friends who were a couple years younger than me, and they thought they were so guilty that they had their own record burning between their houses.

---

[12] Want to know why most people outside Kentucky think that church in our state is just a bunch of snake-handling, speaking-in-tongues hillbillies who can magically heal other members of the congregation? It's because of the Charismatics and Fundamentalists, a relatively cultish branch of Christianity. Unfortunately, their actions get more attention than they should, but hey, maybe they can heal your grandmother's warts. The Baptists just didn't want you to dance.

SHE'S SO COOL

Blaine: That was about a girl that I liked a lot. She was a rich girl, and she'd always talk a big game. She always had the information. She got tickets to concerts, but she'd never go. She'd just tack them to the wall by her bed.

This was me being mad at her – she knows about it. She didn't deserve that, but it's what happened.

Scott: She was one of my sister's best friends, Suzanne. She was hot, cute, smart and cool as hell.

My friend Steve Terrell and I went down to Bowling Green with her to see Jason & The Scorchers. We had this weed we called The Goo. It was this Jamaican press weed, and it was the fucking best shit – we smoked that shit for two years. That's what Blaine started smoking, and it's no wonder he became the world's biggest pothead. It was amazing shit.

We're at this Jason & The Scorchers show, and she was so stoned she kept collapsing. It kept knocking her ass out, and we were kind of worried. We thought we were going to have to take her to the hospital.

We left the show, took her down this hill and she's like, "I'm better. I'm better." So, we went back to the show, and she just fell out again. She was a little scenester who talked a big game, but never really took the plunge.

BYE, BYE, GLENN FREY

Blaine: I hated that guy so much. I remember hearing "Smuggler's Blues" and thought it was the worst song.[13] It was so boring, but somehow he was all over the radio. He was huge. He was like the number-one entertainer, and he was horrible.

Scott and I just laughed at how cheesy it was, but it really wasn't

---

[13] Can confirm "Smuggler's Blues" is a fucking awful song, and somehow the music video is worse.

funny back then. That's how the culture was. Instead of having cool stuff, there was that shit. You couldn't just dial up any music you wanted back then. It was very controlled what you heard and saw – whether purposely or not. People just gravitated towards safe music or they made safe music for big outlets. Either way, it was really boring, and Glenn Frey was the epitome of it all.

Scott: "Smuggler's Blues" and "You Belong To The City," yeah, just the fucking the worst. We beat Mojo Nixon to writing that song. Instead, he did "Don Henley Must Die."

We opened up for Mojo in '87 in Lexington. He heard us play, "Bye, Bye, Glenn Frey," and to his credit, he didn't rip it off. He was like, "Those motherfuckers, Nine Pound Hammer. They beat me!"

LOOKIN' FOR SOMEBODY
Scott: Bart quit the band, and Active Ingredients had broken up – man, we loved them. We played some shows with them in Lexington and one show in Nashville with them on a Sunday night. Drove all the way there. Kept saying, "We're going to Nashville. It's going to be awesome." There were 20 people there, but it was fun. After Active Ingredients broke up, we got their bass player, Brian Moore. To this day, he carries like three songs with him to every band he plays in. One of them was this song called "Lookin' for Somebody."

Blaine: Brian brought that over with him from his old band. They hated to play it. Their guitar player hated that song because it was so poppy. We put distorted guitar on it, and that made it even better.

Every time we'd see Active Ingredients, we would request that song. It was so cool because they'd play hardcore songs, then they'd play "Lookin' for Somebody." It's a great song, and it's just so simple. It's hard to write songs that simple, it really is. I don't know how Brian wrote a song that simple.

We thought we should rip that song off. Then we got him in the band and asked if we could play it. He was kind of a legend to have in the band and to play that song.

He brought in three songs, "Lookin' for Somebody," "Suicide

Romance," "Take from the Poor, Give to the Rich" – and that was a hardcore song that goes, "Take from poor, give to the rich. Reagan regime, son of a bitch." We played all three of those live.

Brian Moore: Scott got it wrong – it's called "Lookin' for Someone." That song was fairly popular, and it made a lot of college playlists. At one point I actually got a royalty check for $2.12. I never cashed it – I framed it.

It's just kind of about breaking up with a girl, then going out and trying to find her at the bar and no one's seen her. The chorus "Nah, nah, nah, nah, nah, nah, nah, nah," Scott embraced that. I was surprised because that's really not his kind of songwriting style. It was his idea to switch back and forth on the vocals.

GEARHEAD BLUES
Scott: That's the first song we really wrote. When I brought that in, Blaine said, "Oh, we're going to write about people we know?"

Blaine: He was talking about these gearheads, which we'd think were probably cool now, but these dudes were just so obsessed with these cars at such a young age. Once again, it was like they think they're so cool because they got so many girls. These dudes would call each other by their engines names, "Oh hey, there's 454 over there." "Hey. Turbo! What's up, Turbo?"

Scott: It's about that culture in Owensboro, the hot rod culture, burning steaks at Sizzler and listening to the Crüe. Blaine probably would have gone more Springsteen, or maybe Lou Reed or gone more ethereal. It was like, "Oh no. Wait? We're going to do this? This is our approach?" It worked.

HATE TO THINK
"I saw two girls dancing that I love the best"

Scott: That's about Tanya Robey and this girl named Robin Woodall. They were cheerleaders. One time in sixth grade I was waiting for the bus, and I went into our middle school band room because there was a stereo in there, and I saw those two girls – who were in eighth grade – double bumping[14] in their Duck Head jeans to "Nothing to Lose" off KISS *Alive!* I was mesmerized by them.

BAREFOOT COUNTY

Scott: There was this place, the Tyler Truck Stop. We'd go out there all the time. It was across the river in Indiana, and we'd go hang out and get milkshakes and shit. Just an old, old hillbilly place in Southern Indiana.

Blaine: One time when I was there, I saw a VHS tape for a dollar, *Hot Summer in Barefoot County*, and I thought that should be a song. The cover of the box said "Hot Rods... Hot Lips... and White Lightning."

So, I said, "Well I'm just stealing this because no one's heard of that." In the '70s there was this whole hillbilly, redneck exploitation thing. It was one of those, and they're usually awful and unwatchable.

The story of the song I made up, I didn't even have a VCR back then.

In the song, there are a lot of references dropped. A lot of it is made up, but one reference is about a former classmate.

I think Robert Dennis was the only person who was real in that song. He was a kid in our high school. He would try to fight everyone all the time. He was an alright dude, but he tried to fight me. It was horrible dealing with him because he was this little, short guy.

I don't know what's worse, beating up a little guy or getting beat up by a little guy.

I didn't like fighting, and you couldn't unleash on a little guy because people would have looked at me like I was crazy. Someone would go, "What are you doing beating up on him?" But if he started

---

[14] The Bump was a popular dance in the 1970s and '80s in America. Basically, two people bump their hips into each other.

hitting you and you don't fight back, "What are you doing? Fight back!"

The Mud, The Blood, and The Beers *came out right around the time the University of Kentucky started its student-run radio station, WRFL.*

Kakie Urch (Associate Professor of Multimedia at The School of Journalism and Media at The University of Kentucky, Co-founder of WRFL): We definitely played Nine Pound Hammer all the time on WRFL. They were an absolute hit on every level of the station. A lot of college radio stations have cliques – hardcore, Brit pop, country, bluegrass, metal. Nine Pound Hammer was the only band that really got everybody to say, "Oh, that is great!" People called them cowpunk, but their lyrics really raised up our everyday reality here in Kentucky.

Brian Moore: It was great we were able to walk that record straight down to the station and say, "Play this!" We sneakingly called every day and kept requesting our songs. Hearing yourself on the radio – it's a magic feeling.

Blaine: It seemed like it took forever to come out, but it was only a few months. I thought it sounded terrible, but once we started getting all these reviews, I let it go. You don't argue with success unless you're foolish. I think Scott's voice was the best thing about that album.

People who liked punk rock really liked the fact that it had penetrated small towns. It was like going into enemy territory. They were glad to see it wasn't just big cities that were latching onto punk, so it was an affirmation of everything we were doing.

CHAPTER 11
KICKED THAT THING THROUGH THE DASHBOARD

From his garage, Len Puch mounted a sizable mail campaign trying to get the album noticed. His hard work resulted in a fair amount of college radio spins, lots of positive reviews and Nine Pound Hammer getting noticed around England and on John Peel's BBC 1 radio show.

Len Puch: I had a really good list of college radio stations. A lot of them would tell you what number your band's song was in their rotation. I also sent out stuff to at least 400 or 500 different publications. The only way I could promote it was to get reviews from all these little punk rock fanzines and magazines – then hope to get one big review.

Their songs would get played, and then once we got a few reviews, I'd send that to distributors and get them to want to buy it. Everything was done by mail. There was no internet, so it was a slow process.

Scott: Len got it out. He worked really hard at helping us get distribution and press. He's a huge part of our success.

Blaine: He sent copies out naively, not knowing if he was going to make his money back, but he got them everywhere.

Scott: It goes over well. We get written up in *Sounds* and *New Musical Express*. We're getting on the front pages of magazines and had these amazing reviews in *Billboard, College Music Journal*

(*CMJ*) and *Goldmine*. I'm like, "Hey, what the hell? It doesn't even sound that good." But that's why some of them liked it. Again, the songs were strong, the lyrics were great, the music was good. It was real.

Blaine: That got the best press I've ever gotten, including anything I've done with Nashville Pussy. I was horrified about how bad it sounded, but the reviews on it were crazy. I don't know if we got a perfect one, but we were getting four out of five stars, nine out of 10, the closest thing they could give us without giving a perfect score.

Before it came out, Scott and I said, "I hope we get one good review." We hoped there was someone out there that was going to pick up on this and understand it.

We got into some pretty mainstream magazines. My mom picked up one, saw a review and was like, "Oh you're amazing. You're in a magazine." That's when our parents thought we were doing great.

Writers said it sounded like Johnny Cash slam dancing or like Clint Eastwood bare-knuckle boxing or this combination or the Ramones meets *Hee Haw*. I thought that was great. I was glad it was taken seriously and no one considered us a novelty.

Everyone thought it was funny. I always say if you can be funny, you should be, because I know all kinds of bands with talented musicians, and they're funny when you talk to them. But when they write songs, they sound like they went to some generic school. I ask them why they're not being funny, and they're like, "I don't want to do that." It's like you're funny all day long, and the least interesting thing you do is singing.

I always thought humor should be part of it. Chuck Berry was hysterical. The Cramps were funny. The Ramones were funny and pushed it to where you didn't know if they were serious or not, or if they were really just crazy.

Scott: Hell, John Peel was playing "Redneck Romance" on his BBC show.

Len Puch: It was expensive to send stuff to Europe, but we sent quite a bit of stuff there.

Blaine: John Peel played it so much that someone mentioned in one of the reviews, "Even though John Peel is playing this to death, we still like it." We were reading this, and I didn't know who John Peel was. We were really isolated in Kentucky.

He played it so much that someone called up John Peel and said he was the drummer for Nine Pound Hammer. So John Peel met him at a bar and realized that he wasn't our drummer. Turns out that guy had a band and wanted to meet John Peel. We were hearing these stories like thirdhand going, "Really?"

Scott: They were looking for anything cutting edge, and I guess they just thought, "Oh my God, these fucking hillbillies! This crazy garage punk shit coming out of Kentucky!" They were loving it, and we're like, "We're going to be rock stars!"

Blaine: We had all these reviews and thought they were going to lead to something. We didn't know you had to follow up. We didn't know what to do. We were out of our league as far as that goes. If we lived in a different city and had a real manager and a lawyer and all that stuff, it would have been different, but we had no idea how to capitalize on that. It's very fleeting. We were in there one month, and the next month, someone else was the next big thing. Then it's like two years have gone by, and you're like, "Oh, we were on the radio in 1989," and it's 1991 and no one gives two shits.

Scott: Maybe if we were on a label, which we really weren't. Len was doing everything he could, though. He just didn't have those kinds of connections.

Blaine: We were waiting for it all to kind of take off by itself because it seemed like it was going to. We thought all we had to do at this point was just play music. Most bands back then wouldn't know what to do either. It was a good few months of surprises.

CHAPTER 12
ON THE ROAD, NO PLACE TO STAY

Not knowing exactly what to do next, the band went back to gigging regionally and tried to put together a proper tour to promote the album.

Scott: We went up the east coast, and that's when we played Portland, Maine. Thankfully, the sound man put us up because the night before, we stayed in the parking lot in Kennebunkport not far from President Bush's compound.

Rob Hulsman: That tour was so tight. We bought a pack of bologna and a loaf of bread to share between us.

Hopefully the statute of limitations has run out, but about that bread, mustard and bologna.

Blaine: We had to steal bologna, I think. I'd never stolen anything in my fucking life. We had to have food.

Scott: Bread, bologna and a thing of mustard, that's how broke we were. We barely made it to a show in Boston. I had worked for Michael Dukakis' presidential campaign in '88. I made friends who lived in Boston, and this guy, he was like, "Yeah, when you play here, I'll put you up." I got in touch with him on a payphone, and he took us to this steakhouse and wrote it off. We ate like Vikings. It was like the first real food we'd had in two or three days.

Rob Hulsman: On the East Coast tour, we played a lot of little weird rooms, but it was great. It was super punk rock, and we met a lot of crazy folks, like good crazy folks.

Scott: We went up to Chicago and played in this Hispanic ghetto. It was this weird showcase for Roadrunner Records or something like that. Anyway, there was no hotel. We didn't get paid, and we had to driveway out in the suburbs to this house.

Brian Moore rode with this guy from the club. I think it was the soundman. We ended up at this modern-looking abandoned house in this crazy, isolated cul de sac. Brian gets out of the car and is looking back at me. He tells me, "You're not going to believe this, but Satanists have been breaking in here and capturing people."

We went into the house, and the guy we followed out there said, "Yeah they tried to get these people that were staying here. That's why nobody stays here." There was this piece of sheet metal over the window, and the front door was beat to hell.

Brian Moore: We were terrified. We didn't sleep the whole night. We kept waiting for something to happen.

Scott: Then we headed towards Madison, Wisconsin, to the O'Cayz Corral. The show was pretty good, and we stayed at Blaine's aunt and uncle's house. Slept on the floor. Then we went to Minneapolis and played with Helios Creed, this crazy-ass guitar player.

Slogging it out on the road, things were starting to change in the band, or at least a couple of the band members were trying to change things.

Blaine: There started to be a kind of division. Before we played a Halloween show, our drummer and bass player wanted to talk to us about how things were going to change or some shit. Rob was a Def Leppard fan. He had a big British flag spread across his big double kick drum. We showed up to play the gig and we were like, "Okay, this ain't cool at all." Rob was solid, heavy, but he wanted us to be a metal band or Bad Brains.

I was like, "Let's just go back to doing the cowpunk stuff please, it's better." It's something we could do that no one else does. It kind of became me and Scott versus them.

We saw the Melvins open up for the Lazy Cowgirls. They just sounded like, "JUUUUUUUUUUHHHH!!!" Me and Scott didn't like that at all. Then Lazy Cowgirls came out, and it sounded like dudes playing early Nine Pound Hammer and the Ramones.

Brian Moore: Rob mentioned an article that described the Melvins as Black Sabbath on Thorazine. That's all I had to hear, so we piled in the van and went to the show. It was a dinky little club, maybe 30 or 40 people max. It was the Melvins' first or second national tour, so I was able to get right up in front of Buzz Osborne, and they just destroyed the crowd – loud, nasty and determined.

Blaine: Then we had a big argument with Rob and Brian about which band was better, and Scott goes, "Hum, one of the Melvin songs. Which was the catchiest one?" That's when Brian was like, "It's not about songs. It's about getting in your face and being heavy."

Scott: Brian, he didn't like me. He didn't think I was good. Blaine and I were moving towards cowpunk, and they wanted to do hardcore. It just wasn't jiving.

So, before a show outside Evansville, Brian and Rob drank a fifth of Dickel.

Brian Moore: I got myself fired from the band. Depending on which side of sobriety you're on, it was either a rock-and-roll crash and burn or something completely dysfunctional. We were set to play in this big VFW Hall outside Evansville surrounded by cornfields. We were hanging out by the van before the show, drinking bourbon from the bottle. The last thing I really remember that night was when I drained the last few drops out of that bottle and tossed it into a cornfield. After that, I was in a blackout mode.

Blaine: He started throwing Rob's cymbals around, and he could barely stand. He was taking his bass and swinging it at these kids while on stage.

Brian Moore: I was out of it. The next thing I remember was waking up in the middle of the cornfield covered in mud and cowshit with the worst hangover ever. It was Sunday morning, and there was no one around. The VFW was deserted. Luckily, I had Scott's mom's home phone number in my pocket. So, I walked about a mile to this little convenience store to use the payphone – I'm still surprised they didn't call the cops on me.

I called Scott's mom's house. Rob Hulsman answered the phone, and I sheepishly asked him to come and get me. When he picked me up, he told me how I had fucked up and that Scott and Blaine were super pissed off at me. He then recounted all the stupid shit I'd done.

He told me that even before we hit our first note, I fell backwards into his drum kit and knocked it all over. I then decided the audience were my enemies. I took off my bass guitar, raised it over my head like an ax, and swung it down at the crowd in front of me. Then, I went headfirst into the crowd. To this day, I still thank that crowd for what they did. They not only hoisted me back on stage, but they also saved my bass, which I still have.

During all the confusion, I slipped away to pass out, but instead of passing out in the bathroom or in the van, I decided to wander off into the cornfields. When the guys were ready to leave, I was nowhere to be found. Scott and Blaine had already left for Lexington, so it was Rob and myself on the long, silent ride back to town.

Shawn Chambers: (Kelly Chambers' Husband and Nine Pound Hammer Fan): I was there, and I remember it seemed like it took almost no time for it to start devolving. You could hear Brian saying shit and Scott yelling at him between songs – they were really getting in each other's faces. My friend Hank was with me. He looks at me and goes, "Are all their shows like this?"

I sort of recollect Brian possibly falling down some stairs or something.

Brian Moore: The main event was me tackling Scott from behind, sending us down a flight of stairs behind the stage.

Kelly Chambers: He tried to hit Scott with his bass.

Scott: If I hadn't pulled my head up, it would've hurt me really badly. Things were not the same after that, obviously.

Blaine: Scott was like, "We can't have this guy anymore." That was the end of Brian. It's too bad, but we found Matt Bartholomy. He played bass like I played guitar. He was in a band called White Hiney from Owensboro.

Matt Bartholomy: I was friends with them, so I went to see them in Evansville one night. I got there late and missed their show, but I heard that it was kind of a wild time. Anyway, Blaine asked me if I wanted to play bass for them because apparently all this shit had gone down.

It seemed to me like they were really going somewhere. They were well known on the underground-ish level. I really believed in it. It was awesome to be in a real touring band. I was always really impressed with the songwriting and the whole sort of a satire of Southern people, but most of them were kind of just real stories. You can't make this shit up. It was really fun music to play. I felt like it was a good fit for me. I really was pretty passionate about playing in that band.

Blaine: Matt was a big part of it. He was so quiet and easy to get along with. Good-looking dude, he got a lot of girls – Scott and him would compete. They had a contest to see who could name the most girls they'd been with. It was ridiculous how good they were at that. It was very frustrating for someone like me.

Rob Hulsman: Then we went up to Canada. That was a big one. There was a band in Lexington called Vale of Tears – they were friends and told us about this Canadian booking agent.

Scott: Tony Briggs from Vale of Tears, rest in peace. He knew a guy named Dave McKeegan, and he gave Blaine his info. Dave was in Winnipeg and had this little empire up there. He ran some clubs and booked us for shows throughout Canada.

I had this shitty, underpowered white Dodge van. The best thing about it, it had one of those Pioneer stereos on the ceiling. That's why I bought it. Otherwise, it was a piece of shit.

Matt Bartholomy: It was a fucking gutted work van. No seats, no nothing. I believe we had a mattress in there to sit on or we sat on the damn wheel well.

Blaine: It sucked. Transportation was always a challenge because they didn't just hand credit cards out to anyone back then, and they didn't have van rentals – you had to have collateral and all that shit.

Scott: We headed toward the border through Fargo, and there was nothing up there. Finally, we met Dave McKeegan at the border, and he took us to Winnipeg.

Winnipeg had this cool little scene, and we immediately won everybody over. All the locals loved us. They thought we were these hillbillies from Kentucky that talked funny with these crazy songs.

So we played three nights at the Royal Albert Arms Hotel, which was like a wino hotel – Dave ran it. The second night we played, we got heckled by this chick making fun of us for being from Kentucky, but everybody loved us. A few years later, we went back and did a three-night stand with Urge Overkill before they broke.

That first tour, we made our way across Canada to Vancouver. As we left Winnipeg, it was October, and there's a whiteout. We can't see, and we're trying to make our way to Saskatoon. It was so cold and windy that the carburetor kept freezing, and the van started losing power. So, we found this garage. We were literally stuffing socks in the engine bay to keep it warm enough to keep going. I look back and marvel that we're alive.

We made it to Saskatoon, rolling in like these ambassadors from Kentucky. People just loved it, man, we were just killing it. I mean, shows of the year and girls and great beer and weed. It was the golden age. We met a lot of good people there. Blaine eventually met Ruyter[15] there.

Then we went up to Edmonton and played there at another hotel wino bar. We met this band called Tankhog. They were from Vancouver, super nice guys. We got to know them, and they said, "Man, Blaine was wandering around the halls of the hotel, and we just didn't know if that dude was a serial killer or what."

He had short hair and was just intense looking. He was not a happy-go-lucky guy back then. When he finally started smoking weed and started getting laid more – well, all that will put a smile on your face.

Blaine: When we went on our first tour up the east coast and across Canada, I realized we were hicks. That's how people saw us.

Scott: So, we were driving back to Winnipeg to get to Toronto – we didn't play any shows in between Vancouver and Winnipeg – we were so broke we had to go back into the States to buy gas because it was cheaper. Blaine got some money wired to him from his mom to help us.

We hung out in Toronto with these folks who had a thing called Fort Goof, this punk rock squat thing. They were kind of assholes, but we played a good show. I think we played with GBH there, this pretty famous punk band from England.

Then we went to Guelph, stayed in another wino hotel, and some guy tried to climb in our window. It was hilarious. We also played in London, Ontario, at a club called Call The Office. Cool club.

The next four or five years, we were the most popular band in Winnipeg. We were celebrities, kind of. That was our first big foray out. We didn't make any money, of course, but it was awesome.

We were young and dumb and just killing it.

---

[15] Ruyter Suys, Blaine's wife and lead guitarist of Nashville Pussy.

CHAPTER 13
OUT COLD ON THE FLOOR

Blaine: It was not a good time. This was '90, '91, we were 27 years old – that was ancient in rock and roll. We had friends who had bought houses and settled down. That's what you were supposed to do, and we were still meandering around.

Scott: Things kind of died off, man. We're like, "Oh, what do we do now?" We're still playing, but a slight pause was going on.

Kelly Chambers: We were feeding each other. It really was a group effort. Scott probably had 120 fucking jobs during this time. He was always losing his job, or he was always quitting his job or too drunk to go in.

For a while, Scott worked at a sandwich shop, and he'd slip us sandwiches for free. Blaine and I went to that sandwich shop every day. It was hard times at that point. We were barely making rent. It was like a bunch of little commie kids stealing and taking care of one another. I know we stole gas at least once in my car to get somewhere. I had never done anything like that.

Blaine: I think our parents were happy at first that we'd gotten together and done all this stuff, but a couple years go by and you're not doing anything and people judge. Especially about money and everything you're supposed to do. We were getting so much pressure, and we weren't happy. We were putting a lot of work into it, but we weren't having fun. It was frustrating.

Scott got lectured constantly, "Where are you going? What are you doing? When are you going to be tired of this? When are you going to grow up? Your friend, he owns a storm window replacement place, and he's got a two-story house out in Owensboro. He goes to our church, and everyone likes him." I just ignored my family.

Scott: We hooked and crooked. We were able to practice in this house in the suburbs for *Smokin' Taters*. We wrote a lot of stuff there. It was another band's house. Rob ended up living there. God, there were cat litter boxes everywhere.

Blaine: I think I'd written "Cadillac Inn" and a couple other songs that were kind of getting better. Then Wanghead Records folded. So, we were just living in Lexington working jobs, hanging out with girlfriends and playing The Wrocklage.[16]

Blaine: Before *Smoking Taters*, we actually went to Dave Barrick's in Glasgow and recorded some demos for a thing that later would be called *Mulebite Deluxe*. We were so frustrated. It was a time when a lot of crappy bands were doing well. Punk rock was still big. Bands on a nightly basis would play Bogart's up in Cincinnati. Hundreds and hundreds of people were in that club, and it was all passing us by.

Scott: We're kind of dead in the water, then Tim Warren of Crypt Records to the rescue – he called out of the blue. Crypt was just this super organic, great rock and roll, punk label.

Blaine: My girlfriend Kelly told me, "You've got a phone call from Germany."

Tim Warren was like, "Hey, I didn't know you guys were still a band. Do you want to make a record?" And I was like, "Yeah, yeah!" He said, "Well, I'll pay for it, and you'll get to tour Europe."

To this day, even though I've been nominated for a Grammy and all

---

[16] The Wrocklage was a historic bar in Lexington for underground and up-and-coming bands at the time. Bands like Soundgarden, The Flaming Lips, The Smashing Pumpkins, Slint, Uncle Tupelo, and The Replacements played there.

this other shit that's gone on with me, that was still the best day ever.

Then I had to go to work, so I couldn't tell any of the other guys in the band. So for eight hours, that was my secret only. That was a big deal.

Scott: I was working at the South Lexington YMCA. I'm literally down there playing basketball with some friends, and Blaine drives all the way out there – again, no cell phones. He says, "Hey, man, I got a call from Tim Warren. He wants to do a record." I'm like, "Cool, cool, cool." Blaine says, "And he wants to bring us to Europe." I'm like, "Oh! Okay." Fire's relit.

With an album full of songs they'd been working on, the Hammer heads to the Big Apple.

Scott: Tim was in New York at the time, so we went up there to record at Coyote Studios with Mike Mariconda from The Raunch Hands.

Blaine: Me, Kelly, and a friend named Jeremy drove up a couple days early and crashed with a guy named Mike Chandler, the singer of The Raunch Hands – he lived in Hoboken. We met tons of people up there, including all The Raunch Hands, had a party, and then Scott came up with Rob and Matt.

Scott: We met this couple Bill and Michelle in Detroit. They moved to Brooklyn. We stayed at their apartment and slept next to cat litter boxes.[17] They lived right by the 9th Avenue and Smith Street subway stop. We would drink Ballantine Ale with them – that stuff would fuck you up.

Rob Hulsman: The second album? We recorded it three times. First, there was a recording studio called the Drag Strip here in Kentucky. I don't even know what happened to that demo. I guess it's kind of lost to history, unfortunately. Scott and Blaine weren't happy with that recording session.

---

[17] Yes, you are picking up on a recurring theme.

We recorded it another time, and that's what became *Mulebite Deluxe*. And once again, they weren't really pleased with it. Then we ended up going up to New York and recording in Brooklyn.

Blaine: Coyote Studios was kind of in the middle of a desolate area. One of the guys who owned it had a brother in the band called The Del-Lords. A lot of hipster stuff got recorded there.

We recorded *Smokin' Taters* in four days – we played most of it live.

Rob Hulsman: That one was a little more professional. Not that Len wasn't professional, but this was a studio in Brooklyn and it was with some of the Crypt Records guys.

Blaine: *Smokin' Taters'* original album cover got rejected. It was a cartoon of us on the train. I thought it was funny, but it was too cutesy for Tim Warren. He said, "It's the worst album cover I've ever seen. You're all sitting there riding this little engine that couldn't. You aren't even going fast."

Scott: The album cover is a screenshot from *Duel,* Steven Spielberg's first movie where a truck is ramming Dennis Weaver's car off the road. It didn't look great, but who cares? It's iconic in its own way.

The second album was infinitely better than the first one, but I think *Mulebite Deluxe* is better.

The first record was released in England, the second one, the whole European continent. It made a lot of noise for us. We got tons of press and reviews in other languages, and they were glowing.

Tim had this great network – talk about another lunatic hard worker. That album sold like 8,000 copies, which was a lot for a band like us.

Over the years, New York City has taken a lot from Nine Pound Hammer – well, primarily Blaine Cartwright.

Blaine: We had a nice time recording. Only thing that was bad, I came back early and the rest of the guys went to the Continental

Club with our equipment in the van, which got broken into.

Scott: The night our shit got stolen, we were at the Continental Club, watching Goober & The Peas – Jack White used to play drums for them. We were supposed to leave town that night after the show.

Well, Joey Ramone was hanging out at the Continental Club, and so was the little guy from *Twin Peaks*.[18]

Our van was parked right across the street, and we were kind of watching it.

Rob Hulsman: I was there for that. That was total chaos. I just remember we were at the club, all of a sudden people ran up to us and said, "They're breaking into your van."

Kelly Chambers: Scott saw the little person from *Twin Peaks* dancing in the club. Scott was convinced it was some kind of weird fucking sign. I think he thought that guy was a distraction. Like somebody told him, "You keep them busy, and we'll steal all their gear."

Scott: It was probably an inside job between the doorman and crew of guys.

Matt Bartholomy: That was our fault, man. We were naive about how you can't leave anything, and they literally stole it in front of my face. I was sitting on a curb across the street from the van, and this girl pretended to lay a blanket down to sell some shit on the street.

These guys jimmied the door, and by the time I realized what was going on, they'd already taken our shit and were gone.

Rob Hulsman: Everybody ran toward the van and started chasing some people. Actually, my snare drum was dropped a couple blocks

---

[18] Actor Michael J. Anderson, who has Osteogenesis Imperfecta, a genetic condition commonly known as "brittle bone disease" or "glass bone disease."

away. I ended up saving that, but Blaine lost his Marshall head. At the time, that was a big deal.

Matt Bartholomy: I remember having to tell Blaine about it when we got back.

Blaine: My grandmother passed away, and I got $800. That was enough to buy a head and a cabinet back then. I always wanted a Marshall, and that one sounded great. After it got stolen, I replaced it, but I've never found one quite like that first one.

It's still a point of contention probably, man. I was pissed off. I was screaming. I might've broken a chair.

Rob Hulsman: I still remember the cry of agony when he heard what had happened. This was the pre-cell phone age. Everybody wasn't in constant contact all the time back then. I can still hear that scream. God, he was so upset.

Blaine: Tim told us, "I've got more money coming to you guys, like $1,800. That's what's left over after I paid for the record."
I said, "$1,800! That's like $400 a piece. My God, we're rich!" And then no, it went to replace my amp.

CHAPTER 14
SMOKIN' TATERS
(1991)

Instead of lifting a lyric from another legendary song for an album title, they pulled a witticism from their own dictionary.

Scott: We were living on Bassett Avenue. This is back when Toby was in the band. Every now and then, we'd have a band meal, usually stroganoff and fried potatoes. That got shortened to smoking potatoes and then just smokin' taters.

Moses Naedele (Lead Singer of Gnarly Love): I remember Toby saying, "They got that from me. I told Scott and Blaine they should call a record *Smokin' Taters*, and then years later they did."

LONG GONE DADDY
Scott: That made a lot of noise for us over in Europe especially. It even charted in some countries.

Blaine: We wanted to be like Jason & The Scorchers – they did "Honky Tonk Blues" and we did "Long Gone Daddy." I had some friends who gave me shit about ripping off The Scorchers. They were right.

CADILLAC INN
Blaine: There are a handful of songs I've written in my life that were a little better than my ability, and that's one of them. It was kind of about one of my first real girlfriends. She might have gotten in a fight at a Van Halen concert.

"With your glitter bandana and your Sammy Hagar T-shirt
You're every trucker's dream
I remember you back in high school, you were such a sight
Then I saw you at the Ted Nugent show, you got kicked out
for starting a fight"

That redneck chick, yeah. Hey, you break my heart, you get in trouble – watch it, man, I might write about you.[19]

Scott: "Cadillac Inn" – true story. Eating late at night at the Cadillac Inn with people saying crazy shit. All real.

Blaine: The actual Cadillac Inn is not where we ate. That place is still there. I think we were actually eating at a place called The Royce – the Cadillac Inn sounded cooler.

We used to dine and dash because we were broke, and it used to be easy to do. We were eating, and all these rednecks were saying racist stuff. We rationalized that we were doing the world and civil rights a good deed by skipping out on our bill. We were drunk, too, that night. When we ran out we were like, "Where's the car? Where's the car?" We were laughing and Scott realized he had left his keys on the table. So, we slowly walked back in, and the redneck waitress was dangling the keys.

We had to go back in, and all of those dudes were just laughing, "Hahaha, You got caught!" Revenge was writing a song about them.

Scott: We went back years later, and for some reason, I threw my keys on top of the roof. Anyway, I dunno how we got out of that one.

EVERYTHING YOU KNOW IS WRONG
Blaine: The title comes from a comedy troupe called the Firesign Theatre from the '70s – that was one of their album titles. I saw their album at the Carnegie Library when I was a kid.

---

[19] When Blaine said this, it felt like it was directed towards me. It might be the nicest verbal threat I've ever received.

I wrote that song when I worked at this place called the Beijing Palace busing tables. A lot of it came from me overhearing conversations every day while I was serving.

IBM was across the street, and their employees came over for lunch all the time. It was mostly yuppies going, "Blah, blah, blah, blah, blah, blah, blah." I just thought, "Everything you know is wrong."

The Beijing Palace was such a shitty job that I could go on tour and come back and it was still there, because whoever they had would quit. People hated working there. I hated it. It was a messy, dirty, shitty job.

I'd go there and sleepwalk through the days, serve tea and bus tables, that's it.

I think the second time I went to Europe, they were like, "You're in a band?" I was this pudgy balding dude. I didn't look like I was in a band at all.

FEELIN' KINDA FROGGY

Blaine: The music is ripped off from the beginning of "Stay All Night, Stay A Little Longer" off a Willie Nelson live record. That was accidental. I came up with that, and Scott said, "Froggy." That song is Scott's family history, basically. I think it means if you're feeling kind of rambunctious and feisty.

> "My Grandpa Doc was a wild old man
> If what I heard was true
> He loved Wild Bird and raised horses
> And he fought in World War II
> He and his brother married the same girl
> And if you're still confused
> My uncle married my grandma
> when my daddy was only two"

Scott: My Granddad, Doc, he was like Archie Bunker combined with Elmer Fudd, just your classic Southerner. He lived in Lexington and was married to Francis, my grandmother, but then they got divorced and Francis ended up marrying Brooks, my grandfather's younger brother – he was the one with the '68 Barracuda.

Legendary feud between them, there were fisticuffs and all that shit. They were pretty infamous around Central Kentucky. My grandmother, Francis, died while still married to my Uncle Brooks.

My dad was the one who would say, "You feelin' froggy, boy?"

DON'T GET NO

American beer commercials in the late '80s and early '90s were either borderline softcore porn or full of former athletes who needed an easy paycheck. Sure, there were giant Clydesdales, but who wants to drink a beer with a horse?

But a pit bull dressed in a Hawaiian shirt with a lampshade on his head? Bottom's up. This Spud's for you!

It was all a mirage, thanks to advertising wizards and big beer companies who preyed on poor and lower-middle class individuals. One ad slogan for Old Milwaukee was, "It Doesn't Get Any Better Than This!" which is where Blaine cribbed the title from.

In Kentucky in 1988, a DUI cost you like $50 and your license was suspended for a month. Those laissez-faire rules and overconsumption came to a head on May 14, 1988, when just outside of Carrollton, Kentucky, on I-71, the deadliest drunk driving crash in U.S. history occurred.

> "Now I'm cruisin' down I-75, throwing my
> empties at the wrong way signs
> I'm so wasted I can't see shit
> And it don't get no better than this"

Blaine: This guy, Larry Mahoney, was drunk on I-71, and he ran into a school bus full of kids. They caught on fire, and he killed more than 20 of them. I said I-75 because it rhymed. It was a fucked-up situation. He was fucked up and drove the wrong way on the interstate.

They wanted to give him the death penalty. Being as progressive as you could be back then, I thought that was fucked up. Everyone drove drunk back then, and we were bombarded with alcohol commercials nonstop. Girls, good times, fun. Drink, drink, drink, drink, drink. This one guy goes out, drinks too much, and this fucking thing happens.

Everyone wanted to kill him, which I understand now more than I did back then. I think he's out of jail now, and I think the community has forgiven him. What choice do you have? There was no way that a pickup truck should have made a bus explode, but driving the wrong way down the interstate is beyond stupid.

FOLSOM PRISON BLUES
Blaine: That's a good version. That was our old-school version. We used to do part of it at normal speed, then part we'd do real fast. I wanted to do more country stuff, and we needed another song.

TURNED TRAITOR FOR A PIECE OF TAIL
Let's pause for a massacre.

Sure, the Ramones and Johnny Cash laid the foundation for Nine Pound Hammer, but the 1986 cinematic masterpiece Texas Chainsaw Massacre 2 *is also responsible for quite a bit of music and inspiration.*

Scott: *Texas Chainsaw Massacre 2* was our *Rocky Horror Picture Show.* I've seen that over 60 times. We would just sit around, get high and drunk and watch *Chainsaw 2.* It's just hilarious. That's one of the first songs I wrote all on guitar.

Blaine: Scott's seen it more times, but I saw it first in 1986 with the girl from "She's So Cool." Then Scott got a hold of it on video, and he was relentless. Anytime we were doing anything, he wanted to watch it – "Let's watch *Chainsaw 2.* Let's watch *Chainsaw 2.*"

Scott: "Turned traitor for a piece of tail" is a line out of *Texas Chainsaw Massacre 2.* It's Ruyter's dad's favorite song. There are so many quotable moments in that movie. My publishing company is called Aching Banana. That's a line, too – "Oh my aching banana."

Blaine: We did a version of "Burning Love" that sounded nothing like "Burning Love." So, we took that and put "Turned Traitor for a Piece of Tail" on top of it.

I'M ON FIRE
Blaine: I saw a Jerry Lee Lewis documentary, and I was like, "What song is this?" It was one of his songs I'd never heard.

There's a live version that's insane. I think it's him playing it in Europe in '64. A lot of people in New York were very impressed that we were covering it, because it was one of those rare songs. It showed that we'd done our homework.

I saw him in like '91. He was doing oldies, but he seemed like he still had that little crazy part about him. He was beloved, especially in the Southeast, man. I loved his country stuff, still do.

WRONG SIDE OF THE ROAD
Blaine: I wrote that about my friend Brent Ford who later transitioned to Suzanne Ford.

Brent was just a very charming, brilliant fuckup. I can't even describe the shit he pulled. I let him live with me in Lexington for months – really good company, great friend.

Suzanne Ford: I remember we were so poor in Lexington that Blaine would let me sleep on his couch, and we'd go get these French bread pizzas. You'd get two for $5, and he'd let me have one – that's the kind of friend Blaine is.

I knew about the song for a long time because I would play it for people when I wanted to brag about how nuts I was. I think I may have even listened to it the first time and thought, "Is that about me?"

I wasn't mad at all about it. It made me feel like Blaine knew where I was headed. I think Blaine wanted a different outcome for me, but Blaine never tried to make me any different than I was.

Blaine: The song was about a person who seemed to get a kick out of fucking up because they were bored when things were going good.

It's an addict thing, a chemical thing. Like the very first Nashville Pussy bass player, same thing. When things were going great, she would get bored. Same thing with Brent. It was more exciting for him to fuck things up, and he had the potential to royally fuck up some situations.

Suzanne Ford: Blaine really changed my life because when I met Blaine in the seventh grade, I was in the KISS Army. That was the extent of my music knowledge. Blaine introduced me to music.

I remember he loaned me *Beggars Banquet* and AC/DC's *Powerage*. I always tell him if it wasn't for him, I might like REO Speedwagon. I wouldn't have known anything about Bruce Springsteen if it wasn't for him.

He took me to my first Grateful Dead Show. He wasn't into them, but he drove me and a bunch of people I knew. I remember him saying, "This might be an answer for you." I did not become a Deadhead. I was somebody that identified more with hippies, and it probably saved my life because I quit doing cocaine for a little bit. I think Blaine knew that that freedom would resonate with me.

Down in Galveston, they tried to take care of me, but you can just hear it in that song – I was a lot. I was always a lot. Blaine might've left me in Texas, but he never really left me.

HEADBANGIN' STOCKBOY
"Jammin' Judas by the Keebler display
Playing air guitar by the Lysol spray
I'm hitting the doob out in the alley
I'm shelving Spaghetti-o's with Mr. Crowley
On my throne I'm never bored
Headbangin' stockboy
Pricing guns and power chords
Headbangin' stockboy"

Blaine: I thought that was funny because I'd go into Kroger late at night, the one in Lexington by the University of Kentucky's campus near where my girlfriend lived, and this dude was blasting metal so loud you could hear it through his headphones. I thought that was really cool.

I had the music already. It was kind of a Ramones-type song. Then our drummer, Rob, his roommate Mark Hendricks – who now plays bass for us – he started working at Kroger. He was stocking shelves and Rob was like, "We can't play that song. Mark will think it's about him." Well, that wasn't popular with me, so I said, "Man, that's not about him."

I've had people tell me that here and there over the years, "Dude, you write songs about crazy shit." I tell them, "If you happen to fit into the lyrics, the problem is not the song. You need to take a good look at your life and why you may be going down the wrong side of the road or why you're a head-banging boy before you get mad at me." Mark thought it was funny.

SURFABILLY
Scott: That's a Snake Out cover, Len Puch's band. We'd wanted to do it. We also needed 12 songs, and it was on the B-side of the *Hangin' Out At The Cadillac Inn* single we'd done before. We'd also played it live a lot.

THE WEASEL
> "There are people around me that don't give a damn
> Thinking of ways to keep those around him down
> He don't care about nobody, only concerned with himself
> Don't let him fool ya, he don't care about nobody else"

Blaine: I didn't write that. Scott wrote that with our old bass player, Bart Altman.

Toby Myrick: The Weasel. That's about me.

CHAPTER 15
BURNING UP LIKE A PAPER CUP

Kelly Chambers: I worked at Transylvania University's library. Tim Warren lived in Germany, and he started faxing weird shit to the library. I was trying to keep that life away from my work, but I ended up being the go-between because nobody in the band could afford to call Germany and a letter would take too long. So, I was the one that would get these weird faxes, and all my bosses at work were like, "What the fuck?"

Blaine: When *Smokin' Taters* came out a few months later, it was the most popular record on Crypt Records. The gigs were packed every night, but there wasn't a lot of money involved. We signed our first autograph in Spain, and we actually had our stuff bootlegged there. That album definitely saved our asses.

Scott: We started going to Europe, that was the real deal – 56 shows in 60 days, crushing it. We did about 25 of those in Germany. We played everywhere – France, Spain, Holland.

We were hanging with The Raunch Hands for the first five shows.

Blaine: The first thing we did in Europe was a live radio show in Holland on VPRO. We played eight songs, and it sounded amazing because of George Sully, the bassist for The Raunch Hands. He went into the mobile recording truck, and he heard how we were being mixed. He goes, "What the fuck are you doing? That sounds awful. Let me do it." Very New York, man.

George got the short end of the stick on that tour. He had to drive us all over Europe, and he got paid jack shit to do it.

Scott: We'd just flown into Amsterdam – we didn't even get a night's rest – and that night we played at this place called the Vera Club in Groningen, Holland. It's pretty much recognized as the premier music club in Europe. Everybody's played there, and it only has a capacity of like 300, 350 people.

In Holland, they had been playing our Baylor Records single with "Cadillac Inn" and "Surfabilly." It was number one for a while. They also really loved "Long Gone Daddy" – that was big on their charts. So they knew us when we rolled in, and it was packed. We're just like, "What the fuck is this? What the fuck have we wandered into?"

They wouldn't let us quit playing. We played for almost two hours. We played every song we knew – all our Ramones covers, and "Train Kept A Rollin'" and "Radar Love." They pounded on the stage with their beer bottles, and it was just a magical deal. That was pretty much the reception almost everywhere.

We're playing every nook and cranny – these roadhouses in the Black Forest in Germany, basically the middle of nowhere on a Tuesday night. Everybody came because that's all there was to do in a hundred-mile radius.

Rob Hulsman: There was a show in Bavaria that was really insane, just a sweaty room full of people swinging from the rafters.

Scott: We're doing Jerry Lee Lewis covers. We're doing "Redneck Romance." We're doing "Feelin' Kinda Froggy" and they fucking lost their shit. These big punks in the crowd are going, "FROOO-GEEY!" "On fire! On fire!" and they were screaming, "Paper cup! Paper cup!"

We were fucking blowing people away. I mean, it's unbelievable the intensity of this thing. The cigarette smoke was so thick, but it was just pure man – beer drinking, smoking hash and playing music. Everybody's sweating. It was just fucking awesome. We're just killing it night after night after night, after night, after night.

People knew Johnny Cash and Jerry Lee Lewis, but they'd never really heard it the way we did. We were the ones that took that music and made it really punk rock. We took it to that level, and it was something different. Jason & The Scorchers weren't hitting places like this. We were the closest thing to this hillbilly, rockabilly, Southern kind of shit.

That first tour Green Day opened up for us in Bremen, Germany. We don't look like they do – we're not pretty enough. There's a poster where our name is big and huge and then there's little Green Day. Billy Joe came out, and we did "Sweet Home, Alabama" and "Rock and Roll All Nite" together. The place we were playing gave us three cases of hot Beck's. Later that night, Tré Cool – I think he was on acid – came up and stole some of our beer at five o'clock in the morning.

Then we played Spain, and we hooked up with this guy named Kike (Kee-Kay) Turmix, who was the leader of a band called The Pleasure Fuckers. He was the godfather of Spanish punk.

He became our tour manager, notoriously corrupt. One night we played in this squat, this abandoned building that people had taken over. They bring out this thing of hash that was the size of a loaf of bread, and Kike cuts almost a quarter of it off and says, "That's your payment." We were like, "Yeaaaaahhh!"

Johnny Evans (SPOILER ALERT: Future, Like Soon-ish, Drummer): Kike was the way you got into Spain. Even the Red Hot Chili Peppers had to use him to play the clubs around Spain.

If you were with Kike, they just gave you free beer everywhere you went. If you knew him, it was a lot of fun going to all the underground bars at three o'clock in the morning.

Scott: Anyway, when we left Europe, we were on top of the world. The show at the Vera got voted the number-two show that year, and "Long Gone Daddy" was top five on a lot of charts.

Blaine: I came back with a new pair of boots and 50 bucks. I wasn't used to having money. I spent it over there, but not on anything big though.

When we came back to America, no one knew who we were. We sold thousands and thousands of copies of our record in Europe, which was a lot back then for a small band. We'd sold a couple of hundred at home in the United States, so we were back to square one.

Back then when you were in a punk band or garage band or a band like ours, the whole thing was to try to get to Europe. That was the goal. It was hard to get over there unless you were summoned. That's where it happened. It really is the rock-and-roll promised land.

But try telling your parents that you're popular in Europe. It's like saying you're popular on Mars.

Scott: We were going to try to record again, and that's when Rob got fired, mostly because he was living with Blaine. They just got on each other's nerves. He dyed his hair blue. Rob just didn't know who he was at the time. We had a lot of fun with him. He's a great drummer.

Kelly Chambers: Blaine liked Rob. That one was painful. We were good friends with him and lived with him, but Blaine just couldn't get him to do what he wanted. He felt like Rob was sneaking in little flourishes and stuff. It was too fancy.

Rob Hulsman: I wanted to be more heavy, and ironically, that's kind of what the songs ended up being later, but I wanted more of a heavy sound. It was kind of an ongoing argument. Eventually it came to a head, and I think at the time I thought of myself more as a band member. I didn't realize it was just the Blaine and Scott show and when you disagree with them, you're out. So that's what happened. They fired me. Oh yeah, it sucked.

Scott: We got a guy named Johnny Evans to replace Rob. Great guy.

Johnny Evans (Former Nine Pound Hammer Drummer): I had a band called Fatman's Dice that would play all ages shows at The Wrocklage. When Rob left the band, I took his spot for one Canadian tour and one European tour.

Scott said, "Well, if you don't do it, somebody else will." That's the one thing you don't say to me. If you were to say, "Johnny, we want you to jump off this building," I would be like, "Well, man, I don't know if I can do that." If you say, "Well, if you don't do it, somebody else will" – I'll probably jump.

Scott: That '93 Canadian tour, I was driving my granddad's '68 Ranch Wagon which would go about 130 miles an hour. I would drag race people in that thing. We called it The White Cloud. It only had like 40,000 miles on it.

Anyway, we got strip searched at the border up in North Dakota, coming back from Winnipeg. I had residue of some sort in the glove box, which I don't think there was anything in there, but they claimed there was. That was fun.

Johnny Evans: They thought, there's no way you can be in a band up here playing shows and making money. "Look at the way you look. Look at what you're driving." So, they took our vehicle into the garage and started searching through it. They did a THC test, and it tested positive for marijuana. Then, they detained us and said it was a $10,000 or $20,000 fine.

So, they pulled me in first and realized it was my first trip up there. They immediately got it into their head, as ridiculous as it sounds, that I was leading the rest of these guys up to Canada to deal marijuana. They were serious about it.

They said, "Well, we think that you're a marijuana kingpin from Kentucky." I said, "No, I quit college to go on this tour and join this band. I had to borrow my brother's underwear to make it for three weeks." No kidding, I did have to borrow my brother's underwear, and he was three years younger than me.

They did a whole cavity search on me. We sat there for hours and hours and hours, and one by one everybody got cavity searched.

Matt Bartholomy: I didn't know exactly what was going on, but I saw Blaine go into this room and when he came out, his face was all red, just angry. I'd never seen him so angry before, just feeling violated, which it was a violation.

Scott: Johnny Evans, he comes back, wide eyed and shit. He was wearing red thong underwear.

We all did the whole spread your cheeks thing. The whole deal. We kept telling them, "We don't have anything." Matt had long hair and at one point they said, "Lookie here, we got Slash!"

Matt Bartholomy: They thought I was on heroin because I was wearing thick socks, and it wasn't cold enough to be wearing thick socks. It was just bizarre.

Scott: They just wanted money, but we didn't have any money. I think we had $240 to our names. They finally relented, and I think my dad ended up paying a $500 fine.

Another time we were driving that white van coming back from Toronto through Niagara Falls. We got stopped again, and they started taking panels off the doors and all that.

I was like, "Do you think we're dumb? What do you think's going on here? There's nothing here. We don't have anything. We're a band, not drug dealers."

CHAPTER 16
A GIRL LIKE THAT

Love was in Canada's air. On one of the tours across Canada, Blaine met Ruyter Suys, which changed the trajectory of his musical career and life. Only one problem, Blaine was still with Kelly.

Ruyter: In Saskatoon we would go see every single band that came to town. It was a small town. We were young and desperate for entertainment. So me and Robin, my high school boyfriend, went and saw Nine Pound Hammer. Robin was a Mötorhead freak.

We'd never seen anything like Nine Pound Hammer. It was like this language that neither of us spoke. It was a revelation. We'd never listened to Johnny Cash or the Ramones. We didn't listen to anything remotely like that, but there was something in the Hammer's music that sounded familiar, and it was good – that's for damn sure.

So when Nine Pound Hammer came back around, probably a year and a half later, Robin and I had split up – they were everything I remembered. Plus, I got to meet the guitar player, and we spent the evening trying to one-up each other. It was great.

At some point Scott says, "You should come with us to Winnipeg. We're going to go see this band from New York called The Devil Dogs." I said, "Yeah, why not?"

Nine Pound Hammer played two nights at this bar called Amigos. The first night, both Blaine and Scott walked me home, and I was like, "Okay, I guess this is how it's done in Kentucky." Then the next day, I took Blaine to the bronze foundry I was working at because

111

obviously we had a connection. Then Blaine and I hooked up, and I wound up going to Winnipeg, and that's where we dropped acid at this horrible, fucking old, just the nastiest hotel in all of Winnipeg called The Royal Albert.

Blaine: We were sitting there together, and I had some visions. I didn't even know Ruyter played guitar, but I just saw me and her going around the world and celebrating for some reason. We were staying in The Devil Dogs' hotel room. They didn't want to stay there because it was so bad. They had left a guitar underneath the bed. She got it out and started playing "Fractured Mirror" by Ace Frehley.

Ruyter: We bounced around that little nasty room for like nine hours.

Blaine: All the other guys in the Crypt bands were fucking around all the time, but that was the first time I had done that. I remember Steve Baise, the bass player of The Devil Dogs, lecturing me because I had a girlfriend back home I was living with in Lexington.

I said, "Why are you lecturing me? You've done it." He goes, "Yeah, and I got caught."

Ruyter: Blaine went to the East Coast with Hammer, and I hitched a ride with The Devil Dogs back to Saskatoon.

He wrote me the most beautiful love letter ever with sections all blacked out. He wasn't going to rewrite the whole thing. He just blacked it out with a pen and rewrote it underneath it. I remember it had the lyrics in the corner to "Two Headed Dog."

> "I've been working in the Kremlin
> With a two-headed dog
> Two-headed dog
> Two-headed dog"

Blaine: Roky Erickson. Yeah.

Ruyter: There were also mustard stains on it, and the return address was 123 Pitty Pat Lane. The whole thing was just a work of art. It was full of intrigue and love and passion and potential. It was beautiful. It was crazy.

Plus, he left me all these messages on my answering machine. I'd left town, and he didn't know it. They went from him being real cool to him being a little perturbed to him finally being a little angry.

First he's like, "Hey, it's me! The man in a hat. I think I've seen you play, and I think you got the goods." Then the next one was, "Hey, it's Blaine calling. I left you a message the other day. I don't know if you got it, but it'd be great to talk to you again." The next day it was, "Hey, I don't know if you're getting these messages, but I'd really like to talk to you again." And then the last one was like, "What the fuck man?!?!?" I was gone for a week.

Blaine: I think I left my version of a guitar solo on there, too. I played "weedle, weedle, weedle" like Chuck Berry.

Ruyter: I was going to rent out my house and take off from work and come down to Kentucky and follow them to Europe. So, I took a train down to Maysville, Kentucky.

Blaine: She followed us to Europe.

Ruyter: Yeah, he had by then got caught by his girlfriend big-time. Kelly exploded and said, "I'm out of here."

Kelly Chambers: Yeah, that was weird. I'm not sure what to say about that. I was at the library when he got back from Canada and me, Blaine and Matt went out to eat. I guess Blaine told Matt, "Dude, come with me." The next thing I know, Ruyter had called our house within a day or two. I'll give Blaine this, he's always very honest.

Of course I was like, "The fuck, dude?" So, I just picked my shit up and went over and stayed with my friend. That's when I think Ruyter came down, and they stayed in our apartment.

I was pissed because I went over there after work to get some stuff, and she had my Sun Records T-shirt in her bag. I was like, "Oh,

fucking no way! You ain't taking my Sun Records T-shirt, bitch."
It's funny, down the road I ended up really liking Ruyter. We get
along now and still send each other stuff on Facebook. I think I like
her better than Blaine.

Ruyter: I was only there for a couple days before Blaine drove his
car up to New York and parked it at a friend's house. Then we went
to Europe.

I remember buying my ticket for three hundred and fifty bucks, and
then I realized that I didn't have my passport. I remember Scott
getting really mad. "This is bullshit, man. Your girlfriend's causing
trouble already. Now she can't even fucking keep a passport."
There's kind of a rule about girls in the band and about girls tagging
along. Basically, any extra person is going to make extra effort for
everybody.

So, I had to go to the Canadian consulate in New York and say an
oath, and I got a new passport instantly.

Blaine got picked up by the Crypt Records people. Then they went
off on their merry way, and I went off on my merry way. We said
goodbye in Rotterdam, and I met them later on the tour at the Vera. I
turned 23 there. I remember that.

Then we said goodbye again, and I met Blaine in Hamburg. I would
hang out in all these towns that they were playing in for a few days,
make friends at the show and I'd wind up finding a place to crash.

I got to hang out with all The Raunch Hands and The Pleasure
Fuckers in Madrid. I stayed at fucking Kike's house for four or five
days. There were no windows, so you never knew what time it was.
There were all these kittens running around and flyers all over the
walls and all across the ceiling.

*After killing it in Europe, it was time for Nine Pound Hammer to
return home. There was only one small problem. Remember when I
said New York City has taken a lot from Blaine Cartwright over the
years? Well, here we go again.*

Johnny Evans: Before we left for the European tour, we mailed a key to The Devil Dogs for Blaine's car. We parked it in Brooklyn. They were supposed to come and get the car and move it to the suburbs of Philadelphia.

So, we go on tour, and Blaine calls back two months later and tries to organize getting the car back to New York City from Philly. You could hear Blaine and somebody from The Devil Dogs on the phone yelling at each other, "You forgot the car?!?" They didn't move it. It sat in the same parking spot in Brooklyn for two months.

When we got back, the car was in the same spot, but it was just the frame. People just took whatever they wanted. There was absolutely nothing left on the car. No door latches. No doors. Absolutely nothing. You would think that the city would've towed it. We were stunned.

Ruyter: I flew back to New York and took a train back to Saskatoon, and then whenever Blaine's tour ended, he landed in New York and realized that his car had been eaten by New York City. So, I said, "Come to Saskatoon," and I bought him a train ticket.

Blaine: When I got to Saskatoon, it was right at the point where Celsius and Fahrenheit kind of just meet. I think it was 40 below. We stayed there for three months. I actually wrote "Skin A Buck" there. I had that riff, and I was doing the same three-chord progression. Ruyter comes in and goes, "Don't do it like that, don't go to that chord. Leave that one out."

Ruyter: And then we got married on a dare.

After a few months back home in the states, Nine Pound Hammer was summoned back to Europe.

Blaine: We went back and played another 50 days.

Scott: Johnny got a job washing dishes right before we left on the second European tour. So all his calluses softened up, and he could barely hold his drumsticks. But the shows went great – we were killing it.

Jean-Luc Jousse: (Former Nine Pound Hammer Tour Manager, Driver and Soundman): I drove them on their second tour. It was something to see, an American band like them in Europe. It was something fresh, and it was something good. When you go to a Nine Pound Hammer show, you see people smiling when they leave the club. It's just good, fun vibes.

Scott: Then there was the Christmas night massacre in Orléans, France.

I was in a bookstore next to the club. Everybody else was hanging out outside, and these Algerian dudes started fucking with them.

Matt Bartholomy: We're getting the equipment out of the van, and these three Middle Eastern tough guys were walking the streets, and they slammed the van door into Johnny. Our tour guide started talking to them in French, and one guy got right in his face. Well, Johnny didn't like that. He took a swing and hit one of the Algerians in the side of the head.

Johnny Evans: One of the club owners had this crowd control mace, and he sprays the Algerian dissidents. It sprayed like 40 or 50 feet, but into the wind. Then that crowd control mace comes gusting back on me. There were at least three weeks of that tour where every time I would sweat during a show or take a shower, my skin would crawl again. It was just like being resprayed. There were a lot of things that happened to me that were inopportune on those two tours.

Scott: They were all mad at me, "Where were you man?"

Blaine: We're doing good in Europe. All I wanted to do was half that good in America. We've still not really had a successful American tour ever. To do good in America, that was going to take some sacrifice, and the days of sacrificing were kind of getting old. Scott was getting serious with his [future] wife, Amber. He was settling down, and he was getting the pressure.

Scott: So, we come back home, and Blaine moves to Nashville.

Blaine: I saw myself being stuck in Lexington. Scott's the kind of guy that would keep his options open. People that have options like to keep them open, but I know how to do this one thing. That's it. The only options I had were failure or success.

Scott: Blaine and I, things weren't great. I was friends with Kelly. There were a lot of hurt feelings because we used to hang out a lot with her. We were all close friends. I just felt bad for her.

Looking back, Blaine and Ruyter were meant to be together, but it was chaotic at the time. They were in love. I mean, it happens, and we thought that him being in Nashville might help things a little bit.

With the tour over and all the mace finally washed off, one more "inopportune" thing happened to Johnny Evans.

Blaine: Johnny was stopping in the middle of the songs. He was out of it. We all knew Johnny was gone. He called me up and said, "When are we going to play again?" and I just started laughing. I just thought it was so obvious.

Scott: Johnny Evans was a good dude and fun to hang out with.

Blaine: Johnny wasn't ready. Johnny's actually a really good drummer now.

CHAPTER 17
IF YOU'RE LUCKY, A REAL FRIEND OR TWO

I tried for about six months to find Tim Warren. The man is elusive. I contacted his (presumedly ex-) wife. I talked to other Crypt Records bands, tried social media, mailed a letter to Santa asking for an interview with Tim, nothing. So, instead of hearing from one of the most fascinating record label execs ever, here are a few stories about the man who helped give Nine Pound Hammer their big break.

Scott: So Crypt's headquarters was in Hamburg, Germany, in an apartment complex.

Jean Luc Jousse: It was above a bar called The Gun Club. It opened at midnight and closed at eight in the morning.

Scott: One of the best bars in all of Europe. I think it was named after the band.

We'd stay upstairs at Tim's over there, which was like going into a museum with all these records, cool hip shit and leopard-print stuff everywhere.

We'd go downstairs to The Gun Club, smoke hash and weed and play foosball. Right down the street was the red light district. Tim's place was near the Star Club where the Beatles played. Jerry Lee Lewis played there, too.

It was all lit up. It was like Vegas for hookers – it's high class, but still seedy. You'd see housewives dropping their husbands off since they didn't have sex with them anymore.

There was this alley, and there were like 30 windows on each side with high-class European call girls, I mean like models. It was the devil's playground. That's literally where I got that song title from. The Deutsche Mark was strong back then, and hey, when in Rome – we would have been fools not to.

Eric Davidson (New Bomb Turks Lead Singer): Tim's apartment was just crazy, and he would do crazy shit. Often there would be pimps walking around the streets. Tim would take an egg, break a little hole in it and put a firecracker in there, light it and then drop the egg so that it exploded right in front of these pimps. He'd throw eggs at people and then turn the lights off and fall on the floor just dying laughing.

We used to joke that Tim had probably seen the New Bomb Turks three times before he ever actually <u>saw</u> a set because he kept passing out drunk by the time we'd come on.

Tim never seemed like a label guy. He just seemed like another musician. He didn't really want to sit around talking about how to promote a record or royalty rates or whatever. He just wanted to sit around and get drunk and put out cool records.

Matt Bartholomy: One time at Tim Warren's apartment building, his wife came upstairs and said, "Oh, there's a dead body down in the lobby," just kind of matter of factly. That was it. Nothing else was said about it.

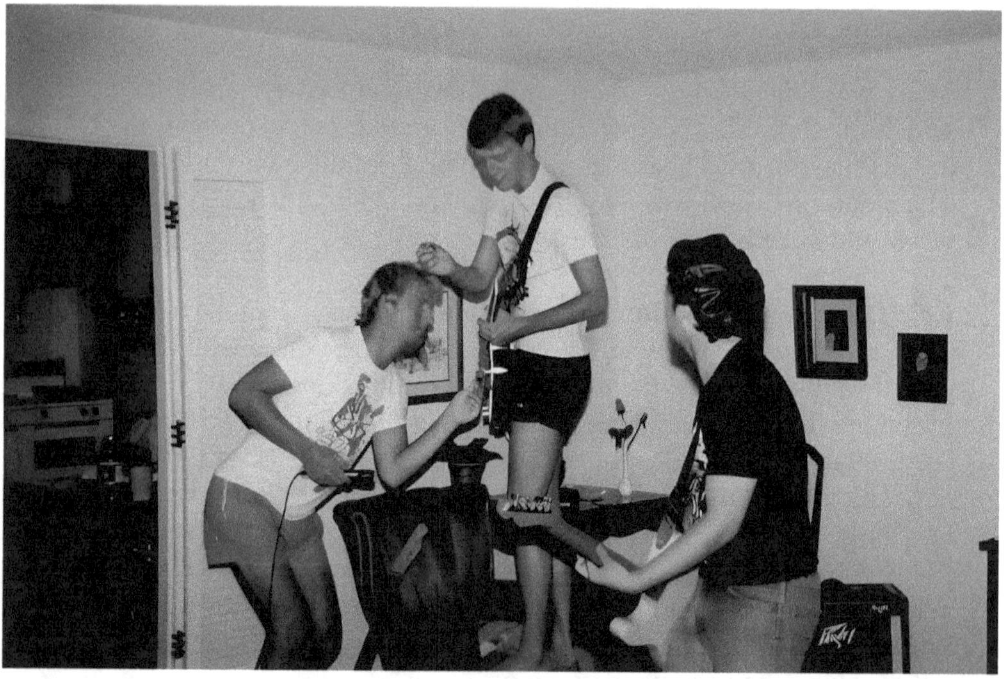

Scott, David Epperson and Blaine's first practice at Scott's mom's house, 1985.

Cranking it out as The Black Sheep at Great Scott's Depot with Toby Myrick on drums.

Great Scott's Depot in Lexington, KY, became homebase for The Black Sheep (Nine Pound Hammer). Depending on who you ask, Great Scott's was either "very miminal," "a little shithole club" or "a cool venue."

Scott on guitar and Blaine singing "Train Kept A Rollin.'" From Scott: "Sometimes it goes on for 10 minutes. There's nothing more punk rock than that. If we play it and you don't get it, you don't get it. It's fucking hilarious, and you get to see Blaine lose his mind."

The lineup for *1987 Revisited* (left to right): Blaine, Scott, Darren Howard and Bart Altman.

Live at Rerun's Lounge in Dearborn, MI. Darren Howard on drums and Kathy Lewellan on bass.

Nine Pound Hammer with Brian Moore, bass (far left) and Rob Hulsman, drums (second from the left) hanging out in The Crawdaddy.

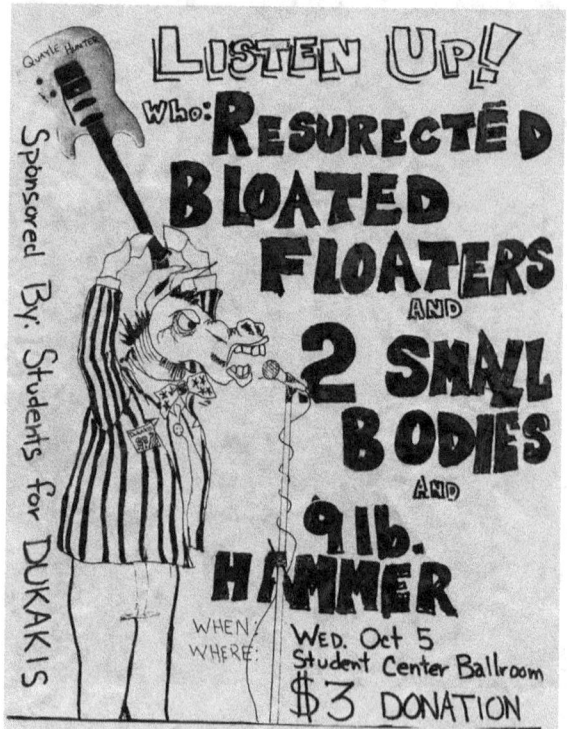

Gig poster featuring two of Lexington's other classic punk bands – 2 Small Bodies and The Resurrected Bloated Floaters. At one point, the latter's lineup featured Lawrence Tarpey, Lexington's godfather of punk, and Brian Pulito, Nine Pound Hammer drummer and producer.

Scott on the microphone in full "Golden God" mode at a 1988 rally for Michael Dukakis at the University of Kentucky student center ballroom.

Above: *The Mud, The Blood, and The Beers* cover shoot. **Below:** Blaine hanging out with the band's friend Lindell Akins with a new copy of Nine Pound Hammer's first album.

Above: Len Puch (left), friend and owner of Wanghead Records, and his band Snake Out.

Right (left to right): Blaine, Scott, Brian Moore and Rob Hulsman hanging out on Scott's "White Cloud."

Billboard

NEWSPAPER

VOLUME 101 NO. 11   THE INTERNATIONAL NEWSWEEKLY OF MUSIC AND HOME

$3.50 (U.K.)

Pepsi denies pulling Madonna's TV spots amid controversy over vidclip *See page 4*

David Bowie catalog goes to Rykodisc *See page 4*

Vestron has more in store for Michael Jackson fans *See page 94*

CD Makers Face Millions In Patent Royalty Payments

BY KEN TERRY

NEW YORK Compact disk manufacturers will have to pay tens of millions of dollars this year and much more over the next 20 years to Discovision Associates (DVA), a joint venture of MCA Inc. and IBM that owns many of the key patents on CD mastering and replication.

Although Philips and Sony developed the CD system, some aspects of its technology stem from Discovision's development of laser videodisk players and software. A number of DVA's patents already have been licensed to CD player manufacturers, and DVA is now focusing its efforts on licensing software manufacturers' use of its more recent patents.

According to Jim Fiedler, president of Discovision and VP of MCA Inc., DVA has already licensed its patents to Philips, PolyGram, Philips Du Pont Optical, Sony, CBS/Sony, Digital Audio Disc Corp., JVC, Nippon/Columbia (Denon), and Sanyo. Fiedler says the company is in the process of licensing and getting back payments
(Continued on page 87)

Warner, Time

BY CHRIS MORRIS

LOS ANGELES The groundwork for the world's largest media and entertainment company was laid March 4, when Warner Communications Inc., parent of the Warner/Elektra/

NINE POUND HAMMER
The Mud, The Blood, And The Beers.
PRODUCERS: Len Puch, Scott Luallen
Wanghead 007

Alternative listeners may be interested in hillbilly punk from a Kentucky quartet that occasionally slips into conventional hardcore fare with tracks like "Little Help" or the Eagle-bashing "Bye Bye Glen Frey." Still, most typical of their Ramones-in-a-pickup stance are such white-thrash melodies as "Redneck Romance," "Drive-In," and "He's Gone." Contact:

Left: The reviews for *The Mud, The Blood, and The Beers* made Nine Pound Hammer critcal darlings.

the u.k./s.a.b. concert committee presents:

mca/curb

recording

artists

"Be there when the cows come home."

the

beat
farmers

with special guests:

9lb. hammer

september 24, 8:00pm
tickets $8
student center box office
general admission-grand ballroom

Above: An opening gig for San Diego legends The Beat Farmers, 1989.

Right: Flyer for the infamous show at Stevenson Station where bassist Brian Moore drank a little too much bourbon and tried to take off Scott's head with his bass – and then slept in a cow pasture.

LIVE FROM
DETROIT!
SNAKE-OUT
PLUS SPECIAL GUESTS
NINE POUND
HAMMER!
(SAT.)
MARCH 25th
9 P.M. $4⁰⁰
STEVENSON
STATION

CHOMP!

BOONEVILLE

BUSLERS GAS STATION
STEVENSON STATION RD
STEVENSON
STATION
1¼ MILES
HIGHLAND PARK
BURKHARDT RD

Above: Nine Pound Hammer opening for Dee Dee Ramone and The Chinese Dragons in Cincinnati at Bogart's in 1990, with Matt Bartholomy on bass and Rob Hulsman on drums.

Left: Scott backstage meeting Joey Ramone and Marky Ramone at King's Island in Cincinnati, OH, on July 18, 1990.

Working up a sweat in Stuttgart, Germany, 1992.

The band pushing their broken-down van in Europe, also the cover for *Live at the Vera*.

Left: Blaine flying like a plane in Spain, February 15, 1992.

Below: Kike Turmix, former tour manager for Nine Pound Hammer and lead singer of The Pleasure Fuckers, throwing Valencia oranges at the band in Valencia, Spain.

Right: Matt Bartholomy at the Vera Club in Groningen, Holland, 1993.

Below: Touring group shot, somewhere in Europe with friend and tour manager Jean Luc Jousse (top left) and drummer Johnny Evans (middle).

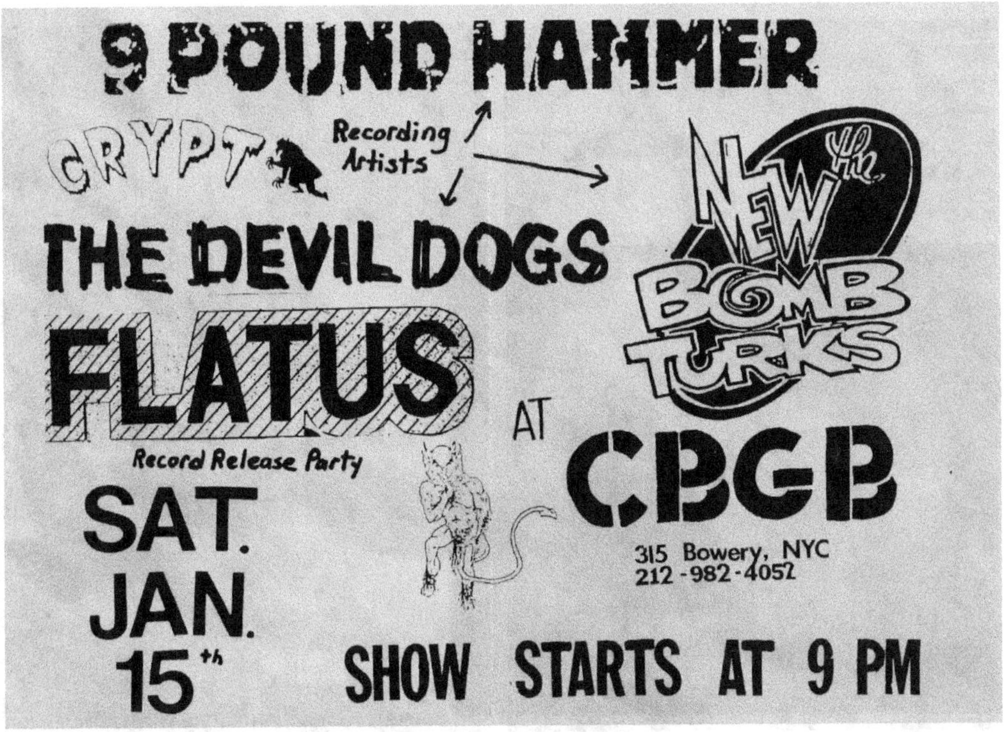
9 POUND HAMMER
CRYPT
Recording Artists
THE DEVIL DOGS
FLATUS
Record Release Party
NEW
the
BOMB TURKS
AT
CBGB
315 Bowery, NYC
212-982-4052
SAT. JAN. 15th
SHOW STARTS AT 9 PM

The band plays the legendary New York club CBGB with a legendary Crypt Records lineup, 1994.

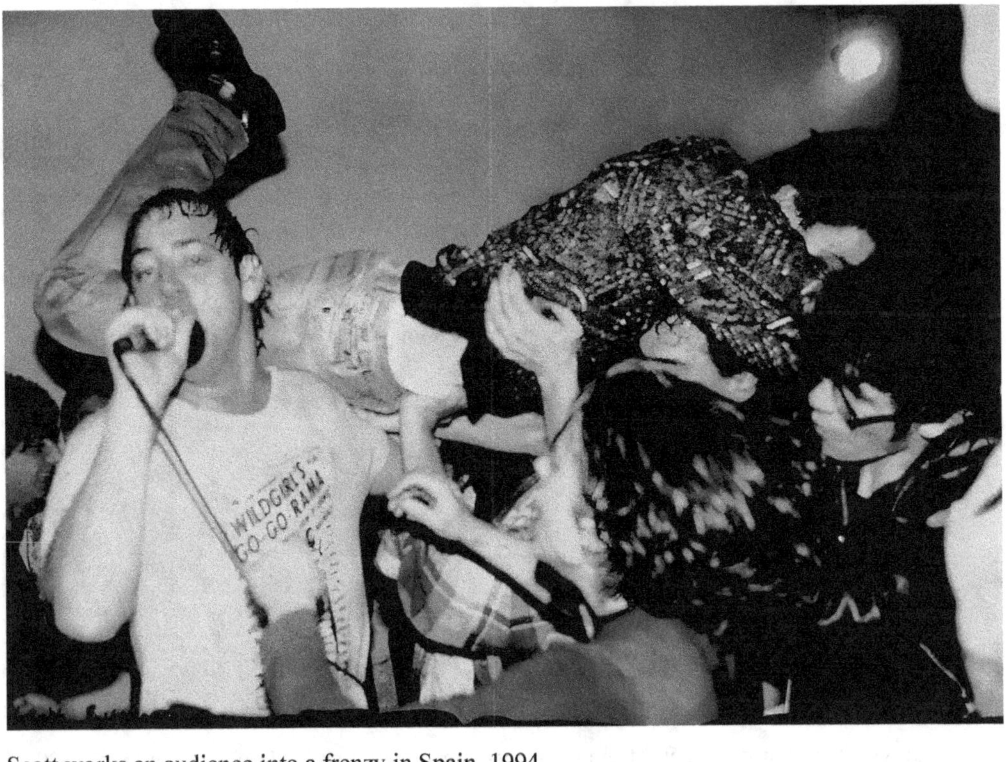
WILDGIRLS GO-GO RAMA

Scott works an audience into a frenzy in Spain, 1994.

Blaine, Scott and Matt Bartholomy in 1994 performing "Train Kept A Rollin.'"

The band with Tim Warren (second from the right) in his apartment in Hamburg, Germany, 1994.

NINE POUND HAMMER

Left: The band in Nashville, beside the infamous chicken car.

Below: Scott and Matt Bartholomy in France, 1995.

SCOTT LUALLEN - Vocals
BLAINE CARTWRIGHT - Guitar

BILL WALDRON - Drums
MATT BARTHOLOMY - Bass

THE GREATEST SHOW ON PLANET EARTH!!! *HEROINA NOVA, Croatia*

"If Johnny Cash had a teenage son that was heavily into the Ramones, Stooges and maybe alcohol." *FLIPSIDE*

"A devastating crazed hoedown of maniac proportions!" *SOUNDS*

"It's Johnny Cash slam-dancing. It's Clint Eastwood bare-knuckle boxing."
NEW MUSICAL EXPRESS

Back together for a Kentucky Breakdown, backstage at Sjock Festival in Belgium, 2003.

Scott singing "Harvest Moon" with Jason Ringenberg of Jason & The Scorchers at Serie Z Festival in Spain, 2003.

Stage view of the crowd at Sleazefest, 2004.

Blaine melting faces on stage, 2005.

The Star Bar in Atlanta, GA, circa 2018.

Sneak Attack Studios, recording *When The Shit Goes Down*, 2020. From left to right: Engineer Jason Groves, Blaine, Scott, Earl Crim, Brian Pulito, producer Daniel Rey and Mark Hendricks.

Left: Kevin Robey, Far Out Fan.

Below: Blaine and Scott on stage at Pitfest in the Netherlands, 2023.

Right: Scott, Blaine and
Mikkey Dee of Motörhead
backstage, 2023.

Below: Mark Hendricks and
Earl Crim on stage, 2023.

Above: Scott "scrubbing one off" with Mark Hendricks and Earl Crim.

Left: Mark Hendricks on stage in Europe, 2023.

Above: Current Nine Pound Hammer lineup, with drummer Josh Love (second from the left).
Below: Blaine and Scott in the studio, summer 2025.

The rest of the
band in the studio,
summer 2025.

CHAPTER 18
EVERYTHING'S BROKEN

Blaine: Scott and I talked about moving the Hammer to Nashville. He's got one of those things where he's not leaving Kentucky, but we'd pretty much done everything we could do in Lexington, and it was boring.

Ruyter: Nashville was a place where neither of us had a history.

Blaine: I always liked Nashville because I thought it was kind of crazy, so Ruyter and I moved there with a pickup truck full of stuff.

Ruyter: My old sculpture boss, for a wedding present, sold us his pickup truck for a dollar. It was this badass '70s Silverado.

Ruyter: You could start it without a key, and you couldn't lock it.

Blaine: Yeah, so needless to say it got stolen in Nashville.

This was around the time Scott had straightened up. He wasn't smoking weed or drinking. He was real thin and was taking things real seriously. He wanted to be a family guy, and he was working towards that, and I was working the opposite way. I'm with Ruyter, and we're trying to make a living doing cool stuff.

When I moved to Nashville with Ruyter, that didn't help matters.

Ruyter: I think Scott's always fought with doing the right thing and doing what he wanted. I think he was mad at us for doing obviously the wrong thing and then having it work out. That was the elephant

144

in the room for the longest time before he accepted me. Even though Nine Pound Hammer was my absolute favorite band in the entire world, I got to see them less than anybody because of the animosity between Scott and I.

It was rough because I wanted to be at every goddamn show. It wasn't like I wasn't allowed. It just wasn't encouraged. It was going to be an issue if I turned up. I've always wanted the best for Nine Pound Hammer. I still want more for them. They're still kind of undiscovered really, but they're definitely my favorite band.

Anyway, when we moved to Nashville, we stayed at Mike Grimes' place for maybe a week while we were house hunting. Blaine was really impatient. He wanted to stay everywhere we found. We finally found the perfect place, which was this spot above a hot sauce shop.

It was right down the northern tip of Vanderbilt University and this record store, The Great Escape. It was right where Music Row basically started. Studio B[20] was like three blocks away. It was a really groovy neighborhood. We were in between two fancy restaurants.

Blaine: Yeah. It was a freestanding house that was between The Rock 'n Roll Hotel and Third Coast Rock on South Street.

Ruyter: Anytime anybody in fucking Nashville made a dollar, they would be next door partying. Townes Van Zandt and Elvis Costello stayed there. Bob Dylan was there. Those places would stay open as late as those people had fucking money. So whoever was the flavor of the week would be celebrating next door. I don't think we even had a TV. We would just sit there with our heads out the window and watch these drunken people getting into cars and making out. It was super entertaining.

Blaine: Ruyter and I eventually started playing guitar together a little bit, and she wrote some little surf songs. We knew we wanted to be

---

[20] Everybody from Dolly Parton to Frank Sinatra to Elvis Presley recorded in RCA Studio B. It's also known as the birthplace of the "Nashville Sound."

in a band eventually, but we didn't know what kind. She was so versatile.

Ruyter: I thought we were going to do more heavy Buck Owens stuff or surf-style, instrumental shit.

Blaine: We liked garage-type stuff, and then I think we just morphed into, "Let's play as hard and fast as we can" at some point.

Ruyter: The first time I ever plugged into a Marshall, it was just like, "Oh!"

Ruyter: Yeah, we were playing little Marshall combo amps in our living room, and nobody could say anything about it.

Blaine: We paid $350 a month, and we worked some of that off cleaning houses that the realtor who rented us the place owned.

Ruyter: There was no way on earth I was going to let him get away with the shit that he got away when he was with Kelly. He used to pay half the rent or whatever. If it was like $240 a month. That's exactly as many hours he would work. He came up with his $240, and that was it. I'm like, "No way, man."

That was when Blaine discovered his work ethic, when he started working for an ice cream company.

Blaine: I went to this ice cream company and interviewed. They said it was commission and all under the table. So, I walked out of there and saw these losers come in and take off in these ice cream trucks.

Well, the Silverado fucked up and stranded me. So, I went back in and said, "Can I actually make money doing this?" and the guy said, "Oh yeah."

So I took the job, then Ruyter and I mapped out our own route – she would go along and help out sometimes. We went to all the daycares around there and said, "Hey, we'll show up here with ice cream." So we'd have a daycare on a Wednesday at 10 o'clock with a hundred kids. Boom! That was the most money I'd ever made. For me to make $350 to $400 in a week, tax-free cash, it was amazing.

The truck played "Three Blind Mice" real loud, but you got used to it. I tried so hard to do such a good job that they gave me a key to the parking lot. They even let me borrow an ice cream truck because our truck got stolen. It was weird to have as a car.

Ruyter: One of the meanest things you can do is to drive around an empty ice cream truck. No ice cream means sad little dejected children everywhere. That was fucking funny.

Blaine: The people who worked at the ice cream place one time said to me and Ruyter, "Y'all are like yuppies, but y'all are cool yuppies." I mean, me and her were barefoot and wearing fucking cutoffs living above a hot sauce shop, but we were the closest thing to yuppies they knew. They said, "Y'all over there on the West Side by that school Vandy-belt."

That job would put me in a good mood. I just dealt with kids all the time. They were cool. I was high.

Ruyter: I was cleaning houses and trying to figure out what the fuck I was doing with my life.

Blaine: I had a habit of quitting stuff early – I got rid of that in Nashville. I saw this paying off, and I thought, "Well shit, maybe I should apply this work ethic to music. Maybe we should start working on music all the time instead of occasionally and stop being mad the rest of the time. At the time with Nine Pound Hammer, I was working 25% of the time and complaining the other 75% of the time.

Scott: We started to write songs for *Hayseed Timebomb*. I'd drive down there. Matt would come down, too. Things were good, but at this point I'm starting to have some anxiety issues, and the seeds were being sewed for chaos.

Ruyter: One time Scott had a panic attack in our house. He was lying in the middle of the floor, arms and legs kind of splayed out like he died. I walked in, and he said, "I can't sleep." I thought he'd had a fucking heart attack.

Without Johnny Evans on drums, Nine Pound Hammer's rhythm section gets its fifth drummer.

Blaine: I found Bill Waldron in Nashville.

Scott: In his prime, Bill is the best drummer we've ever had.

Blaine: We rehearsed in a storage space with a PA and everything. There were tons of bands that did that. That's what half of those storage places in Nashville were being used for back then. You couldn't live there and if you got caught peeing – there wasn't a toilet – you got kicked out.

Scott: We went to Glasgow to Dave Barrick's to record, and George Sully from The Raunch Hands was in tow to produce.

Blaine: He was working with Tim Warren at Crypt Records, so we asked if George could do it, because he had engineered the VPRO Dutch radio recording in Holland. He was also on the outs with The Raunch Hands, and he got to have revenge on the guitar player, Mike Mariconda, who produced *Smokin' Taters*.

We love Glasgow, Kentucky. It's an oasis – there's always a good vibe there. But when we recorded this fucking record, we meant business. We knocked everything out in a short, believe me, really short fashion.

Scott: The session was fine. But Tim wanted more originals. I don't blame him.

Blaine: He said, "You need two more songs, and I'm not putting 'Keep A-Knockin' on there, because it's not cool."

Scott: Blaine brought in "Run Fat Boy Run," and I wrote "Devil's Playground." They were a step up in our writing for sure.

Blaine: *Hayseed* is cool. The songs are great. Song-wise, that might be the best Hammer record. It was better than we were. A lot of those songs we'll play forever. We were very, very, very happy with the way that turned out.

It was fast, but it felt more casual. I'd drive up from Nashville every day. That was like an hour, hour and a half. I wasn't drinking then.

Scott: I was still just smoking weed and drinking beer, no Xanax yet – well I'd done it some, but I wasn't bad. I noticed the variables in the band had changed, though. The honeymoon was over.

Blaine's always looked at this as life or death. Don't get me wrong, it was serious to me, too, but I wasn't ready to say take it or leave it. I was very much wanting to do it, but now there's a bit of pressure that wasn't there prior, just a tiny bit.

Ruyter brought a different dynamic in, it's just true. There was a different vibe going on. It wasn't him and me anymore. It was just the way things happened, and I'm not saying it was bad or anything. There was a new element of some scrutiny and pressure going on, but things were rolling again.

Blaine: Ruyter was really, really into Nine Pound Hammer. She was trying to help out.

Ruyter: For many years, I was Yoko in the band.

Blaine: Scott would call her Yoko, and Ruyter would go, "Yoko's cool. Fuck it."

Anyway, *Hayseed Timebomb* was out, and I thought it was going to make a difference in America because we were distributed by Matador, and I found one copy of it in a Best Buy. Before that hadn't happened, that was a mainstream store and it was out at the same time as The Supersuckers' *La Mano Cornuda*, and they were kicking ass.

They came one night to Nashville and spent some time at our apartment until they had to leave for their next gig. They were living like I wanted to. I wanted to jump in the van and play nonstop.

149

At that point we'd have months where we only did two gigs. Anyway, we were definitely going in different directions.

CHAPTER 19
HAYSEED TIMEBOMB
(1994)

Blaine and Ruyter are living in Nashville, Scott's in Lexington, Matt's in Owensboro, and the world is overrun with grunge. Angst and flannel are rampant.

The Hammer goes back to work and writes an album full of classic songs.

HAYSEED TIMEBOMB
Scott: A few years before "Hayseed Timebomb" came out, we were sitting in Blaine and Kelly's apartment. He was eating Richie's hot chicken, we were smoking weed and Chris Elliott was on TV. I don't know if he was on Letterman or something else, and he said something about a "hayseed timebomb." I think even the trailer and the satellite dish lyric came from Chris Elliott.

> "He's got a one bedroom trailer,
> an' a brand-new satellite dish,
> a warm beer an' a remote control
> in his two clenched fists
> An' he sits in his chair,
> thinking of all the things he's missed"

Scott: That's mostly Blaine creating an absurd environment.

Blaine: It was just exaggerated stuff. It was a good place to ditch a bunch of imagery.

"He's headed into town to try to sell his boots
He spent all his money on a one-eyed prostitute"

Scott: There was a whorehouse/massage parlor across the river from
Owensboro in Indiana. We went in there a few times, and there was a
one-eyed Asian lady there.

"Hayseed Timebomb" is just one of those deals where we're just
looking at each other laughing like, "Oh my God! That's fucking
awesome." It's absurd, it's amazing and fucking funny as hell.

"It's Saturday night, time to go hunt some queers
With his momma's .38, he'll blow away all his fears"

Blaine: The whole thing is, we were making fun of a dude. I worked
with this dude at the Sizzler years before, and I asked him one night,
"What are you gonna do this weekend?" He said, "I'm going to go
down to the river and look for queers. Beat them up, man." He told
me that in 1981.

I kept that for a while because it was one of the most redneck things
I'd ever heard. It was not cool. I was just stunned and lost for words.
I was like, "Ah, okay let's change the subject. Let's go back to
talking about baseball or about how much this job sucks."

No, we were always allies, and I'm serious.

Scott: It's exposing what it's exposing – that prejudice and fear. You
have to be mature and look at it and see what it's really saying. It's
clearly not in support of hate. I know it's shocking that some fucking
suburban rednecks could pull that out of their ass.

<u>SKIN A BUCK</u>
Get ready, we're about to have our first witticism ownership fight.

Blaine: I wrote "Skin a Buck" on Ruyter's Silvertone – that's been
the magic guitar for years. I was hanging out with her, and she told
me, "Just do two chords. Don't do three. Just go back and forth.
You're making it too complicated."

Scott: That's another one of those witticisms that was floating around. I was working on "Skin a Buck," and Blaine lifted that phrase, fucker (laughing)! I did write a verse on that.

> "Last night while I was huntin',
> I fell asleep and had a dream,
> That all the deers had rifles
> And they were comin' after me."

Blaine: "Skin a buck" was a phrase my friend said, because he heard some rednecks say that at a bar.

Scott: For the record, I was saying that phrase when Blaine moved away to Texas. I was hanging around with Steve Terrell and David Epperson and the Owensboro crew.

Sometimes you spend your entire teenage and adult life thinking, "That's a funny story. It has to be made up." Then you learn, no, that's true.

> "I shot my cousin's butt off in a hunting accident"

Blaine: That's true. It was a guy named Marty Owen who did that, and it *fucked* him up.

Randy Ratliff and I knew a dude named Jimbo Courtney. He had a hot rod. It was a $50 Impala from the '60s. He'd drive us around, and we'd egg cars and all kinds of shit.

We were trying to get into trouble one night, and we flipped off a car – it was a dude named Marty Owen. Well, that guy tried to catch us, but Jimbo was such a good driver, he lost them.

So, we found him again, flipped him and lost him again.

A couple nights later, the phone rings. My mom picks it up and goes, "It's some guy for you." I take the phone, and this guy says, "This is Marty Owen, Blaine! You know me?!?" I said, "No, I don't know you."

He goes, "Why don't you think back to the other night when you flipped off some guy in his fucking car. That was me! You know me now, motherfucker?!?"

I was being a smart-ass, so I go, "Oh yeah! Hey!"

Somehow, he found out who was in the car, and he called us all. He was like one of those dudes from *Friday Night Lights*. He was a fucking star in high school and had a cheerleader girlfriend. Then one year out of school, he had a shit job, living in a shit apartment with a baby.

He made us go to his crappy little apartment and apologize. All of my friends were there, including this guy Gene Stroud – he couldn't help but smile.

Marty screams at Gene, "What are you smiling at motherfucker? You've got a shit-eating grin! You scared my wife!" His wife was embarrassed that this was going on. His wife was just like, "I've made the biggest mistake of my life marrying this guy."

Anyway, I found out later from one of his friends that he shot his cousin's butt off in a hunting accident. They were fucking around with guns when they were younger teenagers, and he shot his cousin in the ass. He actually shot part of the butt off, and he hadn't been the same since that.

As soon as I told my friends what happened, they were like, "You should have said, 'Hey Marty, it's not _my_ fault you shot your cousin's butt off.'" So, I guess I always wanted fucking revenge for him being an asshole. I think I added a couple deer hunting stories. I've never been deer hunting.

To me, it sounded like the dumbest thing in the world. I asked somebody, "On Saturday, what time do you have to get up for this? Three? And we've got to sit in a tree all day covered in skunk piss, wearing camouflage?" I did not want to shoot a deer that bad.

STRANDED OUTSIDE TATER KNOB

Blaine: I was bored at the Chinese restaurant one night. I worked on Sunday nights, and this group of 12 people came in. I wrote that song in my head while waiting for them to get finished so I could bus their table, and then I went home and wrote it down. I saw the word Tater Knob all the time. It's a real place in Kentucky.

"Raised on a diet of NoDoz, donuts and diesel emissions"

That made me a legend in Atlanta. If somebody would get mad at me, somebody else would go, "Oh, he wrote 'Stranded Outside Tater Knob.'" That song was their high watermark of redneck culture.

When I wrote lyrics for this song, I was thinking about how very descriptive Bob Dylan, Bruce Springsteen, Chuck Berry, John Fogerty and John Prine were. I wanted to tell a story that created visuals.

"Listening to the wrinkled old men dronin' on and on, about the weather and road conditions"

I always heard old men doing that. When we did the redneck songs, we were making fun of people. When we did trucker songs, like this one, I was a little envious of them. I love just the open road and going out of town. We made fun of the people who stayed in the same place.

Scott: We were covering "Six Days On the Road," and then Blaine just wrote his own trucker song, which is fucking brilliant.

"My ex-wife ran a whorehouse
on the highway out of town,
they used to give special truckers' rates
before the Baptists burned it down."

There was a little fucking whorehouse in Patronville, Indiana.

David Epperson: We did walk in there one night, but we just looked and turned around and ran.

Blaine: They wanted a bunch of money for a hand job, and I had a girlfriend – I wasn't paying for a hand job. I heard that it got burned down by the Baptists.

> "She had a tattoo on her inner thigh, said,
> 'If you can read this, yer too close'
> We used to drive five miles for the nearest cold beer
> and bitch about the lives we chose"

The tattoo on her inner thigh was fucking gold. I joked with someone about a tattoo like that after I saw a "If you can read this, you're too close" bumper sticker.

RUN FAT BOY RUN

Blaine: Tim Warren sent us back to write two more songs. I had that little riff that I'd written for a potential band that me and Ruyter were going to get together as a side project.

At the time, me and her were selling these fake BluBlocker sunglasses for our drummer, Bill Waldron, outside a gas station. While we were selling these sunglasses, we would listen to music. So we had country music playing on the radio, and a Bob Wills song came on called "That's What I Like 'Bout the South," and he just named off food. I'd said, "One of these days, I'm going to have a song that has nothing but food in it."

Scott came up with some of the foods.

Matt Bartholomy: I think I added Goo Goos. Goo Goo Clusters – that's a popular sort of candy bar in the Nashville area.

Blaine: Bill Waldron was like, "Yeah, goat nuts! There's a guy I work with, he gets a goat, skins it, hangs it in tree and cuts the nuts off, and he said, 'My boy loves when I fry 'em up.'"

It was so easy to write because all I had to do was make food rhyme. I thought it was going to take forever to sing. There was so much space in the music – Scott could read them all. I think what's on the record was the first take, honestly. I think he had the lyrics in my handwriting. It had to be one or two takes, and it was done.

156

That song's gotten more attention than our band has. It's had a life of its own. It got into Tony Hawk's *Underground* game, and there was the world's worst movie named after it.[21]

I had low expectations for the movie, and it was worse. I'll go on record – that's the worst movie ever. If I'm on an airplane, and I have five choices, and one is *Run Fatboy Run*, and it's a 10-hour flight, and I can finally maybe listen to where our song got put in the movie? No! I can't watch it. It's just awful. They had a media blitz so everyone would get all their money back the first weekend, because everybody knew it was the biggest waste of talent ever.

It's Hank Azaria and Simon Pegg. Give them a couple of drinks, some pens and paper in a room and they would come up with 10 movies better than that in an hour. I'm kind of glad that our song's not associated with that fucking movie. The movie was off and on for a while, and David Schwimmer from *Friends* ended up directing it. There's a red flag.

At first they claimed that they didn't take the idea for the title from us. So, I called up Nashville Pussy's lawyer and said, "Hey man, they're claiming they didn't take it from us." He's like, "They're lying. It's not a coincidence. Blaine, they're ripping you off." That went on for years.

Ruyter: And then we magically got money for it.

Blaine: I got like $6,000, which isn't shit considering, but I paid the mortgage for a few months with that.

WRECK OF THE OLD 97
Blaine: We always wanted to do that – it was on the best double

---

[21] Run Fatboy Run *was released in the United States on March 28, 2008, more than six months after it was released in the United Kingdom. The budget for the movie was $10 million, and it made $33.5 million at the box office. Blaine was not a fan. Based on his review, I decided not to watch it to see where the song was used.*

album in history, *Johnny Cash Live at San Quentin. San Quentin* is not as iconic as *Folsom*. There are so many songs on *Folsom*, it sounds smaller. *San Quentin* has got five on each side, and it sounded bigger. That album smokes. It's like a punk rock concert.

That was one of the best things we recorded on that VPRO show in Holland. We've searched for it, but back then they couldn't digitally save something.[22]

SHAKEY PUDDIN'
Scott: There's another phrase, Shaky Puddin'. Yeah that's from *White Lightning*, the Burt Reynolds movie.

Blaine: That's the code between Bo Hopkins' girlfriend and Burt Reynolds because they're fucking.

The girlfriend says, "What are y'all thinking about?"

Burt Reynolds replies, "Shaky puddin'."

Scott: That's also about the Catholic girls I grew up with across the street. I mean, just chasing them around, trying to get in their pants. The Hicks girls, there were three of them. I'd sneak out, you know the whole deal.

Back in the day of those big TV antennas, we'd climb up those to get in their windows – this is eighth grade, freshman year. There was a guy down the street who went to Daviess County. I think he was off at college, and he left this old '74 Camaro ragtop. It was open all the time. I'd get in there with a girl and stay there until dawn. Just fun as hell.

Blaine: Scott's girlfriends had friends, so that's how I met girls. He was dating an eighth-grade cheerleader when he was in sixth grade. Yeah, man, they were fighting over him.

Jean Luc Jousse: I drove them, and I remember Scott and Matt were

---

[22] Will trade good bourbon for a copy.

challenging each other to see who could pick up the most girls.

DEVIL'S PLAYGROUND
Blaine: That was the second song we went back to Tim Warren with.

Ruyter: Honestly, the day when Scott and Blaine were writing that in the house in Nashville, at opposite ends of the house, was just one of the most beautiful, creative things I'd ever witnessed in my life. I was sitting in the kitchen, and one was in the living room and the other was in the TV room. They were both writing their own songs, but they were trying to outdo each other.

Scott: *Texas Chainsaw Massacre 2* reference again. I wanted to do a little, heavy swampy thing with silly, stupid, absurd over-the-top lyrics.

Originally I was going to make it a "Sympathy for the Devil" thing, something kind of serious, maybe not political, but it didn't really work.

Ruyter: I remember he'd written some lyrics that were really cutting and really honest. He was telling a truth that he didn't want to tell, but he had to write it down at least once.

STEAMROLLER
Scott: It was an attempt to do a Motörhead-y type thing. I started writing it at a sound check at Babylon Babylon in Lexington. Blaine's like, "What is that?" I'm like, "I don't know? I'm working on it."

It's on *Mulebite Deluxe*, and the lyrics are stupid – embarrassingly bad. It was '89, and Jerry Garcia came out and said voting was like, "Constantly choosing the lesser of two evils is still choosing evil." We were all like, "Whoa, fuck you!"

Blaine: We were more political back then for sure.

The original version of the song was really goofy. It was about the stuff Scott was mad about in 1988 when he wrote it. It was not the same stuff he was mad about in 1994. So, he made it into some kind of a weird story, which I like.

Scott: I'm not a great guitar player, but good enough to crank out some shit. That song wrote itself. Blaine heard that and said, "Oh my, God! This is so hard." I remember him bragging to our friend Mike Grimes, "Man, you got to hear our new song. It's so good." People love that fucking song. We played that one time in Belgium, and there was this crazy slick brick floor. It was like a skating rink. People lost their shit, bodies were flying everywhere. It's three and a half minutes, and people can't hang with it at that pace. It's fun to play, and it gets your attention.

SHOTGUN IN A CHEVY
Blaine: I wrote that pissed off while I was working at the Chinese restaurant.

I was trying to write like Chuck Berry or Springsteen, just a descriptive song about getting out of town and then turning around and coming back. I'd done that before. It just seemed like there's a lot of despair there to tell you the truth.

Whenever I rode in my friend Jimbo's Chevy hot rod, it didn't matter where we were going, if we were going fast. That was it. That's all we needed.

Scott: Jimbo was a senior. We were a bunch of scrawny sophomores. One night, we had one of those fire extinguishers that sprayed water. There was a Sonic Drive-In with all these cars and people. Jimbo drove us by, and we sprayed them all. We got chased all night. Those guys wanted to kill us. It was wilder than hell.

Blaine: I'm very surprised that it's one of the most popular songs we do. It's just two chords, and it's so simple and primitive. It doesn't excite me, but people like it, man.

FUCK PIE
Welcome to the most contested song in the Nine Pound Hammer catalog. Its origins are a bit hazy for everybody. Pull up a chair, get ready for a discussion and have another slice of Fuck Pie.

Blaine: Oh, Jesus Christ, that was from National Lampoon's *Another Dirty Book*. I read that when I was a kid. It was talking about things you don't do. It said, "Don't stand up and yell, 'Eat fuck pie!' in church." I was in my church clothes when I read that in the mall bookstore. It was one of the few books my mom didn't let me get.

That phrase was kept alive within our little clique. The rest of the song is the way I was feeling about things.

Steve Terrell: That was one of my sayings. I was in college, and I had a test or a paper due. I ran into the library, which was going to close at six, and it was like five minutes to six. I asked this older librarian if I could get a copy of this document. She said, "No honey. I am so sorry. We're getting ready to close."

David Epperson was with me. We turned around to walk away, knowing that I was going to fail this test or paper, and I said to David – imitating that lovely older lady – "Oh, before you go though," and I reached behind my back acting like I'm pulling something out. "Here's some fuck pie for you, young man." So that was the genesis of fuck pie.

David Epperson: That was me and Blaine. That came from a book he had, I think.

Scott: Okay, that's another Owensboro witticism, that again, Blaine picked up on. That was something I was saying. I dunno if I said I was going to write a song about it or not. But again, he downloaded it to his subconscious.

It just means everything is broken. "It's fucked. Oh, really? Here, have some more fuck pie." He killed it on that, fucking great, great lyrics.

"Preached from the safety of my bedroom floor"

That's good shit. I've been in that bedroom – I can picture it. I mean that's a Steve Terrell line. I'm pretty much going to stand by that. He didn't get that from *National Lampoon's*, I guarantee you that.

Blaine: I was writing it for me, but I had to have Scott sing it, so I had to make sure he agreed.

> "Turned out to be another scam
> and it seems the older I am
> the closer I get to buyin' a gun"

That was very Scott at that point. He had a very nihilistic, pessimistic view of things. I didn't tap into that often, but for this song I did, and it was easy. I started writing from his way of looking at things – I still do. We agree on more stuff now, but he had more of a bitter viewpoint for a while.

OUTTA THE WAY, PIGFUCKERS
Scott: That's one where I wrote the music to it. "Pigfuckers" is a line from *Texas Chainsaw Massacre 2*.

Here's the thing, not everybody's going to get this one, but if you do, it's brilliant.

Aaron Lee (Former Cut Corner Video Department Manager, Friend of the Band, Former Co-Executive Producer of *Family Guy*): I knew Scott and Blaine through performing music and working at the cool record store in Lexington, Cut Corner. They would come in a lot. They were obsessed with *Texas Chainsaw Massacre 2*. I was too back then. It's very much like if Nine Pound Hammer became a movie. It's very much their universe with The Cramps on the soundtrack and the Southern setting.

Scott was also obsessed with this movie in the adult section, *Butt Man*. He thought the title was hilarious. He was always making jokes about it. I think they might have written a song called that.

Scott: Pigfuckers is just a banger, a good hard driver with great, fucking hilarious lyrics.

Blaine: I was around all this hometown shit. No one talked about anything important.

> "Just a greasy ham stuffed with high school football scores
> I'm hittin' the road, mister, I can't take it anymore"

There were four high schools in Owensboro, and when they'd play each other, people would talk about number 23 this and number 42 that. Who gives a shit?

ADIOS, FAREWELL, GOODBYE, GOOD LUCK, SO LONG

Blaine: I bought *Buck Owens and His Buckaroos in Japan!* and I think that's the only place he played that song. It was just so tailor-made for us, the way it stops and breaks things up. I think I forced that song on everybody. I still think that's a perfect song.

I didn't know Buck was cool. When he was on *Hee Haw*, I thought he was the guy who told bad jokes and didn't play a lot. *Hee Haw* killed him. It was a convenient paycheck, but they would do a whole six months or a year of shows in two weeks with a bunch of cocaine and uppers.

SLAM BANG

Blaine: That's a cover song by a band called Snare and the Idiots from Newport, Kentucky. They grew up white trash misfits in Newport. My ex-girlfriend Kelly, she lived near Newport in Fort Mitchell, and they used to call the high school kids in Newport "Rats" and people in Newport called Fort Mitchell high school kids "Cakes." To me, that's way worse.

The lead singer of Snare and the Idiots, Steve Arnzen, was a Rat. The whole band were Rats. The guitar player, Donny "Tex" Watson, played a lot like Johnny Thunders. It's a shame they only recorded four or five of their songs.

Scott: They had a single, and we were able to parse the lyrics together from that. The song is about OD-ing, but the "pissing on my grave" part is funny.

Blaine: It was a junky song, and "peanut butter" is a sort of speed. That song has had a life of its own, too. It was a hit in Croatia.

People yell for it all the time. We don't play it much.

Scott: Tim Warren loved it. He said, "The biker gangs in Germany are going to love it." I love that fucking song, too, but we've played it soooo much. I've kind of banned it from the set for the last few years, but it works its way back in on special occasions.

CHAPTER 20
WELL, I GOTTA GO, DOWN THE ROAD

Blaine: The German underground rock and roll press loved us. Hammer did so well in Germany when *Hayseed Timebomb* came out, they reviewed it on mainstream German TV. We were there so goddamn much. Our tours would be like 30 gigs – 21 in Germany, three in France, six in Spain, maybe one in Austria and a couple in Holland.

Scott: We go back to Europe. That's the tour where *Live at the Vera* comes from. It was the top-ranked show of the year. We killed it.

Jean Luc Jousse: That show at the Vera was something very special. The shows in Spain were mental as well.

Matt Bartholomy: The Vera was like the CBGB of Holland. A lot of famous American and European bands went through there. We had a really good reception there – you can hear it if you listen to the album.

Scott: It's lo-fi, but the fucking performances are wonderful, just fucking awesome. That record is so great. I loved putting that together.

There's another video we have where we played Ulm, Germany. It was in this old castle. We called it Hitler's bunker. The room was like a dungeon, and it got so hot in there it was raining from the ceiling. Just bam, bam, bam, bam, crushing it.

Blaine: Then Nine Pound Hammer did a tour of the U.S. – Scooch

Pooch Records booked that one, and no one showed up. We played in D.C. to almost nobody – that's how it was night after night. We didn't even have enough to pay for the van rental. We slept in the van a couple times, upright. We played out in Los Angeles to 14 people that we knew. It wasn't good.

We were competing against everything else in the world that people had heard of. No one knew who we were in America. Nobody. We weren't in *Maximum Rocknroll* or *Flip Side* or any of that shit. What we were doing was kind of passé. It wasn't hardcore or thrash metal. It wasn't grunge or pop or noisy crap.

Matt Bartholomy: My first real full U.S. tour? That was humbling. We were taking care of everything ourselves. Renting the van. Rarely staying in hotels, usually just staying at people's houses along the way with days in between shows.

In Europe, you're guaranteed meals every day – sometimes really good ones – nice places to stay and not having to worry about any of the logistics or the monetary part of it. We got paid every day no matter what and with all of us together like that, yeah, things got a little heated. When things got a little desperate or frustrating, I was like, "Oh man, I need to go back to school or something."

Blaine: We didn't have good jobs back home where we could say, "Oh I got it, don't worry about money." That wouldn't happen. It was the same old story, and it was really frustrating, especially for the quality of music we were putting out. I wanted to do it full-time, and we were doing it less and less. Bill quit, then Scott found Adam Neal. He fit like a glove, and we were all excited.

Adam Neal (Former Nine Pound Hammer Drummer): I was a pretty wild little kid. I kind of knew Scott from being in the Lexington scene. I had been in a band called Young Hellions and a band called Jet Jaguar. I got to be friends with Scott around the time that The Devil Dogs played in Lexington. I was into them pretty heavily, and I convinced Scott to get me into an over 21 show that I couldn't get into because I was underage.

Around that time, I played Scott some Jet Jaguar stuff, and I could see the wheels turning in his head. I think he was thinking, "Oh, you drummed on this? Maybe I'll put you on a little list over here of people I might contact if I need somebody."

It wasn't long after that I was working at Cut Corner off and on, and Scott came in and talked to me about drumming for Nine Pound Hammer. He was like, "Hey, I know you're friends with Johnny Evans, but we might need somebody for this U.S. tour thing." And of course I was like, "Whoa! Of course. Absolutely. Whatever you need." In the back of my head, I'm thinking, "Can I even fucking do this? Can I play those songs?"

There was some weirdness to it, though. Johnny was definitely angry about it at the time, but he also encouraged me to do it. That was kind of how I ended up in the seat.

Blaine: Ruyter and I booked a tour for Hammer. A guy named Jeff Clayton from a band called Antiseen faxed us a list of clubs, and we used that. We had a whole list of landline faxes, and we just cold called all these different places.

For that tour, me and Ruyter bought a van from The New Bomb Turks for $3,000. Somewhere in Canada, Scott was driving and had a wreck.

Adam Neal: I believe that it had a dented door. You couldn't get out of the front. Maybe that, or maybe that happened on the tour. I can't remember. But anyway, it was a terrible vehicle, just a mess.

Scott: The wreck happened outside a mall in Edmonton. Some guy came over on us. This was '95. We played shows across Canada and were driving down through Seattle, and then the transmission went out for the third time.

Ruyter: Blaine would be calling and saying, "This went wrong with the van." He's putting coins in a fucking phone, calling long distance, and I'm literally scrubbing fucking toilets, only to Western Union money to some godforsaken town in Washington. Then he would take a Greyhound bus to go back to pick up the fucking money and pay for the alternator or whatever it was to get the van back.

Then Blaine would drive to wherever the fuck Hammer was holed up at, play a goddamn gig, go to the next gig and the van would break down again. It was like that all the way down the West Coast. I think it broke down like four or five times.

Blaine: Five times!

Ruyter: And each time it would require so much fucking effort to keep that thing rolling. Things were falling apart. That van was a metaphor.

Blaine: Nashville Pussy used that same fucking van. No problems.

Adam Neal: I didn't understand any of it. There was a lot of pressure about the vehicle and what was going on, but the real fracture was already there as soon as I was in the band. It felt like, "Is this band over?"

Scott and Blaine seemed to be at each other's throats. Like I said, I was a kid, so I was only seeing 20% of what was real. They seemed to hate each other's guts, and they talked a lot of shit about each other constantly when the other one wasn't around. It was ridiculous.

I thought this was going to be great. Instead, I'm with these two mid-thirties old men just bickering nonstop. It was quite an eye opener to be honest.

Scott: We had to take a bus from Sacramento to L.A. to play our shows. Pulled that off somehow, and then we got another transmission put in.

Adam Neal: Some of the shows were good, lots of 'em were bad. Honestly, they were very lowly attended. We played to absolutely no one sometimes. The shows we did with The Smalls, those were the biggest ones we did.

Scott: We went down to Arizona, played one of the best shows we've ever done at a VFW in Yuma, with this killer band with horns and shit. They were playing this kind of Sublime punk. Had this killer afterparty. We were hanging out with these cool people. Man, it was fucking great.

But tensions were high all around. It wasn't good. Blaine and Adam were plotting Nashville Pussy. It's all fine in retrospect. It was just, we were broke and breaking down.

Adam Neal: Blaine and I hit it off over music. We were both really serious music fans, and we liked a lot of the same stuff. If Blaine went somewhere, I kind of tagged along. I was like, his buddy.

Blaine: Adam breathed some new life back in the band for a bit, but he got sick of it really fast. He was like, "Fuck this band!" He liked Ruyter, and I said, "Ruyter plays guitar." He said, "Really?" So I said, "We should get another band together when Hammer's not doing stuff. Instead of doing country, we'll do R&B. We'll get rid of all the twang, and we'll get a cool singer."

Adam Neal: A lot of it was probably very frustrating for them. The indignities of what they went through were probably very frustrating for both those guys at that age.

I didn't get the Real Scott or the Good Times Scott. I got the beginnings of careening into Bad Times Scott, kind of the Darkness of Scott.

Ruyter: It was not a fucking great tour at all. It was the straw that broke the camel's fucking back.

Scott: The van broke down again, and we're like, okay, everybody's on their own to get home.

Matt and I found this ad in the newspaper. This guy was selling plane tickets for $150 one way. We got those and flew home. The night before we left, I went to this cantina and danced with these old ladies all night. The band was pretty much toast after that.

Adam Neal: There was a mystery if the van could be fixed or not, so me and Blaine had a hotel for a few days. The next thing I really remember was having to call my fucking mom so she could wire me money to get home. After I got the money, I got on a Greyhound bus, and it took like three or four days to get home. And that was kind of the end of it.

Blaine: I got a cheap hotel and talked to the insurance company to try to say something happened in a wreck and that's why the transmission was broken. Ruyter was on the phone with the insurance guy. She started crying, and he said, "Oh man, well, you're going to get money for the wreck." So, I got two thousand bucks, which was enough money to get home. Then we kind of went our separate ways.

CHAPTER 21
NOTHIN' HAUNTS A MAN LIKE KNOWIN' THAT HE'S FREE TO CHOOSE

It's 1996. Not sure what was next, Blaine, Ruyter and Adam decided to keep forging ahead with something new – at least until things blew over a little with Nine Pound Hammer.

Blaine: Scott didn't want to do anything. He was not happy. I think he thought he was over the hill. He thought he should be doing something else. I understand that now. He didn't see Hammer panning out, and I didn't, either. So, two weeks after we got back from that tour, we hooked up with Adam and formed a new band.

Adam Neal: To me, that was a golden opportunity. Pretty quick we were in a basement somewhere working on a few songs. One of them was "Rub Yer Daddy's Lucky Belly" and another one that became a Nashville Pussy song, "Go Motherfucker Go."

Blaine: I was planning on doing both bands, but it just wasn't fun. Even my family was telling me, "You should do something with Ruyter."

We had met Corey Parks back when Nine Pound Hammer played Sleazefest in '94. I saw her sitting on a pool table, and I was like, "Is that a dude? Is that a chick?" She looked like Freewheelin' Franklin from the *Fabulous Furry Freak Brothers*. She looked cool.

Nine Pound Hammer crashed at Southern Culture on the Skids' house. Corey came over, and at one point she was driving me around talking about this band she wanted to form called The Home

171

Wreckers with all women, just badass attitude and rock and roll. I was like, "That sounds great," but I could tell that wasn't going to happen.

Instead of forming The Home Wreckers, Blaine and Ruyter asked Corey to meet them in Kentucky to form something else.

Ruyter: We were supposed to meet at Adam's house in Stanford, Kentucky, and she turned up a day late without a bass.

Blaine: She pawned it.

Ruyter: We didn't know she was a heroin addict.

Ruyter: She made up some story about how the headstock broke, which I was like, "You can't fucking break a headstock on a bass." That was a lie right there. But Adam had a bass she could play, so it didn't matter – and Nashville Pussy was born.

Blaine: Yeah. We wanted to do two-guitar rock and roll like Johnny Thunders, the Supersuckers or AC/DC. So, we started writing and practicing at Adam's house. That house was indescribable. He got to do what he wanted. He'd break down walls when he got mad and spray-paint them.

Ruyter: Pretty much the whole upstairs of the house was Adam's, and almost every single piece of drywall had been smashed with his fist.

Blaine: He was only like 19 or 20 years old when this was going on.

Ruyter: He's a big guy. He would run up and down those stairs. It was like thunder, man. You couldn't do anything wrong in that house. Let's just say that – vomit on the floor, and it'd be fine.

Blaine: We slept downstairs.

Ruyter: The downstairs was more of a hippie home, but upstairs was punk rock terror. It was fucking great. We could make all the noise we wanted. His mom was super supportive and would feed us.

We were sharing riffs and lyrics, too. So the very first Hookers[23] album and the very first Nashville Pussy album, there's little incestuous shit going on.

Blaine: I was originally going to get a singer. We wanted someone like Chris Robinson crossed with Mitch Rider and James Brown, but a punk – that person didn't exist. With Ruyter and Corey up front, we had to get someone who wouldn't be dwarfed. The singer had to get attention somehow.

I sang on a demo of "Go Motherfucker Go," and my friend Jeff Davis from Nashville said, "Whoa, who's that?"

I go, "That's me."

Jeff said, "Oh, that's it right there. That's exactly what you should have been doing all this time."

So, I had to learn how to play and sing at the same time. I would physically scream so loud that I would vomit afterwards and pass out. And that was no drugs, no nothing – probably some weed.

After a few months of writing and practicing, Nashville Pussy played their first shows, Scott got married, and an offer came in to play Japan.

Scott: This was '96. We got a call from this guy out of the blue to go to Japan. We got Bill to drum. He did that with us.

Ruyter: I think it was the weekend after Scott got married, the house we lived in in Nashville burned down.

We got woken up by somebody pounding on our door screaming, "Fire!" We were at the furthest spot from the fire, but smoke had filled the house. Blaine and I were both naked. We had a stack of Nine Pound Hammer work shirts printed up. So as we ran out the

---

[23] The Hookers was Adam's band and where he would turn his attention after he left Nashville Pussy. The Hookers' first album was *Satan's Highway*.

door, we grabbed the work shirts and threw them in front of us. I grabbed one and put it on, and he grabbed the blanket from our bed. Nine Pound Hammer was going to Japan within a couple of weeks. We had everything organized in a desk drawer – plane tickets, passports...

Blaine: ...there was a $5,000 cashier's check that we were supposed to use for buying tickets, too. It took forever for the fire department to get there.

Ruyter: We watched the fire take our house, but it was still intact enough that we were allowed to go back in and retrieve a little bit of stuff. We wound up getting the plane tickets and what was needed for the Hammer tour. We just took out that desk drawer and dumped it in a box, and we were gone. Our beautiful house was super fucking gone.

Scott: Hammer went to Japan, and Blaine and I had our worst fight ever. Ultimately it was about everything. Blaine was doing what he wanted to do. I kind of saw it like, "Okay, we're kind of just a cyclical European band. We tried grinding it out. You want to try doing it without me? That's fine." It was okay. Plus, I was madly in love and didn't really care. I mean, I cared, but it didn't mean I was quitting playing music or anything like that, just different ambitions, man.

Blaine: We started touring and booking stuff – me and Corey booked the first tour with The Pleasure Fuckers.

Blaine: We were lucky enough to have a guy named Peter Davis, who actually kind of discovered Hole and the Melvins and all these bands – L7, Helmet. Peter was a booking agent, but he had such a grating personality. All those bands left him as soon as they had a chance.

Peter started booking Nashville Pussy because he saw us play. That's all we needed. We would jump in the van and go. During the day we'd Xerox flyers for the upcoming gigs, wrap them up and mail them off.

We were putting all the effort in that Nine Pound Hammer should have put in. We were doing, kind of doing, the opposite of what Nine Pound Hammer would do.

Ruyter: This is for real now. This isn't just some fucking lark, and within short order we were playing with Motörhead. We couldn't have done it without Nine Pound Hammer.

One of the big obstacles was all of Blaine's fans. If they found out he started a band with his wife, it would have been like, "Okay, that sounds lame." We had to make sure that we were heavier and louder and more everything than Nine Pound Hammer. We couldn't make anybody second-guess this shit for a second. We had to come out fucking blazing. Just take down all the fucking haters immediately, so they would never question, "Why would you start a band with your wife?"

Scott: I went, saw them. They played in Lexington with The Pleasure Fuckers. It was all right. I put some of those guys up at my house. It was cordial enough. Blaine was now focused on Nashville Pussy, and that was fine. I accepted it and was doing what I was doing with my wife, Amber.

We moved to Ashland, Kentucky, because my wife got a job there. When we moved back to Lexington a few months later, something compelled me to go work at a homeless shelter or something like that. My dad worked in housing, so I got a job at The Hope Center,[24] front desk, second shift. I was not drinking, not doing anything. But if you are a real alcoholic, it's progressive. I was literally textbook. I eventually slowly started drinking again. It was slow, but it was steady.

First year I got married, I went to therapy. I didn't know what was wrong with me. I felt uncomfortable. I was not content. I had no idea what was going on with me? I went to a few AA meetings, but I had

---

[24] The Hope Center's mission is "to provide comprehensive life-sustaining and life-rebuilding services that promote healing from substance use disorder, mental health disorders, and homelessness."

no clue what was really wrong and what was to come.

They would go, "Oh, that's alcoholism," it's a special fucking group. Hell, we're restless, irritable and discontented.

CHAPTER 22
YOU GOTTA RAISE A LITTLE HELL

Blaine: If you were cool around '97 or '98, Nashville Pussy was up your ass and overexposed – we were in every fanzine, some big magazines like *Spin* and also the local paper. We toured so much, we won best local band in Philadelphia and San Diego the same year.

We were on the cover of these magazines, and people would ask Scott about us. It was pretty inescapable for a while. We were very lucky. It was like all the Nine Pound Hammer bad luck changed, and all of a sudden I had nothing but good luck. It was unreal.

We got nominated for a Grammy, and we had record company people throwing money at us. We were basically able to tell people what we wanted, and we did anything we wanted. I met my heroes, our shows were sold out, and we got to play the Leeds and Reading Festivals. I know all that was hard for Scott to deal with.

Scott: A fair amount of my resentment, fairly or not, I was resentful of Blaine and Ruyter, other people and just whoever. I wasn't happy about much. I didn't know I had a "spiritual malady." Blaine and Ruyter and others were just a symbol of my inner shit.

Blaine: Whenever we got written up, I'd mention Nine Pound Hammer right off the bat. On tour, I found there were fans out there, and that helped in America. After the second Nashville Pussy record came out, people started going, "Oh yeah, Nine Pound Hammer, I loved them" and "Man, I like this, but I like the Nine Pound Hammer stuff more." That was cool to me, and I'd tell Scott there were people out there.

There were these little cults that had our records, and they would play them at parties and stuff. There was one in Norway where these guys would play nothing but Nine Pound Hammer all the time.

I've met and talked to a lot of interesting people writing this book. I thought I was a fan until I got an email from Pål Erik Gulliksrud in Norway. Buckle up, gang.

Pål Erik Gulliksrud (Founder of The Shakey Puddin' Appreciation Society): In my record store, Wild Mind, we often sat around drinking beer and spirits all day. Sometimes things got a bit out of hand, especially when we played Cosmic Psychos or Nine Pound Hammer. I remember once when we smashed the entire stereo system in pure ecstasy to "Wrong Side of the Road." Then we hung it from the ceiling as decoration.

There was always a lot of joyful destruction whenever we played Nine Pound Hammer. In 1997, we had a wake for my store. It turned into a wild party that honored the traditions already well-established in my store of smashing inventory and enthusiastic alcohol consumption. When I put on Nine Pound Hammer's album *Hayseed Timebomb*, my store got utterly demolished. We crushed everything – we were so happy. We loved it.

I've lost count of how many pieces of furniture and wooden floors were destroyed as a result of playing Nine Pound Hammer at parties. One time, it got particularly bad. We had a dinner party at my apartment – it was supposed to be a pretty tame dinner with three good friends. The next morning, I woke up, unaware that anything was wrong, but I quickly realized something was terribly amiss when I saw my girlfriend Eli's horrified face after she'd been to the bathroom. The living room was completely trashed – broken furniture, bottles of spirits, shattered glass, vomit everywhere. There was blood, too. Even the ceiling was covered in stains.

Then flashbacks started coming of me diving off the top of the bookshelf onto my friend Kristopher. The armchair being lifted over someone's head and smashed. My dear girlfriend Eli pounding my friend Frode's stomach with her fists. Me grabbing Eli and throwing her across the room into the wall. All with smiles on our faces.

Then on the turntable I saw the culprit, the seven-inch "Radar Love" single by Nine Pound Hammer.

The rest of this email from Pål Erik Gulliksrud features more anarchy. Read the rest of it by scanning the QR code.

Meanwhile Atlanta was becoming Nine Pound Hammer City.

Blaine: Greg Armstrong, one of me and Scott's friends, had moved to Atlanta and was working at The Highlander. He played Nine Pound Hammer in the kitchen, and it spread like a cult all over town.

When Nashville Pussy first played Atlanta, people showed up in Nine Pound Hammer work shirts. I was like, "You're kidding me?" They'd go, "Man, you guys got to get back together and play. The Highlander loves you."

I remember Scott came to a Nashville Pussy show and was like, "We're getting old, Blaine." So, we decided to have a reunion show. I think we just both wanted to do it, and so many people in Atlanta were asking about us. We'd only played there one time to 30 people, and I think that was a free show. That reunion show in Atlanta was probably one of the best rock and roll shows ever.

Scott: We got Bill, and we got Matt, and we played this reunion show at The Echo Lounge in 2000 – and it was fucking nuts! 400 people. It was off the chain. It let us know how important we were in the scheme of things and what we meant to people.

Unfortunately, this was also when I was starting to decline with alcohol and some other things. It didn't affect the night of the show, but the night before when we practiced, I got really wasted. I was nervous, even Bill was like, "Damn, dude. How much are you drinking?" I could drink 30 beers. I'm an alcoholic, and we can drink what would normally kill other people, and it was normal to me.

Jean Luc Jousse: It was great. I didn't expect them to restart the band. The club was rumbling.

Blaine: Atlanta was a big deal. We played really hard and fast, and this local guy I knew, Jim Stacy, introduced us: "This is a band I grew up with and you missed." We did one more reunion show with the same lineup in Lexington at Lynagh's. That was great, too.

Scott: Then there was kind of a lull, and I got a little band together called The Smell Hounds, with Brad Scott and Johnny Evans. We were just kicking around, playing a lot of covers. It was fun. Blaine and Pussy played at Lynagh's here, 2002-ish. The Smell Hounds had recorded a song called "Zebra Lounge." I played it for him, and he was like, "That's really good."

Blaine: Scott asked, "Do you have songs?" I was like, "Yeah. I got some songs."

Scott: So, it was, "Let's do a record."

Blaine: When we got back together, we felt like we had unfinished business. The record came together really fast. At first I called Bill and said, "Hey man, we're going to get Nine Pound Hammer back together." He goes, "Why?!? Is there any money involved?"

I have a thing about having people in the studio who aren't enthusiastic. I think it gets into the grooves of the record. I told Scott that Bill wasn't doing it. He goes, "Well, we can get Brian Pulito. That dude played for Rabby Feeber." I was like, "I remember them being okay."

Brian Pulito: I played in lots of bands over the years in Lexington. I knew Scott through the music scene and being in bands that opened for Nine Pound Hammer.

Blaine: We went to Brian's house. He had this garden shed thing that was part of his house.

He systematically stacked all our amps on top of each other with mics. It was just enough room for us to play in. For us to record,

Brian would walk over and hit a button on the computer, and that saved our ass. I was so busy. I couldn't just go up to Lexington and jam for two weeks. So we'd make demos, and Brian would quickly mix them and put them on a CD. That let us listen to the songs before we went in to record *Kentucky Breakdown*.

Around this time, the band got invited out to Los Angeles to play L.A. Shakedown, which was billed as "2 Nights of Punk, Broken Blues and Primitive Rawk!"

Scott: It was a clusterfuck, but we played our show and Rick Ballard, the owner of Acetate Records, was there. I tried to sell him on us. I basically browbeat him, and he agreed to do *Kentucky Breakdown*.

Rick Ballard: I moved to L.A. in '92. I was at a record store, and they were playing *Smokin' Taters*. I was like, "This is fucking great!" I picked up that record and loved it, same with *Hayseed Timebomb*. I just always liked them a lot, but they didn't come to the West Coast. They were a bit of an exotic beast, and they kind of remained in that space for me – they're bad-fucking-ass, and I love everything about them.

Scott sent me something called the *Smoke Wagon Demos* or *Alcohol, Tobacco & Firearms*. It wasn't all the songs for *Kentucky Breakdown*, but I think it was "Rub Yer Daddy's Lucky Belly," "Drunk, Tired & Mean," "800 Miles" and another couple. I was impressed.

Blaine: We went to Dave Barrack's studio in Glasgow, Kentucky, and did *Kentucky Breakdown* in like five or six days. I thought it was great.

The band was back together, the music was great, but Scott had started to slide into the depths of alcohol and drugs.

Scott: Everything looked good on paper – loving, beautiful wife and decent job – I was still working at The Hope Center, but I'm not great. I think I had two DUIs at that point. I'm bingeing a lot. Benzos and Xanax are involved now because I had gotten to the point where

I couldn't get drunk enough. Xanax just gave me another level of euphoria at first, and I loved it. I sought oblivion. Oblivion.

At that time, what was fucked up was, I was helping homeless addicts get housing and jobs. Meanwhile, I'm sitting there falling apart. It was like, "Why aren't y'all helping me? Do y'all see this? Don't you see me coming into work with these stitches in my head? You're buying my bullshit that I had some kind of accident at home?"

I mean, I would sneak out of my own house on a kamikaze mission. I'd go to a bar and drink people's drinks off their table. Just desperate, pitiful shit like that. Hiding shit, drinking Natty Lights and the cheapest vodka – chugging it straight, snorting Xanax and waking up in the ER getting sewed up. I face-planted all the time – one time I fell in my kitchen, and I hit a corner of this door frame. I just blacked out while I was standing up talking to my wife. It looked like the Zapruder film.

My perception of things was not good. It was skewed. I was sick, very depressed and very anxious. I just wasn't happy and had a lot of resentments. It stemmed from adverse childhood experiences, nothing terrible, just stuff from divorce and some violence. I had PTSD from getting jumped in Lexington years ago. There was stuff at The Hope Center, too, that was very traumatic. It built up, and then when I incorporated Xanax into the mix, it was over with.

I was hooking and crooking prescriptions. I wasn't at ease – I was dis-eased. Xanax put me at ease.

I couldn't do heroin. I couldn't physically – I got sick. It didn't agree with me. Thank God I can't do opiates.

CHAPTER 23
KENTUCKY BREAKDOWN
(2004)

Every Hammer fan has a favorite album. Mine has always been Kentucky Breakdown. *When it was released in 2004, I was living in Chicago, working for an advertising agency writing about tampons, diapers and shampoo all day.*

When it was announced Nine Pound Hammer was going to play The Double Door, I convinced a handful of friends and people at work to go. Those people lost their minds, and by the end of the night they, along with everybody else in the crowd, were drenched in sweat – we're talking log-flume-observation-deck-drenched. It was nuts. It's still the only show I've been to where there were more puddles of sweat than beer on the floor.

Besides it being a phenomenal album, Kentucky Breakdown *hit at the perfect moment. Garage rock was still prevalent on the radio. Hammer seemed to have carved out its own little corner, and they were pulling in new fans. It finally seemed like they were getting the recognition they deserved.*

Blaine: It was cool. I'd be in Atlanta after *Kentucky Breakdown* came out, and people would go, "Man, the album is great."

I'd say, "Really? Where'd you get it?"

They'd say, "At the record store?"

I'd say, "Really?"

Then I'd go into record stores, and I'd see our album would be "Pick of the Week" or something like that. We had good distribution, and Rick from Acetate did a really good job on it. I was really, really happy it got out there.

As far as the title goes...

Scott: The title confuses bluegrass people because a "breakdown" is really associated with bluegrass music. I just thought it sounded cool.

INTRO
Scott: Blaine found that – it's from *The Wild Bunch*. He picked that for getting back together to give us a reunion-themed intro.

Blaine: I've had this Springsteen biography ever since I was in high school, and it had quotes before each chapter that didn't have anything to do with him, just like cool quotes. One of the quotes was from *The Wild Bunch*. It said, "It is not like the old days, but it'll do." So we were like, "That's fucking perfect, man." It ain't the old days.

RUB YER DADDY'S LUCKY BELLY
Scott: That's another Owensboro witticism.

Blaine: That was from our friend Steve Terrell. Our friends would say this crazy stuff, and then Scott and I would go, "We've got to write a song about that one of these days."

Steve Terrell: That was kind of me. I have a fat belly, and I would rub it for luck.

Scott: I brought it into the conversation. Then Blaine runs off and 15 minutes later, he goes, "Here. Is this what you're talking about?" I'm like, "Yeah, that's what I'm talking about."

Blaine: It was such a good line. I thought that was the perfect song. It's quintessential Hammer. I think that may be my favorite song.

"I worked the same job for 25 years
Boss don't know my name
Whether I screw up or tow the line
Things stay about the same"

Blaine: I noticed whenever I had a job that was clock in, clock out –
if I did shitty, they'd offer me more money and a promotion, or I
could work my ass off and they'd not notice and lecture me. They
don't really pay attention. You're just a cog.

"So roll me a joint, fix me a turkey pot pie"

Blaine: It sounds really lame, but there's a quote from *The Breakfast
Club* where Judd Nelson is talking about what it's like at his house.
His dad and mom are fighting, and his dad says, "Shut up, bitch. Go
fix me a turkey pot pie."

I used to eat a lot of turkey pot pies because there was a Kroger Cost
Cutter line of food. The shit was fine, especially if you're broke. I
could get a pot pie for 17¢. We lived on those back in the early days,
but I don't eat turkey pot pies anymore. I eat beef pot pies. I've
gotten kind of snobby about it.

HE DONE RUN OUTTA WORMS

Scott: Well, it's about me, but it's also about this guy who used to
play in our band. He would throw a line here and throw a line there.
Soon he'd thrown a line everywhere. He overextended himself with
the ladies, and when he'd reel in his line, he'd have no worms left on
his hooks. It just means, "I fucked up. I've run out of worms. Now
look at me – I'm empty-handed."

Blaine said, "Is that something your granddad said?" I said, "No,
that's a saying that I came up with." I wrote the music on Kevin
Robey's ridiculous, unplayable acoustic guitar. The strings were two
inches off the neck.

DEAD DOG HIGHWAY

Ruyter: That has some of the saddest lyrics in the world.

> "You can almost hear a steel guitar playing
> As you sing your medley of lies
> I'm like the hound that asked that deadly question
> 'What's on the other side?'"

Ruyter: I've definitely pushed Blaine to make his lyrics more cutting and the line, "What's on the other side?" Like, holy fuck, that's just fucking heart-wrenching.

Blaine: Originally that was kind of a personal song. It was kind of a love song. I drove all the way to Canada to get my wife and bring her home to show my mother.

Then, I switched it because Scott had so much animosity towards Ruyter, he wasn't going to sing that then – he wouldn't say that now. It morphed into this really tragic metaphor about leaving town.

> "Stopped counting the ways that I love you
> Started counting the days 'til I was gone
> I blew up life, went rolling down the highway
> Forgot just how good it feels"

Back before Hammer first formed, I was working at a place called Begley's Drugs. I would deliver drugs to old folks' homes for four hours a day, which was easy. For some reason, Highway 60, between Owensboro and Morganfield, Kentucky, had dead dogs on it all the time. It was sad.

I don't know how well traveled the road is, but obviously these farmer dogs that went stray would get cocky and then, boom! Anyways, there were more dead dogs than I could count, so I called it Dead Dog Highway.

GO-3-GO

Scott: This is another one from Kevin Robey's basement on his shitty guitar. The sample at the beginning is "DW," Daryl Waltrip, he's from Owensboro. Our friend Michael Baker was a huge

186

Earnhardt fan, and he had the video. I just wanted to write a song about Earnhardt. Why not? It was 2004, so it was a tribute.

Blaine: I thought it was dumb back then. "Who? Dale Earnhardt? You're going to write about him?" Now, I love it.

Coincidentally, Scott and I grew up with Michael Waltrip. He was Earnhardt's driving partner. Mike got his first win at the Daytona 500 that year without knowing Dale was dead.

DRUNK, TIRED & MEAN
Blaine: Ruyter and I were in Glasgow, Kentucky, at a FiveStar gas station. We were getting breakfast sandwiches, and there was some guy looking miserable in his car. Ruyter said, "That guy looks drunk, tired and mean," so I wrote that down.

> "I was brought up by desperate fools
> Trying to drink away a small town curse"

That was about my dad to a certain degree. Scott thought it was about him. I was like, "Really? You're not mean at all."

DOUBLE SUPER BUZZ
Scott: I was a huge Jesco White[25] head. I showed *The Dancing Outlaw* to Amber. That was her test. I knew if she liked it, we could get married. Of course she liked it.

Blaine: He was annoying as fuck with that video. He watched it all the time. He kind of drained the fun out of it for us, but he was having fun.

Scott: I wrote that riff smoking weed in my buddy Kevin Robey's basement, again, on the world's worst guitar.

---

[25] If you haven't seen the documentary *The Dancing Outlaw*, head over to YouTube, pronto. It's the story of Jesco White, "the last of the West Virginia mountain dancers." It's a spectacle.

AIN'T HURTIN' NOBODY
Scott: If there's a Mount Rushmore of Hammer songs, that's definitely on there.

It's just a tragic story. Gary Shepard was a disabled Vietnam vet living in Rockcastle County, Kentucky. He had maybe 10, 15 pot plants on his property, and the cops said they were going to cut them down. Now, this is a time when they were flying Black Hawks around the state, repelling out of them and searching for weed.

So cops and feds surrounded Gary's house while he was working on his truck.[26]

I don't know if he felt cornered or not, but the end result was needlessly created, all over some weed. It's one of those bittersweet, tragic comedies that sums up life in Kentucky, and it's the worst form of government overreach and abuse. He wasn't hurting nobody. The war on drugs, man. That pissed us off. It was fucked up.

DON'T REMEMBER LOVIN' YOU LAST NIGHT
Scott: That's a true story about a girl I met when I was working the door at Babylon Babylon. We dated, but there were a few nights that I didn't remember loving her. The rest is just silliness – the keg

---

[26] According to several articles, on Sunday morning, August 4, 1993, Black Hawk helicopters spotted 12 pot plants on Gary Shepard's property. Gary used marijuana to help with PTSD and pain from injuries he'd sustained in Vietnam – he was awarded a purple heart. An officer who knew Gary approached him and said they were going to cut the plants down. Gary allegedly said, "Over my dead body."

That officer left, but called in backup to roadblock all the routes to Gary's house. There were reports he had taken his wife and son hostage and was firing at helicopters. Those reports turned out to be false.

At 5:30 p.m., Gary was approached again by police. Gary grabbed a rifle off his porch and limped out to talk to an officer. He was told to drop the gun. He then raised his hands above his head. A concussion grenade was thrown at Gary, and five bullets were fired from automatic rifles, killing him. One of the bullet fragments grazed his wife's head and covered his son in his father's and mother's blood.

parties, Motley Crüe, the El Camino.

ZEBRA LOUNGE
Moses Naedele: That place was just really a redneck dive. It wasn't even a big Lexington music venue at all.

Scott: My friend Brad, Scott and I wrote that together in The Smell Hounds.

Brad Scott (Friend): We had a little practice space – and Johnny Evans, he was in The Smell Hounds, too. One day, the two of us were just banging around on stuff and at some point, I turned my guitar to open G and had this little one-finger riff. It just kind of came out in the middle of all the mayhem. I recorded it on this little tape recorder, showed it to Scott and he was like, "That's a pretty cool riff." And the lyrics are all Scott.

Scott: That's a true story about a guy who shot his woman at the Zebra Lounge in downtown Lexington. This woman was cheating on her man. She was with another dude, and her man walked into the bar and killed them both.

800 MILES
Blaine: Nashville Pussy was in Cologne, Germany, and we were hanging out with the Backyard Babies on a tour bus. They were playing their record and jumping in my face and shit. I was like, "Fuck this." I went to our van, pulled my guitar out and sang "800 Miles." It just spilled out, and I was like, "Well, this isn't a Nashville Pussy song." That was the first Hammer song I'd written in a long time, and I said, "Well we gotta get Nine Pound Hammer back together for this song."

I love that fucking song. I think I ripped the "Baby, baby, baby, I'll meet you there" part from the Stray Cats' "Too Hip, Gotta Go."

IF YOU WANT TO GET TO HEAVEN
"If you want a drink of water
You got to get it from a well
If you want to get to heaven
You got to raise a little hell"

Scott: We did that cover because of Jesco White in *The Dancing Outlaw*. He's tap dancing across a bridge playing that on his boombox. We play that at pretty much every show – talk about one that hits home.

CHICKEN HI, CHICKEN LO

Scott: Classic Blaine. We have to write songs about chickens and chickens eating chickens. That's just a Blaine spiritual.

Blaine: I love chicken.

Ruyter: It really is continuing a theme. It's in the water in Kentucky – they just have an inherent hatred of chickens.

Blaine: A love-hate relationship with chickens.
Anyway, there's a fiddle player, Doug Kershaw. He had a song, "Diggy Diggy Lo." It's just silly as hell. I liked it. During baseball season, I would sit and watch Braves games on TV and pluck around on the guitar. I kind of fumbled and made a mistake, and I had this crazy little riff. Then towards the end of this recording session, we needed something.

> "Saw the preacher comin' up the road
> Hit you in the head
> Better be dead
> Pastor's knockin'
> He's an ass 'til he gets fed"

Also, I'd seen this movie at the Kentucky Theater years before called *To Sleep With Anger* with Danny Glover. He plays this sketchy guy from the past who comes to visit his friend. At one point, Danny Glover's about to cut a chicken's head off. He goes, "A chicken hates to see the preacher coming to dinner." Then it was like, "Here comes a preacher. It's Sunday, we gotta cook a chicken for him."

As good as the album is, Scott's struggles were becoming a little more apparent.

Blaine: At night Scott would get fucked up, so we had to record him before a certain time. He has a strong voice. He'll do complete fucking takes and nail two or three in a row. I can do two Nashville Pussy songs, then I need a nap and 17 punch-ins.[27]

On the record, at the end of the song, that's real, that's pills. He was fucking wasted, man.

GODDAMN RIGHT

Scott: That was Gatewood Galbraith influenced. I worked for Gatewood on his '95 gubernatorial campaign, and he told me, "Henry Kissinger said, 'There is a they, and they are out to get you.'" And that's always stuck with me.

Gatewood represented a lot of things. He was the last free man in America. What a character. He liked weed, and he was just so anti-establishment. He was a brilliant guy, but he had his own unmanageability, too, unfortunately.

Blaine: We were getting songs together for a new Nashville Pussy record, and I played that for Jeremy, our drummer. He would usually go, "Cool," after I played something, but this time he didn't. So I said, "You like it?" He says, "Yeah. It's a Nine Pound Hammer song, isn't it?"

It's too bad that it's at the end of the record. I think we were going to open with that or "Rub Yer Daddy's Lucky Belly." I think we did the right thing.

---

[27] Basically, re-recording parts of a take that might not be perfect.

CHAPTER 24
THINGS JUST STARTED GETTING WORSE

Blaine: In 2003, we got two offers, one for Sjock Festival in Belgium and one for Serie Z Festival in Jerez, Spain. That's when Matt Bartholomy quit. I get it – it's hard to be in a band. We were just finally starting to get paid, but it was not like the old days. We were all older, and Matt had kids.

Matt Bartholomy: I quit for family reasons, and it was hard. It was kind of funny, too. I remember the moment I decided I wasn't going to do it anymore. There's a picture of us on one of our old posters. We're in front of this car with a big chicken head on top of it – this thing was like fucking seven feet tall or something.

So anyway, I'm in my car at this intersection in Owensboro, and it's just eating at me. "How do I do this? I can't go play this show." I decided I needed to stick with this life where I can consistently make money and provide for my family. Right then, that fucking chicken car rolled by, right in fucking front of me.

I was like wait, "We took that picture of us in front of that chicken car in Nashville like eight years ago, and now that goddamn car rolls in front of me? Right after I decided I was going to quit?" It was just bizarre. So, I called Scott and told him, he said, "Well, I'm going to get drunk tonight." That's all I remember him saying.

Blaine: Scott said, "Well, I can get Earl to play bass." I didn't know who Earl was, but I trusted Scott – it was all about if someone could get along with him.

Earl Crim (Former Bassist and Current Lead Guitarist for Nine Pound Hammer): Back when I was 16 or 17, I saw Nine Pound Hammer play at The Wrocklage. I was blown away. When I walked outside after the show, I saw Blaine sitting there. I said, "Hey, man, if you ever need another guitar player, let me know." He was just kind of like, "Yeah, whatever."

One night I got off work from a restaurant in Lexington and stopped at this bar called The Dame. Scott came in and said, "Our bass player quit. Do you have a passport?" I was like, "Yeah." He's like, "Well, do you want to come try out and play bass with us?

I learned 20 songs on the bass and went over to Brian Pulito's house. We sounded good. It was nice and tight. So they said, "We're going to play a warm-up show at The Dame, then we're going to Belgium to play Sjock Festival."

So my first gig was playing bass at The Dame, and then the next weekend I was flying to Belgium. I'd never been anywhere out of the country in my life. I didn't know what it was going to be like, and it was a festival with 4,000 or 5,000 people. I'd never done anything like that.

Scott: We did the Serie Z Festival in Spain in a bull ring. We were on the same bill with Dan Baird, Jason Ringenberg (of Jason & The Scorchers), The Hellacopters and Twisted Sister. I sang a song with Jason.

Brian Pulito: Serie Z Festival was pretty much my third show. It was a whole different level for me going from playing local clubs in Lexington to getting on a plane and playing in front of thousands of people.

Earl Crim: The Belgium show, that was a really incredible experience, too. I went out into the crowd to watch Twisted Sister. It was surreal. I was watching a band I used to see on MTV, but this time in a Spanish bull ring. It was like, "We're playing here? Holy shit!" But man, fucking Dee Snider was a dick. I went to shake his hand after the show, and he was totally disappointing and dismissive.

Scott: That night after the show at our hotel, we ended up taking over the bar – I ended up bartending all night. They just let us pour beers. That's the way Spain is, man. They didn't give a fuck. There were maybe 20 people there. We just drank beer and did these crazy shots all night.

Blaine: Scott found this guy at Teenage Head Music to book us more shows in Europe. So we flew back over and played 17 days. I was actually coming back home with money.

Scott: 2004, 2005, 2006, we were playing shows around here (America), and we started going back to Europe. I was not doing good, but I could keep it together. It was a period when you didn't know what you were going to get from me.

Brian Pulito: Back in those days when Scott was doing all those pills, he would get extremely – I don't know if it was nervousness or what, but you almost couldn't really be around him. But when the lights go on, man, that guy is a beast. He's a machine.

I don't know what demons he was dealing with in his hotel room before those shows, but Nine Pound Hammer always brought the best out of him in. He never mailed it in. The demons would sometimes come out during a set, but for the most part, he was a force to be reckoned with on stage.

Earl Crim: One night we were in Madrid, and we did "Redneck Romance." That song has got a lot of old references, and it's kind of a spoken song. There were 1,500 people in the crowd that didn't speak English, but they were singing every word. Scott gets down in the crowd, and that was the moment where I was like, "Fuck, man! This is kind of bigger than I thought."

Scott's an incredible front man. He's so good, and you can't stop the smile on your face seeing it.

Scott: We were good then. I mean there was that one show at The Double Door in Chicago, Little Steven and The Cynics. Oh my God, that was great. We had a big clique up there that had carried over from '94 to '04. It was nuts.

Roy Scott (Fan): I remember seeing them in Carbondale, Illinois. It must have been 2004, maybe 2005. Earl got really drunk, and he was playing bass – he was loaded. And on one of the songs, he fell down on stage and his bass case was right next to him. He literally rolled into it, and the case closed on top of a fucking coffin.

Another thing that was really cool, there was a guy probably my age, maybe a little older, and he had his son there – couldn't have been older than 10 or 12. I'm in the front row, and I can tell this kid doesn't know many songs, but when he heard "Feelin' Kinda Froggy," he went completely nuts! It was really cool to see a young kid just really getting into it.

CHAPTER 25
OUT OF MY WAY, I'M DRUNK AS HELL

2004 and 2005 were big years for Nine Pound Hammer. While on tour, they ended up meeting a very animated fan.

Scott: Okay, so after we did *Kentucky Breakdown*, we played Birmingham, Alabama. It was this fucked-up show in this fucked-up neighborhood.

Sara Riney: It was some weird fucking joint that used to be an arcade restaurant or something. The windows were missing, and there were sheets of plywood painted black covering them.

Scott: Nobody showed up, of course, but Matt Maiellaro was there.

Matt Maiellaro (Co-creator and Writer of *Aqua Teen Hunger Force* and the creator of *12 oz. Mouse*): A friend of mine I went to film school with turned me onto Nine Pound Hammer. I was at his house, and he cranked up *Hayseed Timebomb*, and I immediately gravitated towards it. The artwork captivated me. The riffs captivated me. It was the whole hillbilly rock aspect, the lyrics, Scott's voice, and each song had a comedic aspect to it.

When they played in Birmingham, some friends and I drove out there and rented this crappy hotel. Before the show, the band was hanging outside the venue. I'm a big photographer, so I asked them if I could take their picture. Ruyter was there. I started talking to her and told her what I did, and then after the show I really got to meet the band.

Scott: He said, "Hey man, I'm a huge fan. I want you to do a theme

196

song for this show I'm doing, *12 oz. Mouse*."

Matt Maiellaro: Back then Adult Swim was exploding. I'd been doing *Aqua Teen Hunger Force*, and I was putting together *12 oz. Mouse*. It was a weird sort of show – like a David Lynch fever dream. I had this idea of an opening that was this camera flying through a city with shit blowing up. The main character was an alcoholic mouse, and I needed a good original song for this thing – my first thought was Nine Pound Hammer.

After that night in Birmingham, I met up with Blaine at the Highlander here in Atlanta, which was a really cool bar. I told Blaine, "I'm doing this thing – it's fucked up. You guys are fucked up. It makes sense that you would do this song."

Blaine: I said, "What do you need?" He goes, "Well, they did a test for the opening and they used 'Ace of Spades.'" I'm like, "Well, okay. Fuck, I gotta write a Motörhead-type song. Cool. How long does it need to be?" Matt said, "32 seconds."

Ruyter: The coolest part was that they told Blaine, "Just write a song, and we'll edit it to fit 32 seconds." But as soon as you plant a seed or mention something like that to him, it's a personal fucking challenge. He was like, "Fuck that, I'm writing a complete 32-second song."

Blaine: It took two weeks to get it. I had a riff I was trying to make into a Nashville Pussy song that wasn't working. Scott wrote some of the lyrics, too.

Matt Maiellaro: They went away and shot back a demo, and I was like, "Goddamn, this is going to totally work. It was like magic." They were working in a studio in Bowling Green, Kentucky. A buddy of mine and I drove up there, and that night they almost gave us a private concert, which was cool. We were just hanging out, and they were like, "Okay, we're going to play you the song live." They rocked the song, and then they started playing all their other songs. I was screaming the lyrics. It was amazing. I think we wrapped up about three in the morning. We drank a bunch of beers. It was a blast.

Blaine: Adult Swim did these little bumpers before cartoons. One of them was how much we drank that night – it was 144 beers.

Matt Maiellaro: The next day we showed up at the studio, and they went in and recorded all their parts. When I started working on the show, I had this character, Roostre, who was a corn dog farmer. I wanted him to play guitar and I thought, "Man, Scott Luallen has got a great voice. I want to see if he'll do this." I got in touch with him, and he agreed. It didn't take much convincing.

Scott came to Atlanta for the first voice-over session. I told him to bring a guitar and said, "I want you to think of a song about farming corn dogs."

Scott: I go down there, and I'm hanging out with our buddy Billy from the song "Billy Lost His Feet." I was up all night with the drummer from Artemis Pyledriver drinking and doing coke. I was so sick, top five hangover.

During "The Corn Dog Song," I'm coughing and stammering, all that's real. I don't think I knew where I was at, I was so out of it. That song was a blast to write. I ripped it off from a Snake Out song.

Matt Maiellaro: I didn't notice anything. So, if that was the case, he held it together pretty well, or I was just naive. They did a killer job and made my show look better – and sound better – and Roostre was one of the hit characters of the whole show.

Blaine: When I was about 18 years old, me and my girlfriend went to the BBQ fest in Owensboro. I got two corn dogs at this American Legion food truck, and this guy turns to me and says, "Ahhh, the corn dog kid." My girlfriend heard that. She laughed, and the name stuck.

One day I was hitting baseballs in a batting cage, and Ruyter yelled, "Go, corn dog, go!" It's funny, Scott got to be a corn dog farmer on TV. He's a corn dog guy, too. Back when I used to run cross country,

I would eat shit like that because I was running 15 miles a day, and then when I stopped running I got really fat.

The primary reason the Hammer was in Bowling Green, they were finishing off Mulebite Deluxe – *a set of unearthed demos from 1987 with two new originals and a cover. Scott had told Rick Ballard at Acetate Records that he had some reel-to-reel tapes that needed to be transferred. Rick and Scott saw an opportunity.*

Rick Ballard: I think Scott just had some stuff laying around, and being a fan, I'm like, "Yeah, let's dig through it. Let's find something that we can do with this because I want it all." As far as the bands I love, I want the other versions – the alt version, the acoustic version, the half-baked version. I'm the sucker for all of it, man.

I designed the album cover. It looks like an old-fashioned blender at my in-law's house.

Blaine: This album was Scott's idea. I'm not on "The Way It Is" or that version of "I'm Your Huckleberry." That's Earl. But I am on "This Drinkin' Will Kill Me." On the original *Mulebite* tapes, Scott sounded like he was breathing down your neck.

I had no clue what "Mulebite" meant. Here's Scott's explanation of its origins, its meaning and probably where Chuck Palahniuk got the idea for Fight Club.

Scott: "Mulebite" – I love that saying. That's from my middle school. Our coach during gym class would take us all down to this basement – 30, 40 guys – and make us slapbox and wrestle each other.

And if the coach would see you sitting down, he'd grab you by the inner thigh and go "Mulebite! SHEEEE-HAAWWW!" Really loud. They made some poor girl come down there and slapbox, too.

Mulebite Deluxe *gave Nine Pound Hammer something else to promote and tour on. Then Matt Maiellaro decided he wanted the band's help again.*

Matt Maiellaro: I got to work with them again on *Aqua Teen Hunger Force Colon Movie Film for Theaters*. We had money to do a bunch of music at the end during the credits. I wrote Scott and said, "You guys need to do a song for the *Aqua Teen* movie." It was an immediate yes.

He said he wanted to do something about Carl and how badass he was. I told him, "As long as it's loud and in my face and the chords don't stop cranking." No guidance was needed for that.

Blaine: Scott wrote that whole thing.

Scott: It just came out of nowhere. Wrote itself.

Blaine: I made one contribution to the lyrics. I asked Daniel Rey, the producer and fifth Ramone, to tell me something about New Jersey. He's from there. He said, "Well, you're not from a city, you're from an exit." I go, "Well, what exit are you from?" He goes, "109, man, the rock and roll exit."

Ruyter: That's where all the skanks hang out. It's funny, too, almost every time we meet anyone from Jersey and you just mentioned exit 109, they think you know what you're talking about.

Matt Maiellaro: They did Carl's theme, which is I think one of the best pieces of music in that movie.

Blaine: They had a premiere for the movie here in Atlanta. Nashville Pussy had just played a festival in France. We jumped on an airplane, flew straight here and went basically right to the premiere. We bought sunglasses because we hadn't slept. I thought that movie was genius.

Tours, TV shows, movies, 144 beers – the band was on a roll until...

Blaine: It was going great, and then Earl fucks up. He pulled some shit and smashed Brian's Les Paul on stage. It was a bad night. I was upset that everybody wanted to kick him out. Brian said, "I can't work with someone who does that to me, Blaine." And I was like, "Goddamnit!" So, we replaced him with Mark Hendricks.

Mark Hendricks (Current Nine Pound Hammer Bassist): I remember Rob Hulsman responding to the flyer that Blaine had put up looking for a drummer for Nine Pound Hammer back in '87. Rob and I had an apartment together back then, and Blaine came over with his girlfriend at that time, Kelly (Holt) Chambers. We opened the door, and there's Blaine with a biker jacket on, a leather skid lid on his head, and he's just squinting at us – we thought he was a trip.

He just kind of handed a tape to Rob, turned around and walked off. We were like, "Holy shit, dude! We've got to listen to that right now." I think "Redneck Romance," "Gearhead Blues" and "Runaway Train" were on there, and it had us rolling on the floor.

We were into all things metal and making fun of all things that weren't. I didn't really know that much about punk rock at that time, but I knew Hammer sounded different.

After they booted Earl, that's when Scott asked me if I was interested in playing bass because they had another Europe tour already booked that was going to be happening in three weeks. I had just started my own business and was working my ass off. I gave it a lot of thought, but I was like, "Dude, I gotta go to Europe." I'd heard all the songs so much, I kinda knew them already. We had one rehearsal at my house, and it just clicked immediately. It was like I'd already been in the band. We toured Europe, played a handful of shows here in the States and then went into the studio pretty quickly and started doing *Sex, Drugs & Bill Monroe*.

CHAPTER 26
SEX, DRUGS & BILL MONROE
(2007)

Mick Jagger's voice doesn't sound the same way it did in 1971. It happens. We age. Our voices change. When Sex, Drugs & Bill Monroe *came out, you could tell something was different. Scott's voice sounded a little more ragged and raspy. It still has plenty of great moments and a title that's clever as hell.*

Scott: Earl came up with the title, and I had John Haywood do the cover art. John is the last link to a really primal Eastern Kentucky banjo style. We do the album, and I'm not great – my drug and alcohol use was out of hand. I could still be creative and contribute. I brought in some songs, but there was a lot of tension, and I was just kind of annoying. I remember just laughing too much, just overdoing it. I was in my own little world.

Blaine: We recorded that album at Brian Pulito's old studio.

Mark Hendricks: It was an old slave quarters, so it had a haunted vibe. It was a tiny little building with a tracking room and kind of a vocal booth. There was also a storage room and a control room.

Mark Hendricks: Scott would go into the vocal booth to do some vocals. We'd be in the control room, and you could hear him getting drunker with each take. We're like, "How is he doing that? There's no alcohol in there."

Come to find out he would go through the cabinets in there, find a bottle of booze and down it between takes. Scott was so mysterious with his use of stuff, we always wondered what kind of state he was going to be in.

Brian Pulito: He would be on pills and would have a bottle of something back there.

Mark Hendricks: One funny thing that I remember from that session, everybody pretty much smoked pot and instead of smoking joints or doing bong hits, Brian was really into these vaporizers. They didn't create a lot of smoke, and what you get after you vaporize weed is spent weed, but it still looks like weed. So, we'd always keep that in a bag and call that the "Scott Pot" because late in the night, he'd be wasted and want to smoke weed. We'd get that shit out and roll a nasty joint to satisfy him.

I'M YER HUCKLEBERRY

Scott: Earl came up with the intro, Brian came up with that main riff, and I wrote the lyrics and the vocal melody. It's a great saying. I thought it was hilarious.

Blaine: That's from *Tombstone.* At the time, I was worried Scott was watching too much TV. I get quotes from movies and TV occasionally, I just wasn't super familiar with that movie. Oh yeah, Earl plays a solo on that.

Earl Crim: I happened to be down at The Dame again, and Brian Pulito walks in and he's like, "We just went on a European tour. It was okay, but Blaine says it's just not fun without you."

Blaine: I loved being in the band with Earl. He was my trouble buddy. We had a lot of fun together on that first Hammer tour he was on, plus Earl's a badass. I wanted Earl back in the band because I wanted a second guitar player. I think it sounds better, and I wanted to sound as heavy as Nashville Pussy. Earl doing leads and solos broadened what we could do instead of just me doing the same Chuck Berry solo. We could do a bunch of other cool stuff.

Earl Crim: So, after a hiatus, I was back in the band, but I was playing guitar, which I'm much better at than bass. Bass is an instrument on its own, and Mark Hendricks is an actual real bass player.

HOOKERS & HOT SAUCE
Scott: That could have been a Nashville Pussy song.

Blaine: Maybe. I always try to have one song on an album where the other band goes, "Hey! That doesn't fit." It keeps everybody on their toes. I knew we were going to have a bunch of goofy songs. I wanted one that just kicked ass.

BLACK SHEEP
Scott: Blaine brought that in. Robert Altman wrote that for the movie *Nashville*.

Blaine: I remember listening to John Anderson's version on a jukebox somewhere in Indiana a long time ago. I thought the lyrics were amazing, and you could tell whoever wrote it was not a songwriter. They were a writer, because it's a story and Altman made sure to describe everything that's going on perfectly. Where if you're writing a song, sometimes you leave it open to interpretation.

EVERYBODY'S DRUNK
Blaine: I used to say, "Everybody's stupid but me," and when we would do "Train Kept A Rollin'" I would scream, "Everybody sucks but me!"

That could have been about me. Who knows – everyone was really wasted at the time. I thought it was a really clever lyric. I used to write really good lyrics. I've still got some, but I'm starting to feel like I'm competing with my past.

Lyrics have always been really important, and we kind of backed ourselves into that corner. Every time we do a record, we know everyone's going to be paying attention to the lyrics. It can be exhilarating, or it can be exhausting. It's just a daunting task, especially with Nine Pound Hammer songs. There are always so many fucking lyrics.

FIGHTIN' WORDS

Scott: My wife actually wrote that song. I helped her pull it together a little. She's very talented.

Blaine: Scott did 70 takes, I swear to God. Half of them were, "Start again. Start again. Start again. Start again."

He came to the studio drunk, insisting on doing it. He wasn't singing really, and his voice kind of changed because he was struggling.

Scott: That's partly me and partly the technical setup. I'm not singing as much as I'm yelling a lot of stuff on this album. I was just a caricature of myself. This is also the record I started singing differently on. I realized I had another, different register.

Blaine: Jeremy, Nashville Pussy's old drummer, used to describe Scott as, "Singing like he had socks in his mouth." He didn't sound like that before *Sex, Drugs & Bill Monroe*. This should have been a happy record, but for the most part, it reminds me of a lot of turmoil.

MAMA'S DOIN' METH AGAIN

Blaine: I wrote and sang that because it was a novelty song. I had a very specific way I wanted the melody to go, and showing Scott stuff was going to take extra time.

Anyway, Sherri McGee sang that with me. Oh God, she, well, that shit was crazy. She was married to a slide guitar player, but they were fighting. He was accusing her of having an affair with Unknown Hinson, which might've been true.

That song took two days. Sherri and her husband had to come in at separate times because he had a little action figure of Unknown Hinson, and he started hitting it in front of her at home right before she came over to the studio.

Ruyter: She was bonkers, but she did such a good job on that. Her vocals are so deadpan and dry.

Blaine: Sherri had this whole Little Miss Tammy Smith persona. She also had this other persona where she would act like she was Sherri's manager.

She came into the studio, and I said, "Hey, Sherri, how you doing?" She replied, "I'm worried about Miss Tammy. I'm worried she's not going to make it. I haven't seen her in years."

I go, "What the fuck are you talking about? You're not going to play?"

She said, "I just worry Miss Tammy's not going to make it. I talked to her earlier. I think she went on a bender last night."

She's a whole book to herself, man. She's had a crazy life.[28]

Oh and at the end, I burped accidentally. I like leaving shit like that in there. Other people said it took away from the song. I thought that song could have been a novelty hit. Meth was pretty widespread, but it wasn't super crazy yet.

RIGHT TO DO YOU WRONG

Blaine: I had to have stolen that from a country song. There's always those "left hand don't know what the right hand's doing" kind of songs. I was just trying to write a Dwight song, and I'm sure it's got a similar phrasing as some of his songs. It ended up translating really well it into a punk song.

RODE HARD

Scott: There was a skit, "The Last Chance Garage," with Dennis Hopper on *Saturday Night Live* where he says, "I know your type, mister. You like to ride 'em hard and put 'em away wet." I know it's a well-known saying, but that's where I gleaned that from. It's just an outlaw tale. Earl and I wrote that. That's when he and I started becoming song-writing partners.

---

[28] Okay, this took me a second to figure out, but there's Sherri McGee. There's Sherri pretending to be Little Miss Tammy and then there's a third persona — Sherri's manager.

TOO SORRY TO SHIT

"I was born to be sorry, some say too sorry to shit
You need me to feel the pain that I cause
As you sit back and plot yer revenge
Don't waste yer time or tears
On the err of my ways
Cause I ain't wastin' mine makin' amends"

Blaine: Goddamn, Scott came in with that, and I'm like, "Good God, dude. Who are you? Me?"

Scott: That's a saying from my wife's family – she basically wrote that. Her great grandmother who lived to be 103 was from Hazzard, Kentucky. She was a nut that hated men and would say, "He's too sorry to shit." My wife, she just hummed that song in her head, and I helped out a little bit.

When I interviewed Blaine and Ruyter, I said to them, "Scott's pronunciation of 'shit' in this song is maybe the greatest pronunciation of the word ever." Then, at the same time, Blaine and I both said, "SHEEEEEEEIIIIIIIIIUUUUTTTTTT!!!!" Ruyter's response was perfect, "Yeah, that's two or three syllables."

HELL IN MY HAND

Blaine: There was a dude in Vancouver who contacted Nashville Pussy's manager, and he said, "Hey, man, we've got a zombie western. Would Nashville Pussy be interested?" So, I wrote a Western song, and I loved that fucking thing.

Ruyter: I think when the guy first wrote the script, he had Nashville Pussy as actual characters in it.

Blaine: I was a Western fanatic for a while. Back before the internet, I would go to the library and look at books on Western movies and write the titles down. I would do the same thing with movies on The Westerns Channel. I'd scroll along with what's coming up on the cable guide for the week and see titles like, *Hangman Also Die!* and *The Way of the Gun. Hell In My Hand* was one of them.

Ruyter: We'd also buy those bootleg DVDs from truck stops in Italy and Spain. You'd get like 50 of the greatest spaghetti westerns, which was really shit nobody had ever heard of, and the titles alone would set Blaine off running.

Blaine: I was gung ho about the zombie western movie, and then our manager just wrote and said, "Man, this guy's a douchebag. Don't believe a word he says. It's not going to happen." And it didn't.

WHEELS FLEW OFF LAST NIGHT

> "So when my latest lie gets shot down on the fly
> I'll just pop back another pill
> I hope the one who throws my final bail
> Ain't easily offended, when I wind up back in jail"

Scott: That's Brian Pulito and me. This was his song about me. It's fine. I might have lost the battle, but I'm winning the war.

Blaine: I forget what the original lyrics were, but Scott added some.

AIN'T WORTH KILLIN'
Blaine: Mark Hendricks wrote that.

Mark Hendricks: I was trying to be a storyteller and pick from people that I knew, like Scott and Blaine do.

My step-grandmother, my stepdad's mother, was a haggard old woman. She had the weirdest career. She told us she was a cook for 15 men on a train – cooked their meals, their birthday cakes and all this shit. She also worked at a bowling alley before they had automatic machines, and every time somebody freaking bowled, she said she got paid 8¢ to set the pins up – so that's a line in the song.

She had a stroke, which put her mind on a never-ending loop. She was also hooked on nicotine and after her stroke, she could only have four cigarettes a day. It was my mother's job to dole them out. When it was time for my step-grandmother to have a cigarette, she would come over and pretend like she was visiting with us, when really she was just there to ask for a cigarette.

She would also stroll up and down the neighborhood searching for cigarette butts. When she would collect enough cigarette butts, she'd get the tobacco out of them, sneak down in the basement and roll her own cigarettes with pages she'd ripped out of the Bible because it was the thinnest paper she could find.

She did say, "If you aren't working hard, you ain't worth killing." She worked harder than most men, but like I said before, she was a rough, haggard woman. It really is kind of wild to think that somebody would've had sex with her.

Blaine: It's a weird riff that only a bass player would come up with. Mark showed it to me and Scott. Scott didn't like the song, but I was like, "Let's do it anyway." He eventually came around on it.

COOKIN' THE CORN
Scott: That's a great song by Brian.

Blaine: Brian wrote a few songs around this period. He was getting divorced. I guess that's what brought them out of him.

Brian Pulito: My brother-in-law and I used to go fishing and canoeing on the Salt River in Kentucky. We were driving to it one morning, and he looked up as we were driving past the Wild Turkey Distillery. He looked up, sniffed and said, "Oh, they're cooking the corn this morning." So, I just cataloged the phrase "cooking the corn," and the song wrote itself.

Blaine: Pulito sang on the original version, which I thought was cool. Ruyter said, "Wow! He sounds like Steve Earle!"

I wanted to make this song sound different, so I got a little bitty Vox amp and played the guitar through that. For the solo I said, "I'm going to throw it through a Marshall, and we're going to crank it up to 10." Mark Borders, who's now in Mac Sabbath, was the engineer. He was this young kid from Paint Lick, Kentucky. He graduated from Berea College, moved to Lexington, and Brian Pulito gave him a job.

Mark Borders said, "That solo isn't going to fit." I said, "It'll fit. It'll come out of nowhere." So when the solo comes in, my guitar is just

RARRRRRARRR!!! Then Mark Borders went and got a 2 x 4 from a scrap pile around back and taped a tambourine to it and started stomping on it. I was like, "I like this kid."

THE WAY IT IS
Scott: My grandfather really didn't say that. I just attribute it to him because it's something he would have said. Earl and I wrote that. We write well together.

There's a saying about "bankrupt idealists." The world's just not the way it should be. Well, whatcha going to do about it? Set yourself on fire? Are you gonna go burn yourself down?

Blaine: I love that goddamn song, I don't think I even play on it. I think they recorded it without me. That was a frustrating thing. I would come there, and very little shit would get done. I'd tell Brian, "You guys gotta do some shit without me."

I was getting tired of it. Scott was a mess. He would come to the studio, and we might do something to make him mad like say, "You're too fucked up." He'd get in his car, wasted, and he would peel out.

Lexington was a small town. I thought he was going to get pulled over, especially on a Tuesday night at two in the morning. It was an accident waiting to happen. Glad nothing happened. At that point, he had gone to rehab two or three times, I think.

CHAPTER 27
CAN'T SEEM TO SAY GOODBYE TO THIS LIFE OF GETTING HIGH

Scott: We went to Europe again and did the usual routine. First we went to Oslo, and there was this guy, Pål Erik Gulliksrud, who formed The Shaky Puddin' Appreciation Society.

A couple tours before this one, we playing in Copenhagen at this huge squat in Freetown Christiania[29] that these hippies had taken over in the '70s. There were all these buildings with restaurants and a club called Loppen. I mean, a lot of people live there, and they have their own economy. They're kind of an independent community.

Pål showed up in Copenhagen and brought us this big sledgehammer that The Shaky Puddin' Appreciation Society had burned different things into.

Pål Erik Gulliksrud: I painted the hammerhead with three layers of metallic gold paint and burned the words "Nine Pound Hammer made a man outta me" into the handle with a pyrography pen. The security guards at Loppen gave me strange looks as I strolled in with a sledgehammer slung over my shoulder, but they didn't stop us – this was Christiania.

Backstage, I awkwardly handed the sledgehammer to the band. A

---

[29] Freetown Christiania is kind of amazing. In 1971, a group of hippies broke into a defunct military base and made it their own. It's an anarchist commune that allows no cars and no corporations and has very few rules.

couple of hours later, the show starts and everything explodes. No one screams like Scott Luallen. There was a terrifying richness to his guttural Southern roar, like a Kodiak bear on steroids and mescaline chained up inside his Kentucky-fried stomach. We were in heaven.

Scott: Getting that sledgehammer through customs was interesting. Anyway, that Oslo show was sold out, and it was wild as hell. The Shaky Puddin' Appreciation Society was there, too, and everybody was passing bottles around in the crowd. The next day our tour manager, Manny, couldn't drive because he was so hungover. That's a top 10 show of all time, and that was our first time in Oslo. Mark also missed a flight in Germany. First time that ever happened.

Mark Hendricks: It was an adventure, and I didn't care. I was in a weird spot in my life with my first wife. I wasn't happy, and anytime I could go out and just kind of go nuts, I did.

Blaine: That's when I was doing Hammer stuff 25% of the time and Nashville Pussy 75% of the time. It was good, and Scott was fine with that. He could keep his job and do Hammer, and we were actually making money. The only real problem was the drinking and the pills.

That was when Scott would take Xanax before we played, and we'd go through half the set and then the Xanax would kick in. He usually sings a little bit behind the beat naturally, but he would be two sentences behind what we were doing.

We did a couple tours in Europe, and I was basically going over there to get fucked up, hang out, get away from Nashville Pussy and see old friends, but we were partying as much as we were playing. It was kind of getting away from all of us.

CHAPTER 28
COUNTRY CLASSICS
(2009)

We've covered the original Hammer songs on this record, and after talking to Scott, Blaine, Earl, Brian, Mark and Ruyter, there's not a whole lot to report about each individual song.

The major takeaways? Scott picked out a lot of the covers. Ruyter's whistle solo on "I'm Yer Huckleberry" is second only to the whistling on "The Wind of Change." Everybody got the opportunity to take turns on different instruments. And Blaine and crew also formed one, if not two new bands without Scott while recording Country Classics.

This is where Scott really started to slip into some dark territory.

Scott: We came home from that European tour, and that's a little gray area for me from 2008 to 2010.

Blaine: Brian had moved to this nice studio, and he said, "I need to test my equipment out." I was like, "I got a song called, 'One Good Thing.'" It was kind of a commercial song. It's got this kind of Black Crowes-y, Allman Brothers thing going on. We got a young guy, a singer, Andy Brasher, from Owensboro. He was extremely talented and way more mainstream. It was fucking amazing. We just never released it.

Ruyter: Yeah, it's the best thing Blaine and I have ever done.

Blaine: I thought *Country Classics* was a perfect idea. I always wanted to do an album of straight country covers done the Nine Pound Hammer way. But record labels wanted us to do Hammer songs done in a country style, so that's basically the album. You get the best of both worlds.

I don't want to rag on him too much, but Scott wouldn't show up to the studio for two months. He might not even remember that. I get it – he wasn't doing well. At some point we formed another band called Buzzard and recorded all these songs. We all took turns playing. We were having fun. It was like, "Who can play a Banjar[30] solo?" So, we'd all take a shot at it.

Ruyter and I loved that studio because it had a bed. We'd drive our van up from Atlanta, stay there and just record stuff. We were all having fun, but Scott couldn't get out of the house a lot of the time, too. Amber wouldn't let him out and for good reason. I don't blame her what-so-fucking-ever. I remember one time, she dropped him off and started screaming, "Scott's got pills on him!"

Scott: Brian kicked me out of the studio one night when I tried to bring some shit in. He called my wife, "Come get him: I'm not putting up with this."

Brian Pulito: I imagine I kicked him out more than once. This was back in the dark days. I'm sure he dabbled before with Xanax and all that, but I feel like the pill thing really went into overdrive after a car accident.

Blaine: When his partying got more secretive, we didn't know anything about it, and we weren't included. You can see someone drinking and getting drunk. You can smell weed or with cocaine, you know if someone's going to the bathroom too much. But pills are like, someone's fine and then they're not.

As bad as it got, Scott had a lot of good ideas.

---

[30] Aka a GuitJoe. It's like a guitar and a banjo got together and made a mutant baby.

Scott: That was 2009-ish, and that's right before the crash for me. I was operating at 60%. The work suffered. I mean, it's not bad. We were able to pull it off, but it wasn't optimal. I was still managing the band for the most part.

Blaine: I gave a copy of *Country Classics* to everybody and their mother in the late 2000s, and people were like, "You should do really well with this," but nobody knew what to do with it.

We tried to get Acetate Records to release it, but I think they were upset because we weren't touring a lot and we weren't promoting stuff. At the time, record labels were paying so much to artists and other labels per cover song, and we had like eight covers on there. So Acetate said it was too expensive. Rick Ballard offered us zero for it. This is the same time Nashville Pussy was still getting $60,000 to record an album.

We thought maybe Bloodshot Records would want it. They didn't. We didn't mean to self-release it. There just wasn't the interest, man.

With Country Classics *finished, around this point, Brian Pulito decided to hang up his sticks.*

Blaine: It had gotten to the point where Brian didn't want to do it. He'd record, but he refused to go on the road. Brian just couldn't deal with Scott anymore.

Scott: Were all the dynamics and interpersonal relationships in the band perfect? No, and it didn't warrant my response to them by wanting to escape from everything. My attitude at the time was, "I'm going to take my toys and go home and set myself on fire. Hope the smoke bothers everybody."

I was mad about some specific things, justifiable anger. In hindsight it didn't warrant my actions and response, but hurt people, hurt people. No matter how thin you slice it, there are two sides. It wasn't all me, for sure.

CHAPTER 29
KISS THE FACE OF MY MAKER SOON

Blaine: One day Scott calls and says, "Hey, we got a tour in Europe lined up." I asked him, "Does your wife know?" He said, "Yes." She was pregnant, and I said, "Well you can cancel if you want." But he was still planning on going.

Scott: That was 2010. My wife was pre-eclamptic, had high blood pressure and had to go to the hospital six weeks early, so I couldn't go to Europe.

Blaine: We'd already canceled a couple of times – one time so Scott could go to rehab, and another time he booked a tour and didn't tell me about it. I was on the road with Motörhead when I found out about it. I called up the booking agent and said I couldn't do it.

Mark Hendricks: The booking agent said we'd be blackballed from Europe if we canceled. I mean, he was very, very serious.

Scott: They went without me, and that was fine. They did what they had to do. I almost didn't survive that period. I was home by myself, and I wasn't doing good.

Blaine: Rob Hulsman rejoined right before that tour.

Mark Hendricks: Blaine sang the majority of the tunes. I sang like three songs, and we made it through it. I got to see Blaine in his front-man role, which was cool. He was great at it. He was like a redneck James Brown.

Earl Crim: There were complaints that Scott wasn't there, but we played our asses off.

Blaine: That tour was like five or six weeks long with 12 days in Spain, and I always say, "I'll play a kazoo for 12 days in Spain." I thought I was helping out. I was doing more work, playing for less people and loading my own stuff, but we had a good time on that tour. Then Scott starts seeing posts online and commenting on them saying, "You suck." He was hurt, and he was pretty pissed off, which I understood. In my mind, we were saving our asses.

The first gig we did was rough, but it got better by the time we did the live record. At the end of it, I don't think Scott heard this, but I was closing the night by saying, "Hey, man, if you want to make Scott feel good, tell 'em the show was good <u>and</u> tell him we sucked."

I told everyone secretly, "He'll be back, you'll see." Then we made amends, and we planned on playing some more shows.

Mark Hendricks: Two or three months after that tour, I wound up quitting. I had just gotten married again, and I was trying to be a stepdad and start a new life. It was funny because when I told Blaine I quit, he said, "Quit what? We barely do anything."

With Scott dealing with his issues, the gigs became fewer and farther between.

Blaine: We had a really good gig in Atlanta and one in Detroit for Halloween. Scott goes, "I'm fine now. I'm a father. I've straightened up." Then next thing you know, I got an email from his wife: "Scott's in jail. Cancel the gig."

Scott: I had seven DUIs in 20 years. That's a true story.

Blaine: I told Amber, "I'm not canceling these gigs." You can't really do that if the guitar player is a singer, too. They expect you to do something or get somebody to sing, especially if they're paying you. So, I filled in for two gigs. One was too well-paying not to do it, but after the second one I said, "I'm not doing this again."

After that, we did one more show in Atlanta where we did Hammer-okee. We had about 10 different people come up and sing Nine Pound Hammer songs with the band. So, Scott's in jail – I didn't know for how long. I called it. I thought that was it. I thought he was going to die.

CHAPTER 30
SIXTY DAYS IN THE HOLE

Scott: I went to the gates of hell in a suicide suit[31] on the second floor of the Fayette County Detention Center in 2011. That's what it took to have a moment of clarity, and then that had to be followed up with a lot of work.

Alcohol and drug addiction are progressive. For a long time, my relationship with alcohol and drugs was a fucking honeymoon. Smoked a lot of weed, drank a lot of beer.

I remember in '86 or '87 – this is when I knew if I didn't have any weed, I would drink. I was sitting around our house on Bassett Avenue. I'd taken a bottle of Bailey's from my dad's house in Frankfort, and I drank almost all of it by myself. Toby was there, and he goes, "Man! What are you doing? I'm worried about you, man."

Those early tours in '92 when we were going to Canada and Europe, I could handle it. I could drink, and I could stop. There wasn't any morning drinking or other stereotypical, clichéd shit like that, but alcohol and drugs put me at ease.

I could never sleep. I still have trouble with it, but weed worked for a long time. I smoked it addictively, and it was a priority. It's not a benign substance. It changes you and stunts your emotions. Don't get me wrong, it's creative on one end, but it got in the way. I would put

---

[31] These are also known as anti-suicide smocks, turtle suits or pickle suits. They're made of tear-resistant material so the wearer can't make a noose out of them. Typically the person wearing them is naked underneath.

it before family or if I was uncomfortable, I would smoke weed. I'd get stoned in my church basement when I was a senior in high school. I wanted to feel that all the time to some degree, and I went to pretty much any length to do that.

The alcoholic life seems normal, but it's not. I got my first DUI in '85. I was driving everybody home in Blaine's Chevy Nova – the ticket was like $40, and I lost my license for like a month. It was nothing back then.

For 15 years people would see me acting normal and just getting a buzz. Then with pills, it was like Dr. Jekyll and Mr. Hyde. It was baffling, infuriating and frustrating. It really started getting bad later in the '90s and the early 2000s. It progressed, and it changed my personality. I wasn't the same person.

People saw glimpses of it, and it was just sad. I wasn't healthy, didn't look good and just wasn't myself. Blaine was very bitter and mad. He didn't understand addiction – it wasn't his or the band's job to understand it. It bred a lot of resentment and misunderstanding, and I took that a certain way, too. I was like, "Don't you see I'm dying here?"

Don't get me wrong, I didn't want to die. I didn't have a suicide plan. I just didn't want to be living the way I was living. But my external world looked good. I had an amazing wife and a new daughter. It was my perceptions and my expectations that were skewed. And ultimately, it came down to a spiritual issue of sorts.

Now there were some adverse childhood experiences, nothing too terrible – my parents' divorce, some violence, I got jumped once by some guys in Lexington. Lots of violence and mayhem at The Hope Center that I internalized. It all just built up and to be honest, I liked the effect produced by alcohol and drugs – and they worked, temporarily. When I incorporated Xanax into the mix, it was over with.

I remember sitting on my stairs at some point, and I'd run out of Klonopin, Xanax or whatever. I was like, "What am I going to do? I can't go into withdrawal." I was so fearful of that. I remember kind of looking at myself – people talk about that – going, "Goddamn, this is really happening? This is your life now?" It was this weird third-person kind of perspective that didn't seem real. But then it was like, "Oh, well!" and I didn't draw another sober breath for years.

We were able to do *Kentucky Breakdown* and go on those tours, but Blaine didn't want to be around me because I just wasn't myself. I was slurring around and being unpredictable. I wasn't beating people up or doing anything like that. I just wasn't reliable. I would be fucking blasted, and you couldn't really talk to me.

The whole thing reached its crescendo when Nine Pound Hammer was supposed to do this Vegas thing, and I got a DUI. It should have been my fourth in five years – I should have done a year in the county jail. I got off on a technicality for a previous one, so it was only three DUIs. So, we had to cancel the show. It got ugly, and Blaine was pissed. I don't blame him. Again, this disease breeds fierce resentment and misunderstanding.

What flipped it for me was hallucinating for 10 days in jail, having a near-death experience and a moment of clarity – swimming in your own shit in a turtle suit will do that. I don't know how to describe it, but something moved in my mind. I'm still fundamentally the same, but my perception and reaction to things is – I just see things differently now.

It's true that other people were in my mind letting me down. Not meeting my expectations and some definite justifiable anger. But it didn't warrant my response. The other guys in the band pulled their fair share of bullshit, for sure, and had their own issues. I reckon I was the head of the snake, so to speak.

When I went to jail, I was big. I weighed 305 lbs. I lost 60 of it in two months in jail eating oranges to survive. I missed my daughter's first birthday.

I barely survived those two months. I got a staph infection, on top of hallucinating and going through a near fatal detox. Then I went away to Morehead Inspiration Center (MIC) for nine months. The only reason I ended up there was because the former director of The Hope

Center was a lawyer. He helped me out.

They broke me down at MIC and built me back up. It was the hardest thing I've ever done, but it built my foundation. While I was at the MIC, I became a peer mentor, and when I got out, I went to work at The Ridge. Now I'm a certified alcohol and drug counselor. It's kind of natural, man, kind of like the band, just real natural. It's not even work.

CHAPTER 31
WHEN I STOP DRINKING

While Scott was away and Nine Pound Hammer was on pause, Blaine, Earl, bassist Todd Gorrell, and Rob Hulsman formed the Kentucky Bridgeburners and recorded the gospel record Hail Jesus. *The tour went to hell in a handbasket.*

Blaine: It was the worst tour in history. I barely could afford to bring my luggage back.

But just like Leatherface in The Texas Chainsaw Massacre 2, *Nine Pound Hammer refused to die.*

Scott: When I got home, Blaine and I didn't talk for almost two years. I think I was the one who reached out. Again, it felt like we still had unfinished business. So we hashed some shit out and decided to play a show at Lynagh's. So, Rob's back in the band, and we started talking about doing another record.

Blaine: It took a year and a half after that to start recording. It was just hard. Scott had a hard time acclimating to the rock and roll stuff and being sober. I get it – it had to be hard telling his wife, "Hey, I want to get back and play with those guys again," or, "I'm going to the studio," where we were probably smoking weed and drinking while we were working. Or, "Hey, we're going to go play at a bar." We weren't good news, but he became a different person. He was 10,000 times better than before, and he just grew into it.

Scott really bounced back in the studio, too. He was fucking great.

Scott: *Bluegrass Conspiracy* is such a big contrast from *Sex, Drugs & Bill Monroe* vocally. That's probably, maybe, my high watermark.

When Blaine and I got together and carved out that record, we were really collaborating well and were on a new level in a way – friendship-wise and bandmate-wise. We're working together, co-writing a lot of stuff together.

Blaine: That was really cool. We both had songs, and we got Rob Hulsman back on drums and Mark Hendricks was playing bass and Earl was on guitar – that's when we really started having two guitars.[32] That's also when Brian Pulito moved into the good studio.

Mark Hendricks: They started recording that without me. Brian called me and said Earl had done basic tracks, but he's like, "There's a handful of songs on this record that I really think you need to play bass on." So, I went to the studio, and they were very welcoming. Scott said that I rescued a couple of songs that they didn't think they were even going to use. That album wound up sounding cool. Scott came back a new man. It was great. We've never gotten along better, and we've never had any of the problems we used to.

Earl Crim: I think *Bluegrass Conspiracy* is when we started to really become the band that we are now. It's more musical, and we were a little older and a little less angry. We started thinking about songwriting and technical things.

Blaine: That album is like Brian's studio come to life. That's when he figured it out. Brian made it happen, but once again, no luck getting any labels fucking interested in it whatsoever. Acetate offered $0 again. It's like you can't scrounge together $2,500 just to placate us?

I thought for sure, some independent German label would just take it and press a few thousand copies, but I don't know what happened. I made phone calls and sent emails, and I got easily discouraged to say the least.

---

[32] Todd Gorrell plays bass on six tracks of *Bluegrass Conspiracy*.

We weren't touring, so there was that, too, but still it was like, "Here's a legendary band that had gone on hiatus and was back."

The atmosphere was not right for us. We did a GoFundMe and ended up raising $13,000, and it did sell a few thousand copies, but we didn't get one review anywhere. That was one thing Nine Pound Hammer always had back in the day – press kits as thick as a phone book. I thought this would be our last record.

CHAPTER 32
BLUEGRASS CONSPIRACY
(2017)

There's Cocaine Bear *the movie, and then there's the true story behind Cocaine Bear, which was taken from the book* The Bluegrass Conspiracy *by Sally Denton. It's the story of Andrew Carter Thornton II, a preppie drug smuggler from Lexington, Kentucky. After one too many trips to Columbia, with the feds on his tail, Thornton and his partner dumped their cocaine shipment and jumped from Thornton's 404 Cessna. Thornton's dead body was found in a driveway in Knoxville, Tennessee, with 90 pounds of cocaine strapped to it.*

Unluckily, a black bear in the northern Georgia woods found some of the dumped cocaine, ate a healthy portion of it, had a heart attack and died.

The doctor who performed the autopsy had the bear stuffed. Over the years the bear has been owned by several people, including Waylon Jennings – who gifted it to a friend named Ron Thompson. When Ron died, his estate auctioned the bear off.

If you ever find yourself in Lexington, go visit Cocaine Bear at the Kentucky for Kentucky Fun Mall.

Blaine: I didn't know anything about that book, but I knew it was a big deal. I always thought it was a cool name.

Scott: We were paying homage to the book, but also the conspiracy of us getting together again and me coming back.

SIXTY DAYS IN THE HOLE

Scott: Basically I was locked down 23 hours a day. They were taking my blood pressure through the little slit they put the food through. I'd been to jail many times, but not like that.

> "I'm gonna give you 60 days in the hole,
> To burn the fat off your wretched soul."

That was never said, but it was implied, and it sure helped. I almost didn't make it. Few people quit while they still have time.

Blaine: Goddamn, that song is so fucking good. I thought, "Well, this kicks off the fucking record, that's for goddamn sure."

Scott started writing about his experience. It was cool he could do that. It took him a little bit to get back in the studio, but when he came in eventually, he knocked out a bunch of songs in a short period of time, and he had a good scream. He had his voice back on this one.

When he came back, he really came back.

PUT SOME GRAVY ON IT

Scott: It took 30 years to get that one. I started writing it as a country song and then, of course, here comes Blaine. He says, "I've got 'Put Some Gravy On It.'" That's just what he does. I dunno if he recognizes it or not, but that's what happens. It all worked out.

The origins of the phrase "Put some gravy on it" is a hot topic, as hot as, well, gravy.

Blaine: We talked about that title forever. David Epperson used to do all kinds of pranks. One time we were at a bowling alley, and our friend's girlfriend was there. David put his head on her butt and started yelling, "Put some gravy on it! Put some gravy on it!" He was fucking funny.

Scott: So, mid-eighties, we weren't very nice. I was at a bachelor party in Louisville, and a stripper came over to us, and everybody's yelling and being crazy. One of my buddies screams, "Put some gravy on it!" So that stuck, and it became just a little nonsensical phrase. It means everything from "put some gravy on food" to "let's wrap it up, let's get it done."

Blaine: I had the song, and then I wrote the words, "I want it, I want it, I want it. I'm going to put some gravy on it." I just put that in there as a placeholder. That was not meant to be the song.

So, I recorded that, sent it to Scott, and he was like, "Oh, those are the lyrics?"

"You want some, you can't have none."

I kinda stole that from a Mr. Show skit. They had a commercial that goes, "Brought to you by Glauman's Custard," and the camera focused on this old lady, and there was a caption that said, "None for you, dear." I took that from there for sure.

Scott: I saw Clutch a few years ago at The Palace in Louisville, and I swear when the lead singer left the stage, he said, "Put some gravy on it." I swear. I wouldn't doubt if they were fans or knew of us.

COUNTY MATTRESS
Scott: That's about two things – a woman who's a "county mattress" and also sleeping on a county mattress in jail. It's really just the inner switching of alcohol and drugs for a woman. The tune is a bit of a rip-off of "The Corn Dog Song."

Blaine: I think Scott and Rob argued about how to play the drums on it forever. Scott was right, and that's the first song Mark Hendricks sang backup on.

FREE AT LAST
Blaine: I wrote the sad part when I was happy and the happy part when I was sad. There's one great line in there that I fucking made up: "Watching my greener grass quickly turn to hay." I was really happy with that.

DEEP IN THE GROUND
Scott: That's our Tom Petty song. It just has the feel. It's not the

Ramones. Blaine had the lick, and I liked it. I just expounded on his phrase. It's a real dark horse.

Blaine: For a while, it was me, Rob, Earl, and Todd Gorrell on bass in the studio. They asked me if I had any other songs. I'd had this song for years. I didn't think it was very good, so we started playing it. We got halfway through it twice, and I go, "This song sucks. It's terrible."

They said, "No, no, it's good."

When we start getting into my throwaways, it's like, "No, let's just write something else." So, I did a scratch vocal with those lyrics, and then Scott came in and just nailed it.

DEATH EATIN' A CRACKER
Blaine: Oh goddamn, that's another *Texas Chainsaw Massacre 2* reference, and I think Scott said his grandmother actually said that.

Scott: My meemaw would say that if her hair was messed up.

Blaine: It's been explained to me, but I still don't understand why you would say, "I feel like death eatin' a cracker."

Scott: That's my metal tune. I had that riff a long time ago. I was just hanging onto it. Then when I was working at The Ridge, three patients were planning this big road trip to Michigan to go get a bunch of Oxycontin. I'm just sitting there going, "Kiss the face of my maker soon."

That's what it's about, a suicide trip – not to see Jack Kevorkian, but to go doctor shopping, or to take the "Pain Train" down to Florida, same deal.

TWO DRUNKS DOWN
Scott: That's all Blaine. I think that's the best song he's ever written, and it's a song that adds another dimension to Hammer. It's like our most nuanced, sophisticated song in my mind. I don't know where he got that one.

Blaine: There was a Dolly Parton song called "Two Doors Down." I tried to write a Nashville Pussy song called "Two Drunks Down" in the style of AC/DC forever.

That song is about people being gossipy. I remember a story from when I was a kid going to Pizza Hut. My friend's mother was a teacher, and she was fucking gossipy. She was talking about some teenager who had gotten pregnant. The teacher got up from the booth, and the teenager was sitting behind her.

That always made me look around when I bad-mouthed somebody. I still look around, because you don't know who's going to walk up.

"Don't they know that assholes have feelings too?
It makes me wonder what I ever did to them."

That's what people say when they're drunk and they're getting bad-mouthed. It's like, "Well, what did I ever do to you?" Instead of, "Hey, wow! Why have I gotten so fucked up that people are talking about me? Other people I can understand, but why the fuck is that person talking about me? I didn't do anything to them specifically."

WHEN I STOP DRINKING
"When I stop drinking, they'll have a big parade,
and give me the key to my hometown.
They'll put me on their shoulders,
and carry me around.
That'll be me.
You'll all see.
When I stop drinking
And everyone will wonder what I'm thinking."

Blaine: That's based on a Dwight Yoakam song, "Since I Started Drinking Again," except it's the opposite. The thing is, in the song, "he's" not stopped yet, but they're going to carry him around on their shoulders. I also ripped some of that off from, "I'm Just An Old Chunk Of Coal (But I'm Going To Be A Diamond Some Day)." I don't think we've ever played that live – I don't know why.

MOON UPSTAIRS

Blaine: We always wanted to cover that song. That is The Dictators' version of a Mott the Hoople song. Scott insisted on us doing that one. Everyone else had it down. I was the one that had to be taught how to do it again and again. We jammed on that song for a whole night, just learning it and having fun. I was happy we did that one. We made sure The Dictators heard it. They were impressed.

Scott started screaming on this record, and he sounds fucking great. He's got a few where I'm like, "Whoa!" He's got more lung power than I do.

Earl kicked ass on the solo. We played it live some, and I think I fucked it up to where we stopped doing it and once Rob was gone, we didn't play anymore.

Scott: Great song, great lyrics. I had been banging that around at practice for 10 years. Rob killed it on that. And yes, I outscream Blaine!

ALMOST AIN'T BUTTERED TOAST

Scott: Blaine silliness. Classic.

Blaine: A long time ago someone would say, "Almost." And I would say, "Almost ain't buttered toast," just because I'm a weird guy, and I say weird shit.

We were on tour with Nashville Pussy, and I came up with that riding in the van because Nine Pound Hammer needed another fucking song, and I was getting frustrated. So, I was like, "That's it! I'm writing the dumbest fucking song I can think of."

> "Betsy Ross, George Jefferson and good old Abraham Lincoln,
> All got together behind the barn and started drinking.
> Abe pulled out a knife and said, 'This will come in handy.
> Let's go to every house in town and steal some candy.'"

Blaine: Yeah and the last verse has Colonel Sanders in it.

"The old king of Kentucky, Colonel Harland Sanders,
Found a pile of dead birds and fired them up in flour.
Mashed a bunch of taters 'til he made, he made a killing,
Bought a fancy house with a fridge full of pudding."

*This is one of my favorite Nine Pound Hammer songs because it
comes out of nowhere. It has also single-handedly redefined how I
look at people and judge them because it's all based on what I like to
call "Blaine Cartwright's Pudding Theory."*

Blaine: There's a reason for the pudding.

I used to babysit. If you babysat at a rich family's house, they would
say, "Help yourself to some food." You'd open up the fridge, and
they'd always have pudding. Poor people didn't have pudding. They
might have Fritos or something like that.

My mom's parents had a house in the suburbs. They always had
pudding. It was just lying around.

My grandmother, my dad's mom, very poor, they just had beer and
RC Cola.

That always goes through my head in a really nice house when I see
somebody's fridge. I always, always think, "I bet they've got
pudding in there."

Some people take pudding for granted.

MOUTH OF THE SOUTH

Scott: I got a little payback on Blaine with that one. That's my ode
to him – porno mags and chicken bones. I read the lyrics to the band
and asked, "Should I do this?" They said, "Do it, do it. He's written
so much stuff about you and other people." Anyway, I wasn't being
mean-spirited.

Blaine: Yeah, he's describing me. I was like, "Dude? I'm like riding
around with chicken and porno mags, and I don't know where I'm
bound?" I was like, "Dude, I'm on a fucking tight schedule. My
schedule is on the internet."

I think I also had a shirt that said "Mouth of the South." It's a cool song, and the way it sounds is great.

After the recording of Bluegrass Conspiracy, *touring and shows were limited. Scott was still adjusting to sobriety and being in a band. But finally, the band headed back to the "rock and roll promised land."*

Blaine: For Scott to go to Europe around that time was hard. I was over there with Nashville Pussy, and people started asking, "Where's Hammer? Where's Hammer? Where's Hammer?" So I said, "Hey Scott, man, we've got to do this." He's like, "Man, I got a good job – we have health insurance. I can't be touring." I said, "You've got to figure out some way because we made this connection with these people."

I understood it, but the proper Hammer lineup hadn't been to Europe in 10 years. We had this amazing record *Bluegrass Conspiracy*, and we were just doing a Christmas show in Lexington every year.

So, I convinced him, and we did seven shows – two festivals and five clubs – they were packed. It went fucking great.

Scott: We played Sjock Festival. Went back to Norway, played The Vera and it was great, just smooth. Everybody was getting along. Everybody was mature, and financially, everybody had money. It was all gravy, solid as hell. No drama.

Rob Hulsman: When we were recording *Bluegrass Conspiracy*, that's when Scott got involved again. A lot of those songs were recorded before he did. Actually, that was a kind of point of contention. He sang like Christian lyrics over top of something I didn't know was going to be on there.

Anyway, Scott was back. We did the record and did a tour, and he said a few things on stage that were uncomfortable to the point where Blaine convinced me not to talk to him while we were on tour.

Scott: I haven't got a clue what any of that is about. We all got along great.

CHAPTER 33
WHEN THE SHIT GOES DOWN
(2021)

After Bluegrass Conspiracy, *touring and shows became a little more regular, but after a few years, it was time for more new music and a dash of Covid.*

Blaine: When we went to Europe in 2018, Scott was like, "Well, we can do this one more time and maybe that'll be it," but we've gone back five or six times since then. Somehow he got the bug. I think he just realized that playing music is probably the most fun thing you can do.

We started talking about doing another album, and we said, "What should we write about? What do we really have to say anymore?" We were seriously thinking, "What's the point? We've written all the tater songs you can write and all the chicken songs – we've already done *all* that."

I had read an *InFlight* magazine about fentanyl – I didn't even know what that was – this was maybe seven or eight years ago. The article was about three people dying in the same month that worked at the same restaurant. That's fucked up. That doesn't happen anywhere. Scott was like, "Yeah, that's opioids," so we started talking about fentanyl and how he was dealing with the drug opioid crisis in Lexington. We'd go back and forth and just have these conversations about what Kentucky was like and how it was getting bad. When I would go back to jam and hang out with anyone in Lexington, there'd be a new fucking funeral. "Remember so-and-so?" He's dead." It was young people, too.

234

When I'd visit Lexington, I didn't expect to see that many homeless people walking around. It was like a ghetto with grass, and it wasn't like that a few years before. I was also driving around a lot of two-lane roads, and then I saw all these little towns that had gone to shit. I had no idea all this shit had gotten that bad.

Finally Scott and I said, "Why don't we write about the stuff we're talking about?" It usually ends up like that, so we decided to make *When The Shit Goes Down*. I originally wanted to call it *Hee-Haw & Fentanyl*.

Scott: We had this window, so Blaine and I said, "Let's do it. We've got to keep moving. There are no guarantees. Who knows what's going to happen?"

Blaine: When I headed up there in 2020 to do pre-production, Trump was on the TV shutting things down. I was going to turn around because if I went up there, I thought I was going to get stuck. Rob had already rented a hotel room, and he wanted to go. So, we started rehearsing, and two days later the whole country was shut down except for Tennessee, which was great – Cracker Barrel was open.

Scott: Rob started being super paranoid about Covid. We were like, "Hey man, do you mind if we go ahead and record? You'll still be the drummer when you're ready and willing, but we'll just have Brian Pulito play drums on it." He was like, "Yeah, man, sure." He didn't mean it. He was mad and bitter and cut us off.

Blaine: He was being irrational about Covid. I mean he was even refusing to text me. It was bad.

Rob Hulsman: Without putting too fine a point on it, it was a good time to break away from those guys. Scott is kind of the de facto leader, and I just wasn't comfortable with some of the stuff he was saying.

Blaine: We still thought we were going to do this record in Brian Pulito's basement. Then Nashville Pussy's old tour manager Dez said, "You guys should get some unemployment." We're like, "What are you talking about? We're in America. We don't get that." So she applied for us, and all of a sudden we got back pay, too. We had $11,000 in the bank, and I was like, "We should hire a producer."

Scott: Years ago I had been listening to Joey Ramone's solo record and suggested to Blaine that Nashville Pussy use Daniel Rey. So, I said to Blaine, "What about Daniel Rey?" He was like the fifth Ramone. It was a dream to get him with us!

Blaine: I called Daniel, and he was in Germany. He's a liberal dude, but he just didn't like the restrictions. He said, "When I'm in New York City, they make me wear a mask when I walk down the street. I'm in Germany where I can smoke a cigarette in the bar and live."

I negotiated with him, and he agreed.

Earl Crim: That was kind of a dream for me because I'm a huge Ramones fan. That was kind of like a bucket list for me.

Blaine: The good things about Covid – the studio wasn't booked, AirBnBs were cheap and so were plane tickets. I think round-trip for Daniel from New York to Lexington was like $150. So, I lined up everything for November, which is when everything in Kentucky started shutting back down. It worked out though because certain businesses didn't have to shut down, and the studio was one of them. Everybody was still cool to do the record.

Right before we recorded, Daniel says, "Okay, we've got to have a talk about this Covid thing. It's only us in the studio. No parties." And he looked right at me. "No going to bars. No girls. No nothing. Just us." We kept it tight-knit and started recording.

I'd always wanted to do a record with Nine Pound Hammer this way. Nashville Pussy gets three weeks to record, and it's great. I wanted to do something concentrated like that.

Ruyter: It was beautiful to have those guys in there for a finite amount of time. You can't dick around. You've got from this day to that day to complete all this really important shit. You've got this master who's going to tweak the shit and get the best performance out of you.

Daniel got an excellent performance out of Scott, and I think he taught Scott a better approach to singing. Just to have Daniel in there makes it more official.

Blaine: My stuff was done fast, so I was basically going to get food every day for everybody. I'd go get pizza or Cajun food, and if something needed to be done before people got off work and came in to record, I'd do that, too.

They worked a long time on the vocals. That's one of the reasons we got Daniel.

I remember Daniel saying, "He's doing a good job. By the time we make him do everything over again, it'll be great."

It went really, really, really smoothly. Daniel was really good about encouraging us to do one more vocal take or to make something we played better. Everyone loved the experience. It was amazing, the whole thing.

I'm really proud of this record. I just wish it got out there better because I've run across people that still haven't heard it.

Hey you! Yes, you! The person reading these words. Go buy a copy or at least crank it up on Spotify.

WHAT KIND OF GOD
Blaine: Scott wrote the lyrics to that. It's from the point of view of this dude who'd just rather be numb – eternally numb – where oblivion seems like a good option.

Scott: I work at the needle exchange now. I'm down there twice a week. There was this guy who played drums in a local band. He was talking about sleeping out in the park in the rain on a couch and the drama that goes along with living that life. Just fucking tragic, but to him it's normal. So, I wrote a song about that and threw in some *True Detective* shit.

<u>**WHEN THE SHIT GOES DOWN**</u>
"Uncle's got a barn full of AR-15s,
Gives them all names, keeps 'em real clean
He's crazy as hell, doesn't like'm comin' 'round
Head to his house when the shit goes down"

Blaine: I wrote that because that's what was going on. I thought it was very of the moment.

Scott: I helped tweak that. It's hilarious. It's kind of "Feelin' Kinda Froggy 2.0" in a way. It sounds similar.

We've got a buddy, Brad Scott, that's really about him. He's got a bunch of Ars, and all he does is work on them. He's ex-military. Wouldn't hurt a fly. Good dude.

Brad Scott: I didn't know he was talking about me when he wrote those lyrics. There was a time when I sent him an email with a picture of my AR-15s, and the title of it was, "Gives them all names. Keeps them real clean." So, maybe after that happened, he associated that line about me.

Just for the record, none of my guns have names, but I do keep 'em real clean.

Blaine: We know Ted Nugent. He likes our band, and we got our name, Nashville Pussy, from one of his songs.

Everyone bitches about his politics, but when shit goes down, I'm going to his house.

People ask me, "If something happens, what are you going to do?" My answer: I'll be on a hill, watching. I'm not joining any fucking cause – that's for sure.

One time we were in Cincinnati, and Lemmy[33] was talking about history and fighting until you die. I said, "Fuck that!" He said,

---

[33] Yeah, we all know which "Lemmy" he's referencing.

"Yeah, I'll fucking fight until I get knocked down."

Ruyter: Lemmy also said, "Don't vote. It only encourages them." Politicians are the only people who will just lie straight to your face. They're the worst fucking people possible.

Blaine: When I was writing this song, there was a riot down the street here in Atlanta. The city was getting trashed, and there was a moment where shit was on fire.

They mostly attacked the AT&T store, Target, CNN and Starbucks. I was like, "That's kind of cool." People were saying, "No, it's a protest." I thought it sounded fun. I always thought my generation missed out. It's like, "We had a protest? What'd you do?"

"Oh, we got up there and sang a song."

"Wait, you didn't break anything?"

"No."

Nine Pound Hammer was actually in a soccer riot in Barcelona. I've been in a soccer riot twice. They both were a blast. The cops were like, "Let's just let everyone do what they're doing and hope it's not too bad."

Man, we're spoiled. I think people would just surrender if someone hid their cell phone. I know the city folk would.

Ruyter: You don't even have to do that, just cut off their fucking WiFi.

Blaine: Well, if the shit ever does go down, I'm hauling my ass back to Western Kentucky. You'll find me on Kentucky Lake saying, "Fucking city folk."

A GIRL LIKE THAT
Scott: That's Blaine's Beach Boys tribute, total Ramones rip-off.

Blaine: For some reason when I was writing this, I was watching musicals. I guess because I saw Larry David on *Curb Your Enthusiasm*. He was always watching Broadway stuff.

My buddy David Cross is married to Amber Tamblyn. So, his father-in-law is Russ Tamblyn who's in *West Side Story*. I watched it and thought, "I'm going to steal something from this." Then Rita Moreno and Natalie Wood are in different places, and they're both singing about the same boy or some shit – "A Boy Like That."

That's so smart. That's clever as shit. I go, "I wonder if there's a song called 'A Girl Like That,'" because that seems really obvious. I looked it up online. There wasn't one.

I had the hardest fucking time writing those lyrics. I knew it had to be simple like a Ramones song. I thought, "Who are the Ramones like? The Beach Boys." So, I wrote a goddamn punk rock Beach Boys song.

The Beach Boys, the thing about them, they were singing about shit that they wish they could do. It was more of a fantasy, kind of idyllic thing. I was trying to think what kind of chick Scott would like because he's got to sing it. So,

> "I met her at Old Hickory BBQ.
> Eating a pulled pork plate,
> Sauce all over her face."

And

> "Cruising at the Southland Drive-In show
> She was sitting on her hood,
> And singing Status Quo.[34]"

After that, it was simple.

DRUNKS, BABIES AND FOOLS

Scott: That's an old saying from recovery: "God loves drunks,

---

[34] Status Quo is a legendary British rock band who made it big all over the world except America. They have released 33 albums.

babies and fools." That riff is something Earl had from back in the day.

Blaine: Earl carries these songs around forever, and Scott finally made this one into a song. Scott wrote a lot on this record. I was kind of glad. I kind of enjoy listening to some of these songs because I'm not as familiar with them. It was nice not to be carrying these fucking songs in my head for two years and then finally getting them out and being overly critical about this or that.

I do love the way my guitar sounds on this one. It has a really thick Ramones guitar tone that I got from the amp I use on stage with Nine Pound Hammer. It was so good that when I walked into the studio one day, Daniel Rey gave me a high five. I rarely high-fived anyone, but it was like the greatest tone in the fucking world.

Blaine: When the guy who was the fifth Ramone, from the band where guitar tone changed everything, yields to me when setting up an amp – that was cool.

STREET CHICKEN
Scott: Fucking hilarious! Just another silly chicken song. Mark brought that in.

Mark Hendricks: I wrote that song with Blaine in mind. Whenever we're on tour and we come into a town, he's always been there before. Son of a bitch has been everywhere and has friends everywhere. We'll get out of the van, and he'll just start walking like he knows where he's going – but really he doesn't. He's really just looking for some kind of weird place to eat.

We'll go into the venue, check it out, load in and be hanging out in the green room or whatever. He'll come in with some takeout that he's found and go, "Man, two blocks down there's this killer Indian place." He's always looking for chicken to eat – chicken on a stick or fucking fried chicken or spaghetti. He loves spaghetti and fried chicken.

He loves going to Amsterdam, and where he stays is in a section of town that's kind of away from the touristy part, but it's still on the canals. There are a bunch of Italian restaurants there where you can get cheap spaghetti. He'll just stay there a week, smoke pot and eat spaghetti.

Want to know a few more things about Blaine's eating and listening habits?

Jean Luc Jousse: He doesn't care about the catering stuff or the hospitality rider at shows. If we were at a festival, he'd go out and eat at a food truck or a booth. It was also surprising a couple times that I found Blaine in the van listening to disco music. I don't know if he likes disco or not, but you could hear it outside the van, and he wasn't turning it off.

2 LEGGED DOPE
Scott: That's about my brother who would just substitute women or men for a drug – it's the same behavior. It's also about folks – not only in recovery – but people that prioritize something over their family and their own kids to get that "feel good" from a person, place or thing.

We brought in our first piano player on that one. We're highfalutin. I was trying for a Stones jam.

MAMA LIED
Blaine: I remember looking on the internet to see if there was a song called "Mama Lied." Turns out, there wasn't. I started thinking, "Well, what'd she lie about? Hard work will get you ahead?" Sometimes hard work puts people in their grave. I don't know if the answer is to work harder, especially if it's a shitty job.

So me and Scott started going back and forth about that. I tossed in,

> "Mama said, gonna ruin your eyes sitting so close to the TV."
> "Mama said, most important thing is to get married and settle down."

Scott: Blaine wanted to play that as a rocker, and I'm like, "No, man, that's country. Let's slow that down." My mom and dad divorced when I was a kid, so I threw in some lines like,

"Come meet your new daddy.
This one might just stick around."

Blaine: That's a great line.

Ruyter: That's fucking great.

Blaine: Daniel Rey's singing background on this one. He's so good. I think he might've ripped that idea off from an old country song.

BILLY LOST HIS FEET

Mark Hendricks: I'm kind of a songwriter, too, but I'm not nearly as prolific as Scott and Blaine. I can come up with riffs and put a song together musically, but when it comes to subject matter and words, I struggle. But I was inspired by a dude that I met on my very first outing with Nine Pound Hammer, Billy Bell. He lost both his legs in a car wreck – he has no legs from the knees down.

Ruyter: I think he crashed into a train drunk out of his mind. He passed out and woke up with his pickup truck on fire, and he had third-degree burns all over his body and his feet were just scorched.

Blaine: Billy was crazy. He lived in Atlanta and was a huge Nine Pound Hammer fan. When I met him, he worked for CNN. He would get free Atlanta Hawks tickets and a parking spot right by the door of the CNN Center. I remember one time at a Hawks game, he was like, "Let's go out to the car and smoke a joint." I said, "They're not going to let us back in." He said, "Watch." So he goes up to the woman taking tickets at the door and says, "Ma'am, I gotta go adjust my legs. I'll come right back." She turns to him and says, "Go ahead, baby." So, we go out back and smoke a joint, and he turns to me and says, "Hey man, I'll sneak some cocaine back in, in my leg." The cocaine went really well with the basketball game.

Mark Hendricks: My first experience with Billy was wild because he was driving us through the Blue Ridge Mountains in North Carolina at like 90 miles an hour playing some punk rock shit on the stereo – just air guitaring and beating the shit out of the wheel. I was just sitting in the backseat going, "What the fuck?"

We stopped at a rest stop, and he just took off running up this hill in cutoff shorts and tennis shoes with his titanium prosthetic legs. I think he was trying to show us that he was not impaired, but he was higher than a fucking kite.

For a while, I ended up rooming with him in hotels on the road. We'd get ready to go to bed, and I'd look over and there were his prosthetic legs with shoes on them and his shorts down around the ankles – just in case he needed to jump up and hop into those things. Sometimes in the middle of the night, he'd go to the bathroom and would just be crawling around the room like a spider.

He's an absolute character, just a trip, man. After the tour he drove us on was over with, I just kept thinking about that dude and this song came to me pretty quick. I shelved it for a long, long time because I played it for Blaine and Scott, and they were like, "Dude, we can't do that! He's a friend, and we don't want to offend him."

When we did eventually get around to doing that song, Blaine and Scott were like, "We can't tell him. You gotta do it." I sent him the song and wrote him a long email about where it came from. He came back with, "I played that song for my dad. My dad said, 'It's going to be a hit.'" He wasn't offended at all.

ONE LAST MIDNIGHT
Scott: I wrote that in the break room at The Ridge on a guitar that was lying around. That was about *True Detective* – that whole "life is a dream, time is a flat circle" thing. That show rocked my world and changed my perception of things. It really did. I was early in recovery, and that show fucking jolted me out of my kind of pink cloud that I was on. It was like, "This is reality, motherfucker."

The landscape of that show in Louisiana. That was kind of the star of the show and just the bleakness of it. I remember one scene that shows all these young girls hanging out smoking cigarettes. They were so vulnerable, and there's a fucking killer out there running around?!?

It was just fucking nuts, and that's some of the best dialogue ever on screen. Matthew McConaughey had a lot to do with that, those monologues. I don't know what can top those and that show.

The Johnny Cash mariachi horns on this song – I put them there for better or for worse.

GET THE HELL OFF THE FARM

Blaine: Originally that was about my grandfather. He was the one that got off the farm and got a job at Dr. Pepper. I'm glad he got the hell off the farm. One of my cousins who stayed on the farm got shot and killed by his stepfather in a trailer arguing over nothing.

Scott: It's about our friend Randy Ratliff. He lived on a farm in Utica, Kentucky.

Randy Ratliff: My dad was a workaholic. That's how he dealt with life. By the time I was nine, I had my own tobacco crop. I didn't play sports, but I told my dad I wanted to play football, and he said, "You can't play football because practice is when we cut tobacco."

My dad would roll me out of bed at five o'clock in the morning to go do whatever needed doing depending on the season – planting, spraying crops, hoeing tobacco, picking weeds.

Blaine: He had to be on the farm all the time. It wasn't like working at Sizzler. It wasn't a job – it was a way of life. Occasionally during the summer he'd have one night where he'd come into town. He had tons of friends and went to parties, but he missed out on a lot of stuff.

Randy Ratliff: Sometimes I'd run around until two or three in the morning with friends and get up at five – still drunk – get on a tractor and go. Blaine and Scott would come out and sometimes help me. I paid them a couple of times to help cut tobacco.

POSSUM KICKIN' FRIED SQUIRREL EATING SON OF A BITCH

Scott: Now that's a true story. My roommate in rehab at Morehead was this dude from North Carolina, big ol' dude named Jade. Loud as hell, country witticisms coming out of his mouth left and right.

He told us a story about partying one night in North Carolina. He said there were all these big trucks, and they had cornered this poor possum. They had spotlights on it and were messing with it, poking on it, just being mean to it. My roommate felt bad for the possum, so he came up and kicked it off into the woods to help save it. So, his nickname was Possum Kicker.

Blaine: There was one point where I was writing songs – I think it was a GoFundMe for the Kentucky Bridgeburners record – and I wrote a song for this guy named Ron for $250 – it was called "Fried Squirrel Eating Son of a Bitch." Scott added the possum-kicking part.

DAVIESS COUNTY TRACTOR MASSACRE

Blaine: Once again, me and Scott were sitting there talking about this stupid party we went to in Owensboro where this guy, Rudy Yeagle, was showing off drunk. He was driving this tractor around, and he started smashing these cars.

We both looked at each other like, "Oh, there's a song." It was a graduation party maybe a year or two after we were out of school.

Scott: Earl had played the riff during pre-production, and I really liked it. I marinated on it. Then I could hear the words of tractor party starting to fit in. We tweaked it some to fit, and I wrote the words.

That party was legendary, surreal. You had to be there! It was me, Randy Ratliff, Steve Terrell and some other friends. We had a case of Heinekens and other shit in the trunk. I had just caught this girl stealing some of our beer when Rudy rolled by on a tractor and just started climbing on top of those cars, just smashing and flattening them.

Randy Ratliff: I kind of remember saying, "Oh, here's the farmer coming to break up the party." As this tractor is coming over the hill, it hits a car on the right side, then he overcorrects and runs between two other cars. The left side tires go up on this bank, and the right tires go right up in the middle of a Chevrolet Camaro IROC-Z.

Then, bam, bam, bam, the tractor starts smashing cars like a monster truck. Then it got really quiet for a second, and then everybody went apeshit. I'm thinking, "Oh my God! Were there people in those cars making out?"

Scott: It was surreal. We took off and came back later. When we did, our friend Theresa was crying on my shoulder saying her dad was going to kill her. It was his Chrysler Cordoba!

Blaine: This is the song that got recognized by the Frazier Museum in Louisville.[35] That was a good day. We went to that presentation and when I got there, the first thing I saw were these people in these old-timey dresses and suits. They were acting like they were down on a steamboat or something. I'm going, "Where the fuck am I? I know it's a museum, but still. What the fuck have I gotten myself into?"

The dude who picked the songs was great. He had the greatest selection of music from across Kentucky. The Nappy Roots were there. He also had this band that was from Louisville that formed in prison in 1983.[36] A lot of people showed up. It was really cool and probably the best thing that's happened as far as acknowledgement and recognition for Hammer.

Scott: The Frazier Museum thing was sweet. Blaine and I also were on KET.

LIZARD BRAIN
Scott: I wanted something fast. Something like Dee Dee Ramone would write, like "Weasel Face" or "Wart Hog." I had this old Hammer song called "You'll Learn" that never made it on anything, so I pulled that out. Then I thought, "Lawrence Tarpey, the godfather of Lexington."

---

[35] Daviess County Massacre was recognized as part of the *120: Cool KY Counties* exhibit at the Frazier Museum. Communications and research specialist Simon Meiners chose a song from each Kentucky county to honor. The songs included everything from jazz to jug bands and Appalachian folk to yodeling.

[36] The band Risk was formed during its members' incarceration in the Kentucky State Penitentiary in Eddyville.

Blaine: Lawrence is the greatest. He wrote the lyrics and sang it.

Lawrence Tarpey: It was during Covid, and Scott asked me, "Hey, you want to sing a song on this record?" I said, "Yeah, I'll do it." Then I kind of forgot about it until he kind of mentioned it again in passing. He said, "Daniel Rey is in town. We got this time booked at the studio. We need you to come in and sing."

Well, I had some lyrics I'd written, but we'd never played the song. Scott calls me, "Hey are you coming in to do this?" So, I just went in there and did it on the fly, and what you hear on the record is me singing it for the first time. When I hear it now, I kind of kick myself in the ass. I think I should have sung it in half-time, but I sang it double-time.

I think it's the weakest song on the record personally. I think I dropped the ball on it. But anyway, that song is super fast, probably the fastest beats per minute of any song on that record. I think the chorus is good, and Daniel Rey was right there singing it with me.

Scott: Lawrence took it in a slightly different direction, but it worked out. I was going to go with the fact that everybody on Earth is lizard braining with the brainstem instead of the frontal lobe.

BEST OF ALL POSSIBLE WORLDS
Scott: This song came in on the radio in my car. I took a photo of it on my phone, sent it to Blaine and said, "We need to cover this." He was like, "Hell yeah!"

Blaine: That was one song we got to unleash Earl on.

Earl Crim: Daniel Rey did tell me, though, the biggest compliment I've ever gotten. He said my right hand was like Johnny Ramone's.

Blaine: Daniel, Scott and I had a little meeting about the solo and this one part we didn't like. Scott and I started kind of arguing about how we're going to tell Earl he needed to come back and fix some things. Daniel goes, "What? We just have him come back in. He's a guitar player. He loves to play guitar. What's the problem?" I think it's unfortunate that on vinyl the solo gets cut off a little bit because of time. Earl kicks ass. It's always cool to show him off because he's like a secret weapon.

When The Shit Goes Down came out in 2021 to very little fanfare. Covid was still around, so touring and promoting it was even more difficult. It's a shame. Front to back, it's a solid album, and it showed another level of growth from a band that had been around over 35 years at that point.

It should have been way bigger. It should have gotten more press. It's a damn fine record that feels like it deserves the equivalent of a Kate Bush "Running Up That Hill" moment in a few years.

Ruyter: It came out to a whisper.

Blaine: I thought the quality was so good. Me and Daniel Rey were sitting there listening to mixes, and he was like, "Great record. Real good." Talking about Scott, he goes, "Got a great country voice, but he's still a punk."

I sent it to my punk rock friends in California, and nothing happened. I thought because Acetate Records is out in L.A., they would get stuff out, but Rick is just one guy who has a full-time job.

The record industry is really weird, because there's always this reputation among the independent world that once you get to the corporate level, the big labels rip you off. It's like, well, they probably will, but also they're more likely to pay you something.

We used to have an economic incentive to make a record. Labels used to say, "Hey, we'll pay you for a record. We'll pay everybody a weekly wage or wages and get you a nice hotel." But when *When The Shit Goes Down* came out, whatever reviews we got were from *Brave Words* and Don Jamieson's heavy metal show. He didn't even know Nine Pound Hammer. This was the first thing he'd heard.

Anyway, it came out on Acetate Records, and Rick made a video of "Drunks, Babies and Fools." I thought that was the most commercial song we'd ever done. I thought for sure we'd make our money back one day, and that still hasn't happened.

CHAPTER 34
ROCK 'N' ROLL RADIO
(2023)

After some touring in the states and Europe, Cleopatra Records asked Nine Pound Hammer to record a covers album that would hopefully make some noise in a few movies.

Scott: Blaine knew somebody who knew one of the VPs or the owner of Cleopatra Records, and they wanted us and Nashville Pussy to do a cover record – the whole idea was to get on soundtracks, and it still hasn't. I don't know why.

Blaine: You don't have to pay Cheap Trick. You can use us.

Scott: We did that whole thing in Brian Pulito's basement, and he ended up playing drums on it. We did "Do You Remember Rock 'n' Roll Radio?" because it's the Ramones' tribute to music, and that's our tribute to their music.

Blaine: At first they wanted us to do a yacht rock song and some novelty covers. Then we're like, let's do a whole covers record. It sounded so good, and everybody in the band is so accomplished that instead of doing punk rock versions of songs, we did the songs pretty much like the original recordings.

I let Scott pick all the songs. I'm probably on that album less than anything we've done. We nailed it. We spent a lot of time on that record. We were in the studio for a year, I think.

DO YOU REMEMBER ROCK 'N' ROLL RADIO?

Blaine: I was kind of the punk, but that's where Scott and I met in the middle. He liked the Sex Pistols. So did I, and we both loved the Ramones. I like our version, but the original's got a sax on it that plays the main riff and the guitar is playing bar chords. On our version, the bass is playing the sax riff.

Scott: This was chosen because it covered a lot of bases. I knew it could be cool live, too. We played it at a village festival in Spain, where they filmed *The Good, the Bad and the Ugly*. Those people flipped out! Maybe the best moment ever on stage. For us to pay homage and get that response was special. Blaine and I were looking at each other with Cheshire grins. Surreal.

ARE YOU READY?

Scott: That's so hard to play. We wanted to do a Thin Lizzy song. All the other stuff is too complicated. That was the easiest song we could do.

Blaine: Scott picked all these songs because he had to sing them. I think Cleopatra Records thought, "They'll do punk rock versions of songs." But our band is so talented that it was either we're going to do a punk version or we're going to do it exactly like the original. And I think the reason most people do a punk version is they can't do it exactly like the original.

Ruyter: There's a sense of proving yourself, too, that Nashville Pussy and Nine Pound Hammer both do. We don't tend to stray from the original cover, because we want to prove that we can play it.

Blaine: I agree. I remember specifically Nashville Pussy did a cover of "Highway to Hell," and I think The Donnas did an interview reviewing it and they said, "Oh, we put our own spin on it." I love that band, but I'm like, the punk version of putting your own spin on it is just playing it like the Ramones.

Doing this record was cool. I got to learn how to play different songs, and the band had to teach me how to play some stuff. There are certain parts of "Are You Ready" that Earl had to overdub because I couldn't do it. That is such a great Thin Lizzy song.

HEADING OUT TO THE HIGHWAY

Scott: Judas Priest is a top five band for me. It's not even metal. It's just a great anthemic rock song. We had the legendary Ben Lacy play the solo, which we combined with Earl. It sounds great.

TAKE A LONG LINE

Scott: "Take a Long Line" is a very obscure song. It shouldn't be.

Blaine: That is by a band in Australia called The Angels, but in America they're called Angel City or The Angels from Angel City.

Scott: They're as big or bigger than AC/DC in Australia. Their record and our love of that band goes back a ways. We heard them at New Attitude Records in Owensboro.

Blaine: I think it was Earl who was like, "Man, what's that band from Australia you used to play all the time?" I was like, "What are you talking about?" Then finally it was like, "Oh yeah, them."

Scott: I think our version is better than theirs, honestly.

2000 MAN

Scott: That's the best song off KISS's *Dynasty*. We wanted to do a KISS song, but this song is actually a Rolling Stones song that Ace Frehley revved up. It's nothing like the Stones' version. Ace's version is amazing. Covering this was a little bucket list thing for me.

Blaine: I grew up with the KISS version. I was a Stones fanatic, but I always knew enough to stay away from *Their Satanic Majesties Request*. Back before music was free, it was like, "Don't go mow two yards just to buy that album. You'll be upset." I still really haven't really listened to *Their Satanic Majesties Request* because what I have heard, I didn't like.

Ace Frehley fucking nailed this song. His guitar tone on that was amazing. We couldn't replicate that. I ended up getting this monster cabinet from my cousin Adam. It was an empty cabinet for two 12-inch speakers, and I was like, "I want to get the heaviest possible speakers you can put in there." It's so heavy, it just sits in the studio.

GIMME SHELTER

Scott: So, you're going to do "Gimme Shelter"? Good luck. I heard this version 10 years ago by an English band called Thunder. They kind of did an AC/DC intro, so I'm like, "We can do that." I showed that version to the band, and they wanted to try it. I think it turned out great. We brought in Heather Parish. She killed it.

DID YOU NO WRONG

Blaine: That song should have been on *Nevermind The Bollocks*. I think that was a song the Sex Pistols had written for the next record.[37]

Scott: The Raunch Hands covered this, and we loved their version.

CALIFORNIA MAN

Scott: Although not a Cheap Trick original, it's a classic. Another bucket list song.

Blaine: Me and Scott saw Cheap Trick in high school. The Romantics opened up. We were sophomores, and he took a girl that we both liked, but she liked him.

It wasn't really a date, but he was kind of making it a date. There were other people there. We went to Evansville with a pile of people in the car.

We were dropping everyone off and Scott's about to drop her off, and she was going off about all these people who were sluts. She said, "Did you hear what happened to so-and-so? She let Jim Jackson finger fuck her." Scott's like "Later," and he drove off.

DOWN DOWN

Scott: Blaine is a huge Status Quo guy. He got me into them and thought we could rock this.

Blaine: We discovered Status Quo because of something we called

---

[37] "Did You No Wrong" by the Sex Pistols is the B-side to "God Save the Queen." It was not included on their debut album but was released as a separate single.

"The Pot Tape." One of Ruyter's old boyfriends made for her this tape full of all these obscure seventies rock bands. I knew who all of them were, except for one song.

Ruyter: If you don't know them, Spinal Tap is based on them. They started off as this kind of boy band in the late sixties. Then they became the pub rock boogie band. Basically AC/DC saw them when they were kids and were like, "We're going to be like this."

Blaine: They were the biggest band in England for a while. When they played some reunion shows in 2003, they played at Wembley Stadium in England, but in America, they played much smaller places like The House of Blues in Chicago.

COVER OF THE ROLLING STONE
Scott: I'm a YouTube guy – a little politics, some civil war, some spirituality. I'm in my little loop of music, and this song by Dr. Hook pops up. Those are the best lyrics. I forgot how fucking clever this song was. It already sounds like the Georgia Satellites doing Hammer.

Blaine: My father has been up my ass since 1988 for Nine Pound Hammer to record that song.

I was there a lot, and I jammed on all this stuff. I don't think I did any solos except for "2000 Man."

The whole thing took forever because people would listen to the original song and say, "You didn't do that one part." Or, "You missed that." I thought it'd be fun to be in a cover band. Then I'm like, I don't think I want to be in a cover band. That's the whole thing – we had to prove that we could do it, but it was easier to just write a song.

NOBODY WANTS TO PARTY WITH ME
Scott: That's by Natural Child. Cheap Trick made "California Man" their song. "Nobody Wants To Party With Me" is our "California

Man." It's hard to play, more complicated than you would think.[38]
Great live song for us now.

---

[38] "Nobody Wants To Party With Me" was released as a single and was not on *Rock 'n' Roll Radio.*

CHAPTER 35
THE BARS ALL CLOSED, BUT THE NIGHT'S NOT OVER YET

No killer was captured. Long-lost loves weren't reunited while reaching for the same corn dog at a drive-in on a hot, summer Kentucky night. But, the time has come to blast some Ramones on a jambox in the front seat of a 1975 Pontiac Grand Ville as we rip up a cornfield and drive into the sunset. We've reached the end of the line.

Ending a book when the story isn't over is an odd problem to have, but that's where we're at.

As I write this, the band is hard at work on another album, possibly two. By the time this comes out, they'll likely be on tour in Europe, again. Not to be too Dude-ian, but I take comfort in that. It's good knowin' they're out there. Playing music for all us sinners.

Speaking of which, when you interview a bunch of people about a band that's been around for 40 years, you hear all about their sins. You also hear all kinds of kind things.

Lawrence Tarpey: One of the biggest takeaways from Nine Pound Hammer was just how tenacious they are. That's never changed.

Mike Grimes: I don't know where the drive came from, but there are not that many people from Owensboro who had their drive. I think you can count them on two hands.

Toby Myrick: Being in Nine Pound Hammer was a great experience. I couldn't even begin to tell you. It got me out of the house. It got me into something. It allowed me to become a musician.

Darren Howard: I can't say enough good things about Scott and Blaine. I'm still playing in a band, and I owe it all to them. Blaine calling me on the phone all those years ago and asking me to play in Nine Pound Hammer kickstarted my musical journey.

Brian Pulito: For me, it was kind of a personal journey with Nine Pound Hammer. They helped me get through a rough part of my life. It gave me a chance to do things I would've never gotten to do. So, I have nothing but appreciation for them. They're all great friends, man. They're all my brothers.

Earl Crim: I joined the band in 2003, and from then, on it's gone through many changes. We're like brothers. We get along, and we don't – that's the way things are in a band. I mean I feel lucky. I was just an introverted kid who sat in his room and played guitar all day. I would have never traveled the world without them.

Mark Hendricks: When Scott asked me if I wanted to be in Nine Pound Hammer, I was like, "Holy shit." I'd heard their songs so much, I already knew how to play a lot of them. We had one rehearsal at my house, and it just clicked immediately.

I'll say this, we're lucky enough to still be doing this, and have people still want to hear us. It also feels like we haven't reached that ultimate plateau as a band. We just keep getting better as players, and the songs we come up with are always good. It's just still a lot of fun, man. So, I don't like looking in the rearview mirror as much as I like thinking about what the next few years are going to be. I'm excited to keep doing it, man.

Kevin Martinez (Friend of the Band, DJ for WRFL and Colonel Paco's Rocketship Roundup): I've gotten to be friends with a lot of musicians outside of Lexington who always talk to me about their appreciation of Kentucky and the music that comes from here, like Merle Travis and Bill Monroe. I wouldn't have listened to any of those artists if it wasn't for Nine Pound Hammer.

Those guys have definitely left their mark on Lexington. I'm pretty sure they're the longest lasting band in our scene.

Ruyter: They're the greatest band in the world that nobody knows about.

Rob Hulsman: I loved playing music with those guys, especially Blaine. He's a really, really, really good musician and songwriter, and he's just always fun to be on the road with. He's a smart guy, good conversationalist and knows a lot about music. Those are my favorite types of folks to hang around with.

Elwood Francis (ZZ Top Bassist, Blaine's Former Neighbor): Blaine is a vision guy. You wouldn't think of him as a visionary when you say it out loud, but he is – and Nine Pound Hammer is still pretty fucking cool.

Lawrence Tarpey: One of the things that stands out about Blaine, when I first saw him play guitar, he was like a man possessed. His stage presence was because of the intensity he played with, and he's still got that to this day.

Brian Pulito: Blaine, they broke the mold with him. He is one of the most unique people I've ever been around. He's an encyclopedia of knowledge when it comes to music. God, he knows more about music than anyone I know. I don't think Blaine could do anything else other than be a musician. He's all in, and he will always be all in.

Roy Scott (Vice President of Nine Pound Hammer, Inc.): They're just so approachable and relatable. They make fucking good music. They have risen in my top five to number two, and I've told them this – it's the Ramones, then Nine Pound Hammer. That's how much I fucking love this band.

Mike Grimes: Their lyrics are fucking poetry for the state of the union of Owensboro, Kentucky, in the mid- to late-eighties. They put their observations into lyrical genius in those early songs. I'm not kidding. I listen to 'em now, and I'm kind of in awe. I really am. Blaine's the real deal, and so is Scott.

Adam Neal: I still have a lot of respect for Scott. Great frontman. Great, great voice. I got Scott in his worst drug time, and I would say if I met Scott now in real life, we'd probably chat and chum it up.

Jason England (Vice President of Nine Pound Hammer, Inc.): They sound better today than they sounded 20 years ago. With Scott's voice, I hear it, and I think of Kentucky. There's just something about it. Whether it's Scott from 30 years ago or Scott right now. That's the thing that makes them cowpunk to me.

Don Garragio (Friend, Executive Producer of *Bluegrass Conspiracy*): I'm so proud of Scott. He's overcome so much adversity.

Rick Ballard: Scott's trajectory, to me, is the hero's journey. He embodies the things that I really respond to in this world. He's a free-thinking, individualist, counterculture guy who is flawed and wild and just out loud about it. And, he's a kind and respectful person.

There's also nothing in this world more satisfying than getting an email from Scott Luallen with demos attached, and you put the first song on and it's "Drunk, Tired & Mean." Give me that day every day.

Lawrence Tarpey: One of my takeaways with Scott, he was able to get his shit together and continue to keep being creative. It's a testament to his strength of character that he was able to pull his ass out of that shit and not die, because so many people have fucking died.

Kevin Robey (Friend): Hell, Scott DJ'd my wedding. I've known him a long time, and he's evolved into the perfect person that he should be. His emotional intelligence and what he is able to do outside of music now because he's been through that. It's inspiring to see him helping people.

Scott is currently the Overdose Prevention Coordinator for the Lexington, Fayette County Urban Government. Part of his responsibilities includes administering Naloxone. Since 2024 he has distributed over 5,000 kits, which has led to a massive reduction in fatal overdoses. Dude saves lives.

Brian Pulito: What he does to help people that are in that state – in some ways it's probably a bit therapeutic for him. To me, that's the best part of his story, that he overcame it and is helping other people overcome it. I've seen him go way out of his way to help people that are dealing with it.

After spending hours and hours and hours with both Blaine and Scott, I knew I had finally run out of questions when I pulled out the job interview trope, "Where do you all see yourselves in 10 years?"

Cringe, but necessary.

Blaine: I hope we're all still together. We always talk about quitting at some point because, well, physically. I go back and forth because I see some of these older bands, and it's just not what it was. 10 years from now, me and Scott will be 70. That's a little much.

I tend to ignore what people say in their seventies because they don't have that filter, and you're going to show your age every time you open your mouth. If you try to be cool and young, you're just going to look even stupider.

I lucked out to where I looked old when I was young. So, I think I'll pretty much look the same when I'm 70. I don't know, we'll see. If there's a demand for us to go play, then I can't imagine saying no.

Hopefully we'll have a couple more records. Hopefully we're all collecting some royalties from some songs that are in movies and shit like that. You know, sitting in our mansions drinking iced tea out on the porch or something.

If someone calls up and says "I'll pay your plane fare and give you guys like 10 grand to play Japan at a festival," we're not going to say no, as long as it's me and Scott.

Scott: We still have meaningful songs in us, so hopefully we can get them recorded and play them out live. Blaine and I have a creative and personal tension that produces interesting music. It kinda has to be that way. It hasn't been pretty, but again, that's what creates the rich soil. The band was meant to happen, and all the drama is just the backdrop. I wouldn't have it any other way!

None of this, however, would have been possible without the extraordinarily important contributions from everybody who's been in this band. Especially in the last 10 years or so – Brian Pulito – and more importantly Earl and Mark. Both of them bring a level of musicianship that allows us to write and record the music that fully expresses our unique experiences and upbringing.

EPILOGUE

When I started writing this book – of all people – my mom asked me, "Why did you choose to write about them?"[39]

After telling her and my dad, "Because they write songs about chicken, one-eyed prostitutes and tractor massacres. Duh!" My serious answer was, "What they do matters."

They're amazing storytellers and observers that discovered some secret formula that melds bluegrass and honky-tonk together with punk's speed, volume, irreverence and energy. What they do is singular, and they're a greatly underappreciated part of Kentucky's music heritage and punk rock history.

Nobody writes songs like Blaine Cartwright and Scott Luallen, and nobody plays them like Nine Pound Hammer – whether it's with the first drummer and the second bass player or drummer seven and bass player five.

Album after album they've showcased the oddness and oddballs they've come across in Kentucky and around the world. Often giving a voice to those marginalized by society and creating anthems about the rowdy, the restless and the written-off.

Plus, they're still out here teaching us valuable lessons, like you can tell if somebody is rich or not if they have pudding in their fridge.

---

[39] Her tone made me feel like she Googled Nine Pound Hammer, read a little bit about them and then discovered the words "Nashville Pussy." As a fairly religious woman, she probably said a prayer or two.

And finally, if you don't like Nine Pound Hammer, you don't like rock 'n roll.

***

I want to thank everybody that gave up nights and weekends to make this book happen. Major thanks to everybody I interviewed. You were all a delight. To those I asked for help and advice, thank you all.

The biggest thanks go to Scott and Blaine. Thank you for the opportunity, for being open and honest and, of course, thank you for the music.

P.S. The book might end here, but if you want to see handwritten lyrics, old concert posters and photos, read a few more stories and who knows what else, use the QR code below.

www.ingramcontent.com/pod-product-compliance
Lightning Source LLC
Chambersburg PA
CBHW071631140626
46555CB00022B/2059